IMAGES
of America

Show Low

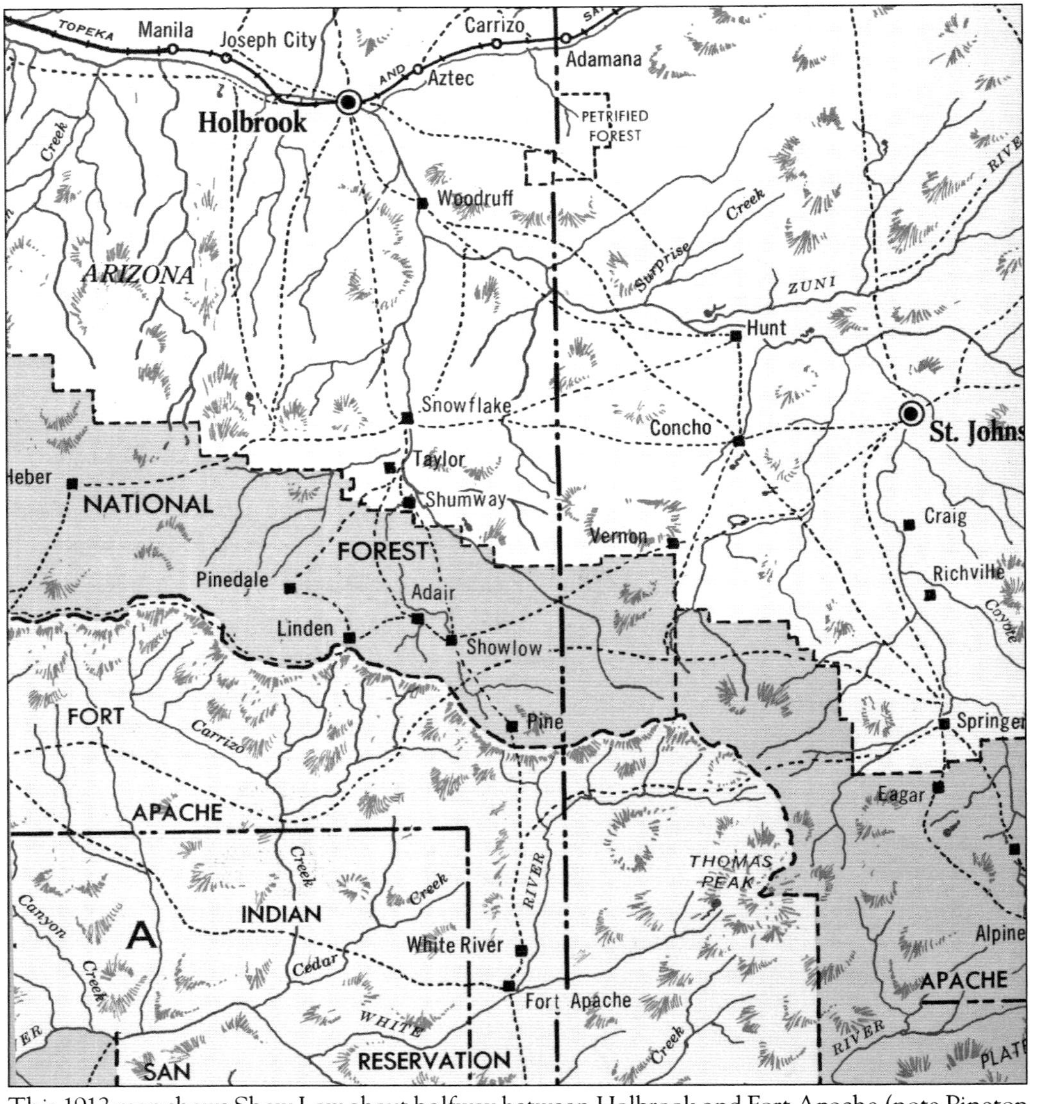

This 1912 map shows Show Low about halfway between Holbrook and Fort Apache (note Pinetop is listed as Pine). After the railroad reached Holbrook in 1881, all supplies, fresh troops, and payroll for Fort Apache came by rail to Holbrook. Then local men, usually with double wagons and six sturdy horses, hauled food, clothing, and hay south for the army. The 90-mile trip took eight days in good weather. (Ellis Collection.)

ON THE COVER: In the 1950s, visitors to the Paint Pony Lodge were the famous and wealthy wanting to escape to a cool, out-of-the-way mountain location. Community celebrations were also held at the Paint Pony, including this eighth-grade graduation of 1952. Part of the class included, from left to right, Bobby Potts (back), Renee Owens, Marcia Earl, Lavell Owens, Judie Standlee, Suzanne Petersen, Roy Chlarson Jr., Gary Wayne Wakefield, and Carl Malone. (Show Low Historical Society Museum.)

IMAGES
of America

SHOW LOW

Jani Huso and Catherine H. Ellis

Foreword by the Show Low Historical Society

ARCADIA
PUBLISHING

ISBN 978-0-7385-7138-6

Published by Arcadia Publishing
Charleston, South Carolina

Printed in the United States of America

Library of Congress Control Number: 2008941569

For all general information contact Arcadia Publishing at:
Telephone 843-853-2070
Fax 843-853-0044
E-mail sales@arcadiapublishing.com
For customer service and orders:
Toll-Free 1-888-313-2665

Visit us on the Internet at www.arcadiapublishing.com

To William "Bill" and Irene Huso, who lived community service, and Charles Whipple, the best principal a teacher could have.

Contents

FOREWORD

History is a second look. It isn't what happened but a story of what happened.

This book is a second look at the history of Show Low, Arizona. It is not the literal past, the "facts" of history, that will impress you during your journey between the book's covers but rather the stories invoked by the camera's images and the personal recollections of those who lived it.

Historically speaking, there are always different versions about the same events. And like stories, each of the different versions contains different lessons. That is a feature of history. So we invite you to consider the evidence as it has been collected herein and judge for yourself.

An ancient Greek writer stated, "History is indeed the witness of the times, the light of truth." Fortunately for us all, images of light have been preserved as photographs to witness that history. But this book has collected pictures, not just photographs. Photographs accurately depict people, things, and events at the moment the shutter was opened and light entered. Pictures, however, tell stories that stimulate our imagination because they are seen with the "new eyes" of you, the reader.

As you ponder the pictures, imagine the stories they tell. What led up to the picture? What likely happened to the subjects after the camera was stilled? As you read the narratives, reflect upon the circumstances being portrayed. What are the lessons there for us today?

The study of the past has never been static. Likewise, the history of Show Low is still being written and interpreted as new evidence is discovered. Conjectures continue to be converted to facts, and contradictions are still being resolved. Our historical society is proud to be a part of that progress.

We thank the contributors to this book for their willingness to give us a "second look" and commend the publishers for their commitment to the preservation of our heritage that we might have a better understanding of the present. Enjoy the journey!

—Show Low Historical Society, Inc.
2009

Acknowledgments

Ardell Ellsworth, in his book on the LDS Globe Stake, wrote, "For those who would write future histories, let them profit from our mistakes, but also build upon our successes. Our tomorrows need to be recorded in a more perfect manner. Now is the time to begin." We hope that our efforts to capture Show Low's history in photographs meet his criteria.

Many of the photographs here come from the Show Low Historical Society Museum (SLHisSoc Museum). The historical society was incorporated in 1991, and the museum opened in 1995. Of particular interest are the photographs from the Paint Pony Lodge scrapbook. We encourage all to visit the museum, enjoy the displays, and contribute photographs and artifacts of interest to the community. Additional photographs have come from the Arizona Historical Society in Tucson (AHS/Tucson), the Arizona State Archives in Phoenix, and the Navajo County Historical Society in Holbrook.

However, our most important resource was photographs from families who settled the area. Emma Adams, Georgia Adams, Ardell Ellsworth, Hilda Frost, Beatrice Jarvis, Neola Mills, Elizabeth Nikolaus, Jackie Solomon, Ruby Stock, and Ione "Babe" Whipple have been particularly diligent in historic preservation. We wish to thank family members who have shared these photographs with us. Credit for each photograph is in parentheses at the end of the caption.

Finally, we express our thanks to Christine Talbot and Jared Jackson of Arcadia Publishing for their commitment to the preservation of history across the nation.

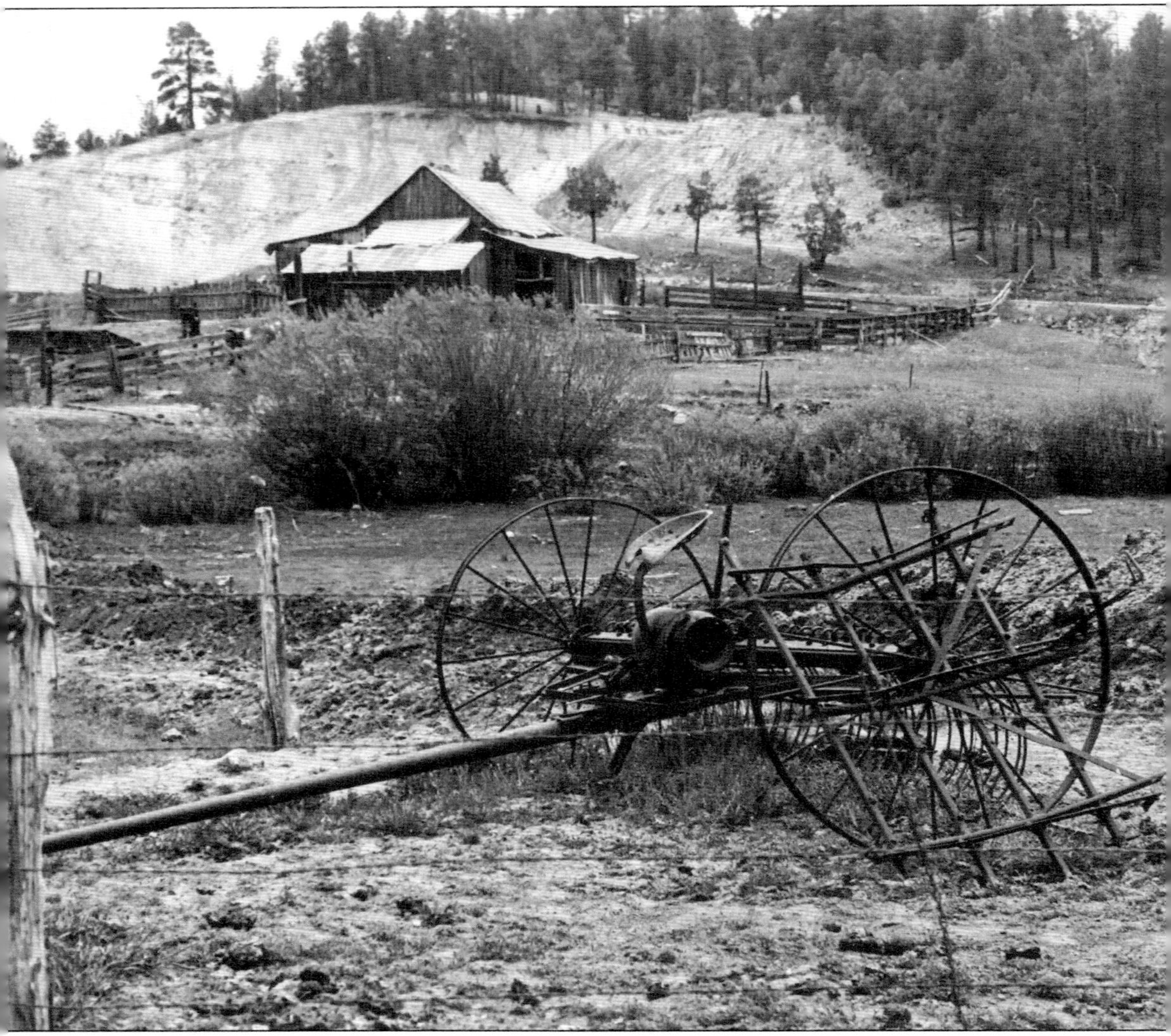

The Ellsworth barn, south of Show Low, has probably been the subject of more photographs and paintings than any other structure around. Deborah Austin in this photograph caught the light to show the weathering and beauty of the barn. According to Morley "Pete" Ellsworth, the barn was originally built in the 1920s. During the great snow of 1932, his father, Whittie, was inside the barn when he heard the rafter split, sending half of the roof to the east and half to the west. The tall posts were not involved, so it was possible to rebuild using the same framework. When Whittie was transporting lumber for reconstruction from the Mahonri Fish sawmill, his foot slipped while the horses were pulling the wagon up the wash. He fell backward on a double-bitted axe, causing a deep gash on his buttocks. His aunt, Edna Merrell Ellsworth, promptly poured kerosene on the wound, preventing infection and almost killing the patient. (Photograph by Deborah Austin.)

INTRODUCTION

The lush valley Corydon E. Cooley encountered as he entered the Show Low Creek area in 1870 looks much the same today because many pioneer families have retained ownership of their lands. The Owens, Adams, Reidhead, Ellsworth, and Whipple families still have well-bred horses and cattle, and an occasional elk, grazing in their pastures. These descendants of the early pioneers have remained faithful stewards of the land and should be commended; no matter what else may have changed, this part of Show Low is still recognizable.

In the 1940s and 1950s, Show Low's main street (before it was named Deuce of Clubs) began an awakening in the form of many mom-and-pop businesses. A log building for the post office and Tanner's Variety became a new state-of-the-art brick post office on Old Linden Road and Main Street. Myrtle Mills Loveless opened a teenage hangout called the Snak n' Yak. At Christmastime, the window of Kay's Drugs contained Kitty's Christmas Village, with mirrors for ponds and lots of angel hair for snow. The Show Low Drug had a full-service soda fountain where a lettuce-and-tomato sandwich was 25¢ and additional ham was 10¢. Suicide Cokes were the rage with the teens; Virginia Hall drew the line at adding marshmallow and butterscotch cream because these syrups caused them to foam all over the counter.

Before the advent of Interstate 40 fifty miles north of Show Low, many commercial trucks came through Show Low. Navajo Freight Lines, Yellow Freight, and Watkins Brothers used Highway 60 to Phoenix. At the Butler Trucking Yard, employees could recognize the sound of their drivers' rigs and knew who was speeding and who was grinding gears. Most drivers were ready for some home cooking by the time they reached Show Low. Many local teenagers waited tables and washed dishes and were on a first-name basis with drivers from all over the country.

The city of Show Low was incorporated in 1953. Show Low then was a one-blinking-stoplight town with the stoplight at the intersection of White Mountain Road and Deuce of Clubs. There were portable signs on wheel rims in the middle of the street alerting drivers to slow down. In the 1950s, summer and winter nights were spent "cruising Main," from the White Mountain Café on the east to the Show Low Café on the west. Teens were usually joined by Ross and Georgia Adams and Eph and Nell Mills.

In the 1950s, there were no car dealers in Show Low. If someone wanted a new Ford or Chevrolet, they had to drive to Holbrook, Globe, Springerville, or St. Johns. From the 1940s through the 1960s, when each year's body style was modified and recognizable, there was always competition to be the first to see the new models. But, although Show Low lacked car dealers, there were garages. Ray Butler, Jim Stock and his boys, the Woolfords, and Al Hansen had garages in the center of town. Church's Garage and the White and Jaeger Garage were on the west end of town. With this many garages in a town this small, it is apparent there were many older cars and trucks requiring a little assistance.

In 1957, C. I. Robson built the Malapai Inn Steak House and Bar for his friend Ann Encke to showcase her culinary abilities. Working men ate at the Show Low Café, Ross' Café, and the White

Mountain Café. The Sportsman Café was a local hangout, especially after the bars closed and partyers were seeking bacon and eggs. When Mitchell and Garland Bushman built the two-story Show Low Hotel west of Show Low Creek bridge, the Hashknife Restaurant in the southwest corner was run by Alta McNeil. The basement had a pool hall, which Janene Bushman, Mitchell's daughter, ran. She became quite a pool shark, and it was said that she subsidized her stay at Brigham Young University by engaging unsuspecting newcomers with a friendly bet on a game.

Dancing was important in Show Low. Bill's Bar and the Navajo Inn (owned by Joe Baird and Dutch Kay) were the preferred places for adults to dance, or if people were willing to drive, they could go to the Ponderosa Club in Pinetop. Most teenagers learned to dance at the Latter-day Saints (LDS) Church and spent many Saturday nights enjoying the hardwood floor of the Cultural Hall while listening to local bands. In summer, the cement slab with a chain-link fence, called the Pavilion, was the place to be seen. Garth Nikolaus and his Westernaires were popular with locals and summer visitors alike. Because the music wafted all over town, parents expected teenagers home soon after the music ended.

In the 1950s, the Show Low Elementary School was the only school in town; high school students rode the bus to Snowflake. Show Low teachers were excellent and dedicated, with very little turnover. Students listened for the first bell at 8:00 a.m., which announced the time to depart from home. They met in groups to make the journey to "school house hill." They walked or rode bicycles; in winter, sleds were often used to go down the two hills leading to school. At the steep one on the east, "Aunt" Sarah Mills often came out of her house to supervise the fun. Automobiles also used the north road, so sledding (or driving) was a little tricky on snowy days. As the students approached school, they could usually smell chili beans and hot rolls in Jessie Chlarson's school cafeteria, a lean-to on the south end of the Quonset hut gymnasium. Jessie and her crew provided nutritional and economical food. Many students worked for their meals and a small stipend.

The north end of the gymnasium contained a stage and served as a music room. An annual event was the Christmas operetta. In 1953, Janice Vance and Perry Bassett were to ride in a sleigh, similar to one seen in *The Nutcracker.* A few minutes before the planned appearance, Perry refused to participate. There were pleas from the third-grade teacher, Ione Pearce, and threats from his parents. Finally, he decided to join the fun. Fifty-five years later, while researching for this book, it was discovered that Perry's change of heart came when his father, Walt, bribed him with a $10 bill. Ten dollars was a fortune for a nine-year-old in 1953.

During the time that Show Low students went to high school in Snowflake (Show Low High School was built in 1972), there were also many Navajo students living in dormitories and attending school there. One of the Navajo students said that the elders of the Diné (or the People as they call themselves) reminded them to *hoozho naninaa doo* or "walk in beauty." A walk through Show Low's history is a walk in beauty.

One

The Legendary Card Game

The name Show Low is generally believed to be from a card game played between Corydon E. Cooley and Marion Clark sometime in the 1870s. The men were partners, farming and ranching along the creek at the edge of the forest where ponderosa pines are replaced by junipers. After a disagreement, they decided the area was not big enough for both of them, so ownership of the ranch was to be decided with a game of Seven-Up. They played through the night, and in the early morning, the game was tied. Whoever could show the low card would win, and Cooley turned over a deuce of clubs. Clark moved farther south.

However, there is a bit of disagreement with the name. In 1877, Prescott's *Arizona Miner* had a note about C. E. Cooley, "now a resident of Sho Lou, 40 miles north of Camp Apache." Early maps generally show the creek as Show Low Creek (although an 1879 map has Show Low Creek and Silver Creek reversed). This map also has the creek labeled "Chiloe Creek," and Franz Huning (brother of Henry) wrote about an 1851 trip, "This little river is a confluent of the Little Colorado and the Indians called it Shothloo, pronounced short." Cooley himself was a consummate storyteller, and sometimes the details of his stories varied. In fact, Sen. Carl Hayden, when living in Washington, D.C., in 1950, sent copies of documents to Robert Cooley and wrote, "I did not state with whom he played the card game at Show Low because the stories about it are conflicting."

Regardless of the origin of the name, Apaches were using the Show Low area, albeit lightly, when settlers first arrived about 1870. Later Col. H. B. Wharfield wrote, "The Sierra Blanca people were mostly friendly toward the whites. Such hostility as existed was usually caused by irascible individuals or at most by a few wild ones. . . . The early day soldiering at Fort Apache, located in the White Mountains, was chiefly engaged in conflicts on campaigns into the other areas of Apacheria."

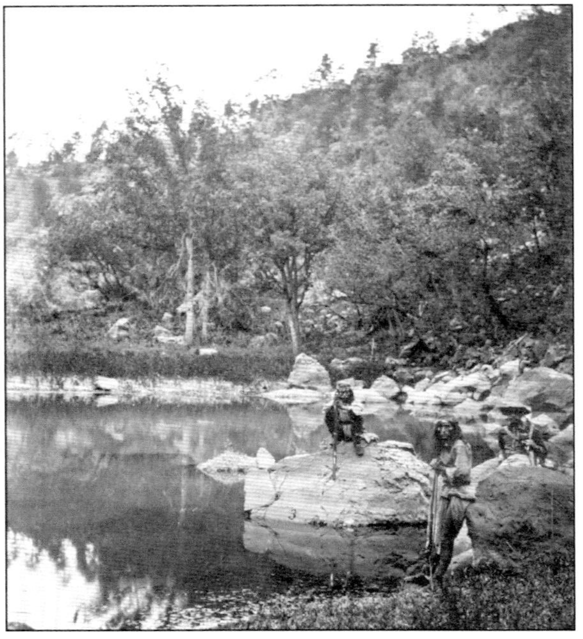

Apache Lake is an ephemeral pond that Timothy O'Sullivan, traveling with Lt. George M. Wheeler in 1873, listed as 35 miles east of Camp Apache at an elevation of 10,500 feet. It shows two Apache scouts and a member of the expedition in the foreground. The Apaches were a nomadic Athapaskan tribe that came into Arizona between 1300 and 1500 AD from northern Canada. Their language is closely related to Navajo. (National Archives 77-WF-7.)

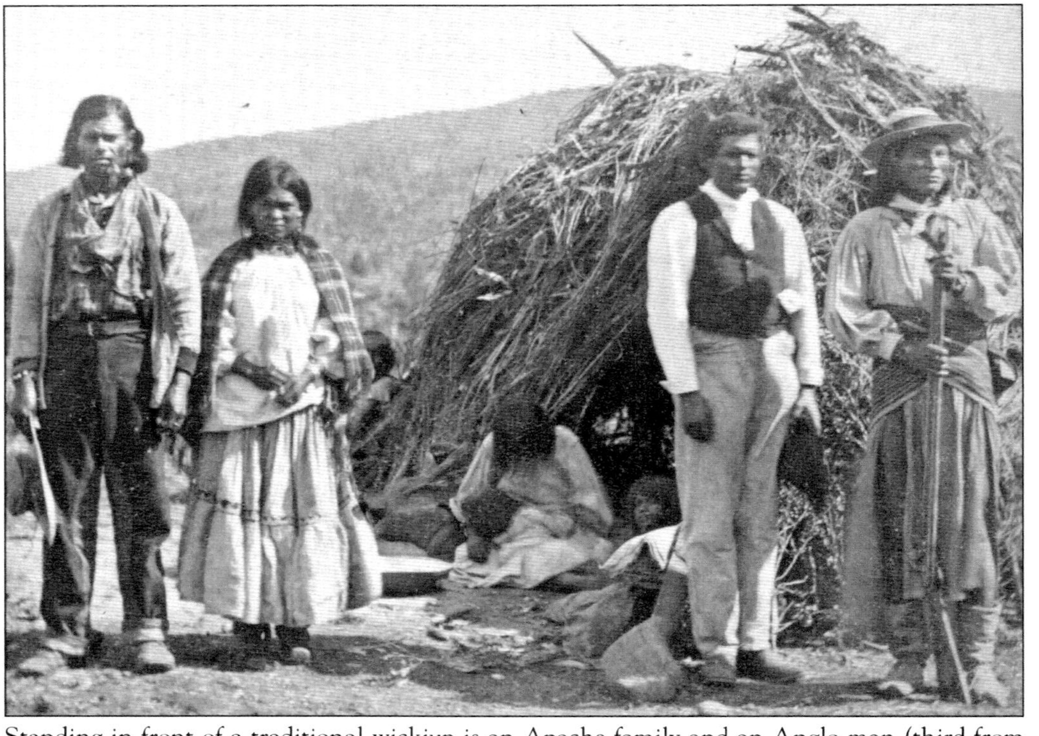

Standing in front of a traditional wickiup is an Apache family and an Anglo man (third from left) who may be the Indian agent. Both the military and the Apaches often had problems with the agents. Martha Summerhayes, after meeting one, said, "Heaven save us from a Government which appoints such men as *that* to watch over and deal with Indians." (Photograph by Timothy O'Sullivan, Library of Congress.)

Two important White Mountain Apache leaders in the 1870s were Miguel (right) and Pedro (below), both of whom Col. H. B. Wharfield described as "peacefully disposed toward Whites." In June 1872, Miguel and Pedro were part of a group that traveled by train to Washington, D.C., to visit Pres. Ulysses S. Grant and other officials. They stayed at Howard University (a historically African American school), were given army uniforms (which Pedro is wearing below in 1873), and were vaccinated for smallpox. The photograph of Miguel was taken while in Washington. Earlier letters sometimes refer to him as "One-eyed McGill," and while in D.C., Miguel was fitted with a glass eye. (Right, photograph by Alex Gardner, National Archives 75-ID-24B; below, photograph by Timothy O'Sullivan, Library of Congress.)

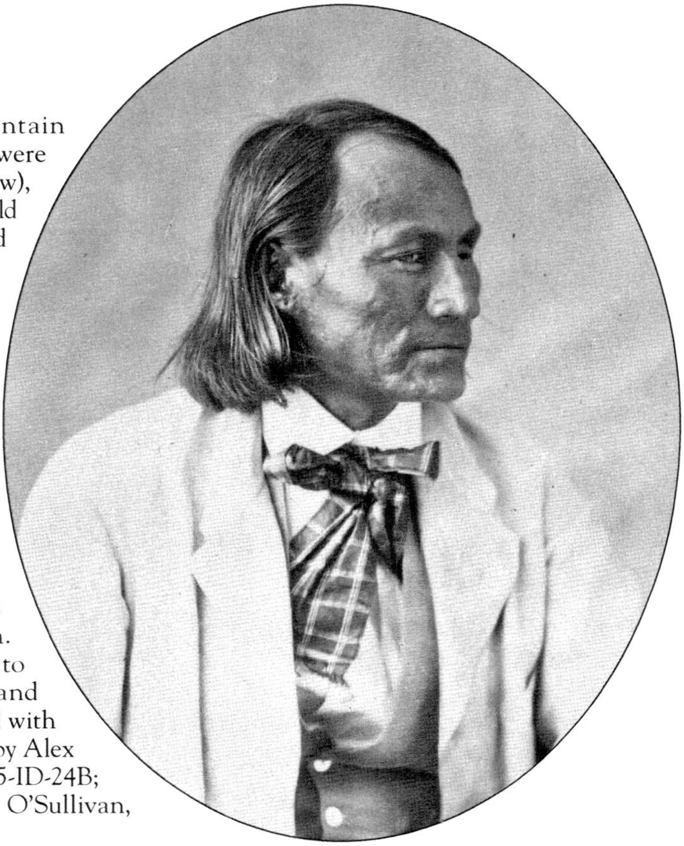

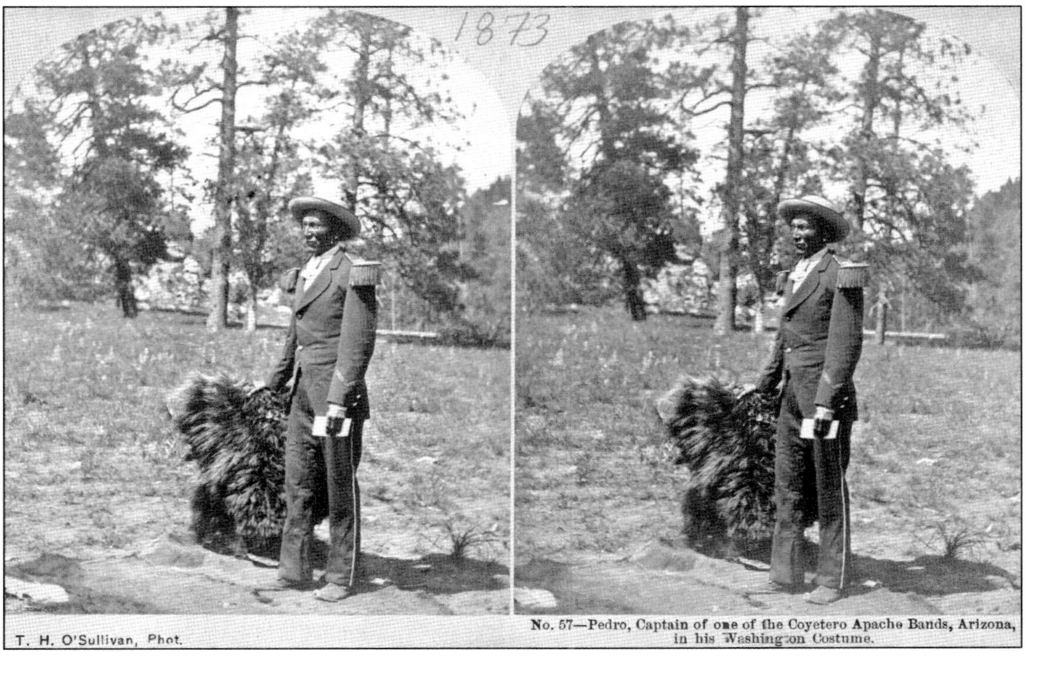

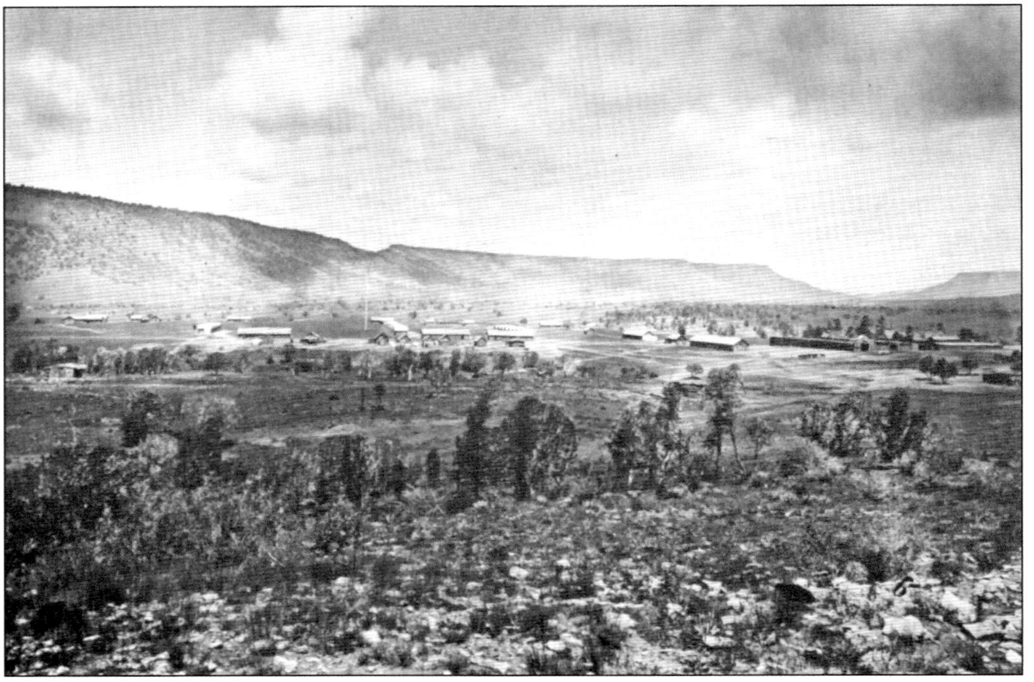

In early spring 1870, a military camp was established at the forks of the White River and named Camp Ord. Two months later, the name changed to Camp Thomas, and in February 1871, it became Camp Apache (the designation Fort Apache came in 1879). Both cavalry and infantry were stationed there. Col. H. B. Wharfield called it "one of the best and loveliest [assignments] in all Arizona." (Photograph by Timothy O'Sullivan, National Archives 106-WB-101.)

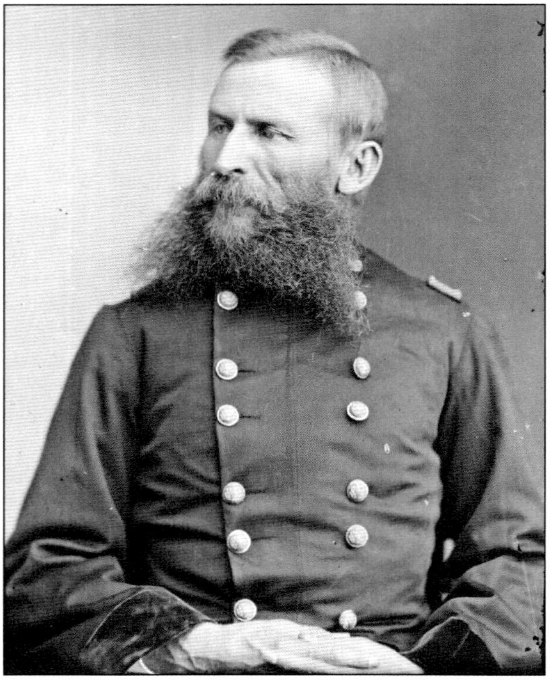

With the influx of white settlers, Apache/Anglo conflicts demanded a solution. Gen. George Crook came to Arizona with a plan. He sent White Mountain Apache scouts with enlisted men on hunt-and-kill forays against other Apaches, mostly Tontos and Chiricahuas. His plan, as stated in an 1873 report, was: "when day-light came they might attack the enemy and secure the advantage of surprise." By 1873, most of the fighting was over. (Library of Congress.)

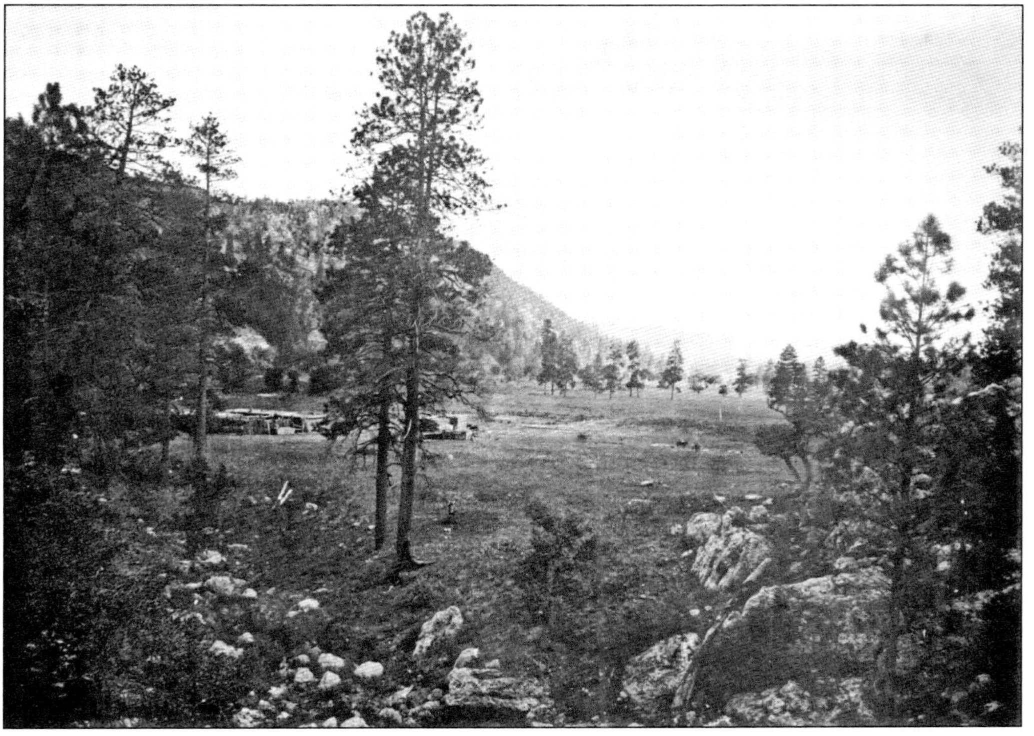

In 1873, O'Sullivan photographed "Cooley's Park, about 10 miles east of Camp Apache" (above). Corydon Cooley, born in Virginia in 1836, was in Santa Fe by 1856 and joined the Union army in 1861 to help defend New Mexico from Texan Confederates. Cooley came to Arizona about 1869 looking for gold. He came to Camp Ord in 1870, farmed, learned the Apache language, was a guide and interpreter for the U.S. Army, married both Mary "Mollie" and Cora, daughters of Chief Pedro, and settled at Show Low. On August 18, 1879, the *Arizona Daily Star* reported that Cooley had about 200 acres of grain, "which looks fine and is almost ready for the harvesters. Friend Cooley . . . has set out a great variety of fruit trees, also strawberries, currents [*sic*], blackberries, etc." (Above, National Archives 106-WB-347; right, Arizona State Archives 96-1392.)

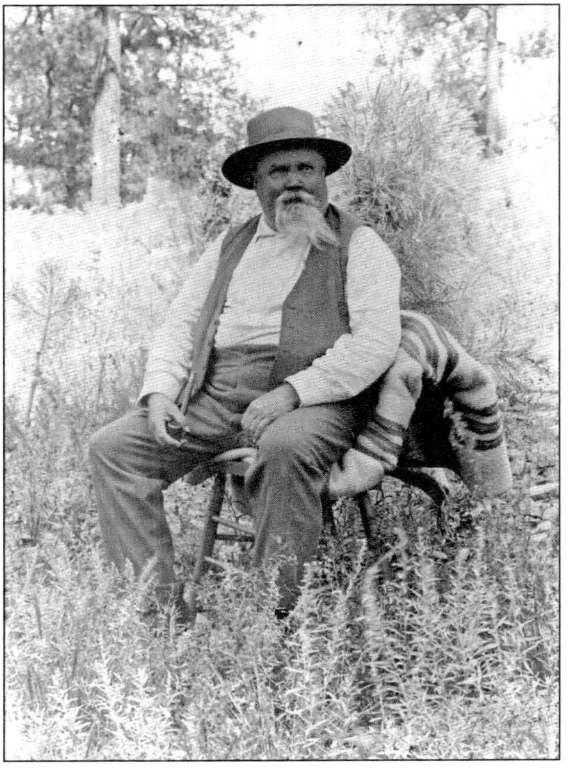

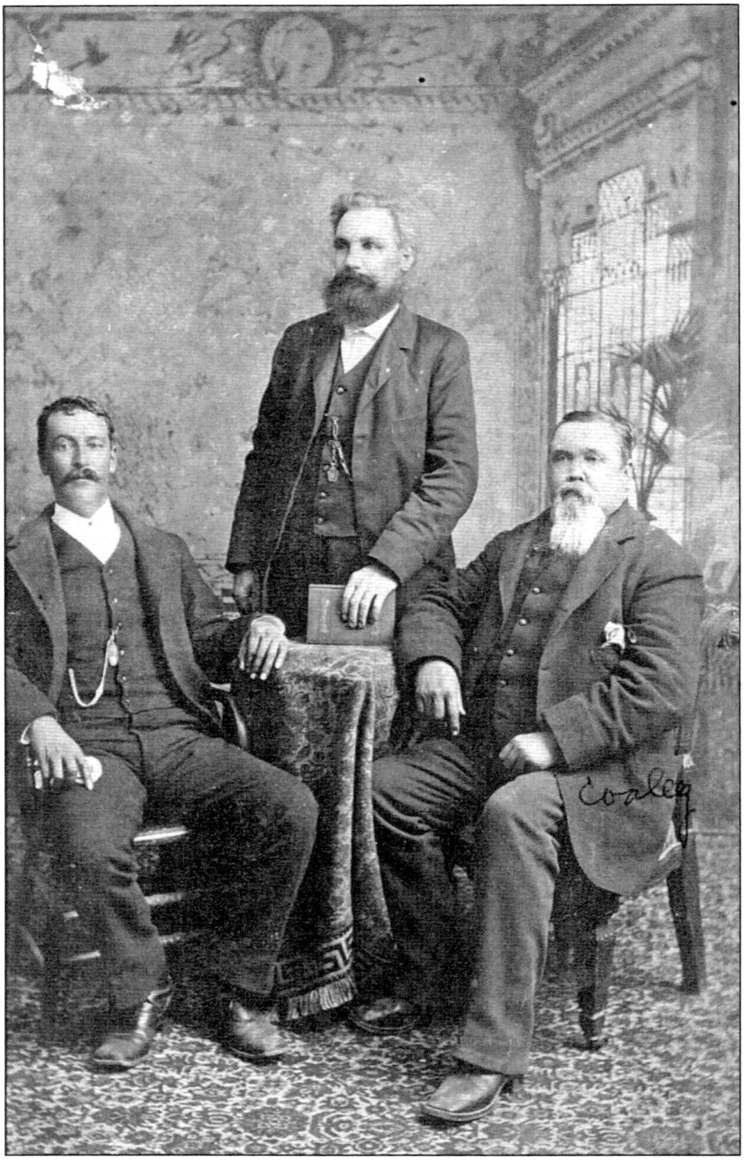

The German brothers Louis, Franz, and Henry Huning became prominent New Mexico businessmen and by 1876 were sending supplies into Arizona. In 1879, Henry Huning was the lowest bidder to furnish Camp Apache with flour ($5.50 per 100 pounds). About 1880, he formed a partnership with C. E. Cooley and settled in Show Low. Two years later, he abducted Juliana, the wife of Holbrook store owner Berardo Freyda (or convinced her to come freely because she brought her children). They lived together in Show Low until 1888, when a lawsuit was brought against them (so the judge simply granted a divorce and performed a marriage). Huning, a wealthy cattleman, was president of the Navajo-Apache Bank and was on the finance committee for statehood. In 1898, he purchased the entire bond ($15,000) for the Navajo County courthouse and jail. Finally, in 1903, Huning sold his Show Low property to William J. Flake and moved to California; he died in 1922. Above from left to right are Donica Baca, Henry Huning, and C. E. Cooley, probably when they were Apache County supervisors. (JoAnn Finney Hatch.)

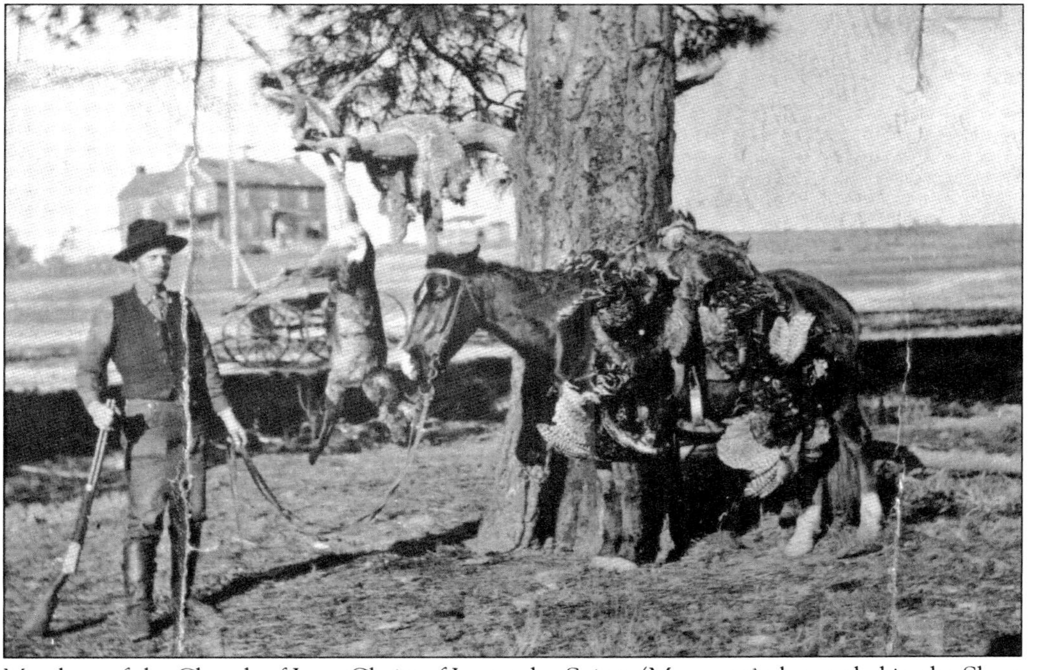

Members of the Church of Jesus Christ of Latter-day Saints (Mormons) also settled in the Show Low area, as early as 1876. Above is George M. Adams after a hunting foray into the mountains, his sheep hanging in the tree and several turkeys hanging on his horse. In the background is Cooley's White House. (Helen Adams Capps.)

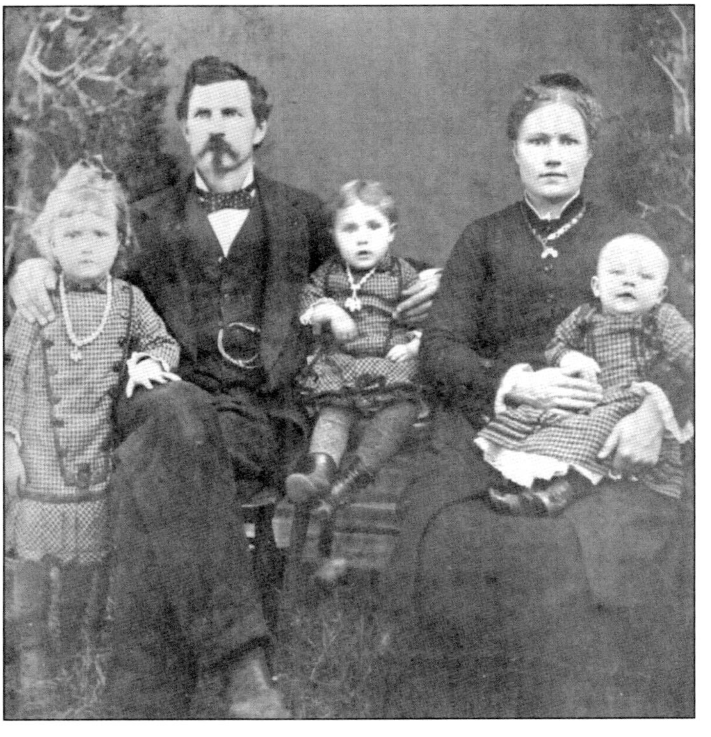

One Mormon family that came to Show Low early was that of Sanford Jaques (at right with his wife, Anna Christina Hansen, and children, from left to right, Anna Christine, Sarah, and Sanford). Jaques built the White House for Cooley in 1882. Other men who worked as carpenters included John Bull (for Huning), Joseph Sponsellor (who designed and built the White River covered bridge), and Hans and Jens Niels Hansen (at Fort Apache). (Lois Adams Lemons.)

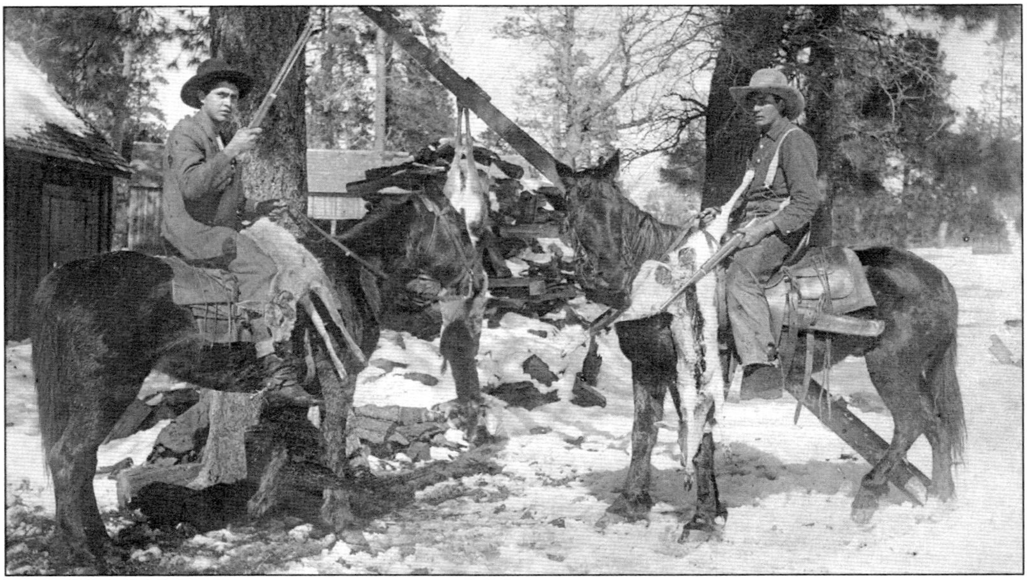

C. E. Cooley's influence was noted by Hans Hansen when, in 1912, he wrote in Cooley's guest book, "To one who has been a friend to me and all. And will always have friends and be long remembered for good." Cooley's children included Cora's child Lillie (who married Delbert Penrod) and Mollie's children Belle (wife of Abe Amos); Cora (wife of Charles Pettis); Charles; Fredric; Corydon "Don" (above left, possibly with brother Albert); Albert; and Ernestine (who died young). (AHS/Tucson 42,605.)

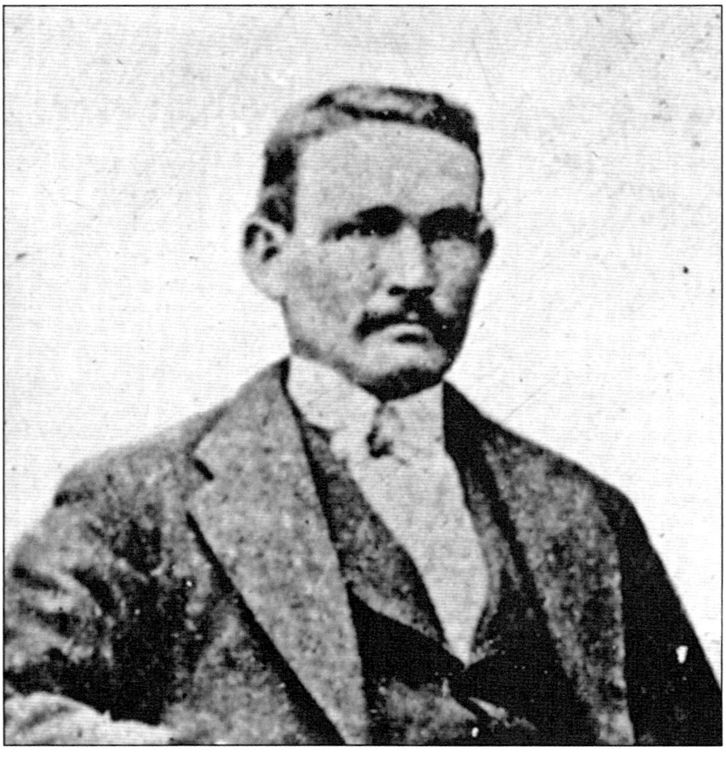

The winter of 1881–1882 was a period of Apache unrest. Many settlers gathered at Cooley's place for defense; others moved to Snowflake or Taylor for safety. Forestdale was eventually declared reservation land. Nathan Robinson (at left) was the only casualty. While searching for missing cows, he apparently happened upon Apaches who killed him and dumped his body into the creek. (Arizona State Archives 03-0120.)

Sarah McNeil Mills was honored Mother's Day 1958 for civic deeds, storytelling, and kindness. But as a child in the 1880s, she lived at Forestdale. One day, her father, John McNeil, jokingly told the Apache chief Petone that he could have Sarah as his wife. Thereafter, she would hide whenever Petone came to the house. Later Petone and Alchesay, another Apache, settled an argument with guns, leaving Petone dead, and Sarah wrote, "It was a big relief to know he wasn't going to have me." (Elizabeth Nikolaus.)

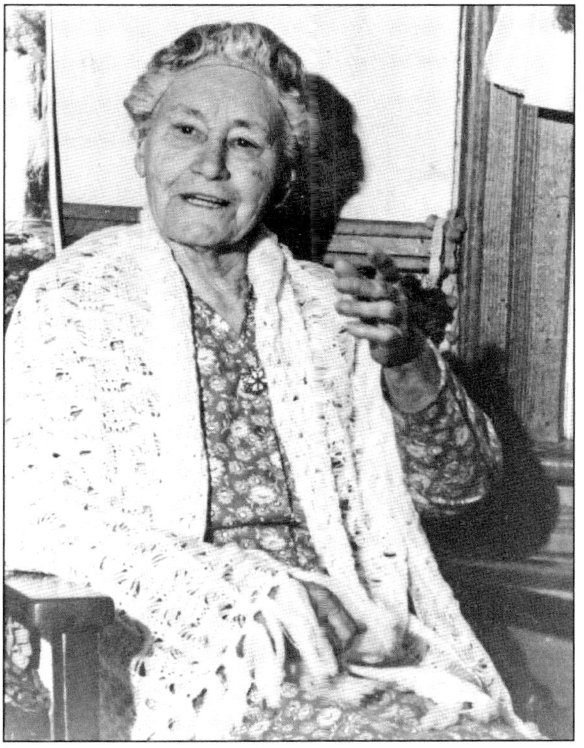

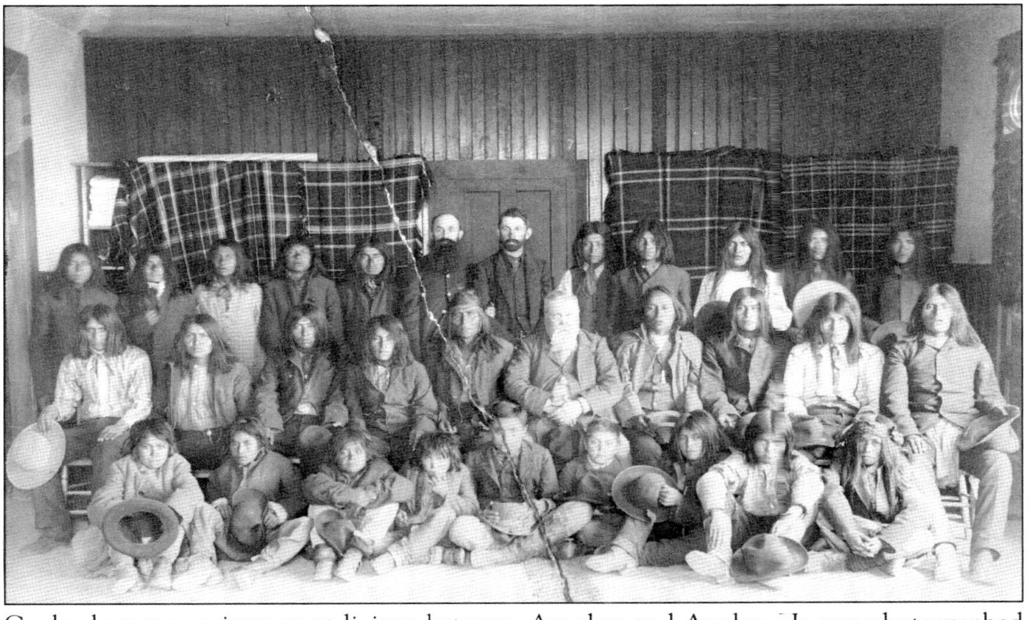

Cooley became an important liaison between Apaches and Anglos. He was photographed December 13, 1892, with the first group of Apaches to leave the White Mountains for school, meaning to the Manual Training School for Indians at Albuquerque, New Mexico. Cooley is seated in the center, and two of the boys in front are probably Cooley's sons, Fred and Charles; Fred died while at school in Albuquerque. (AHS/Tucson 49,900.)

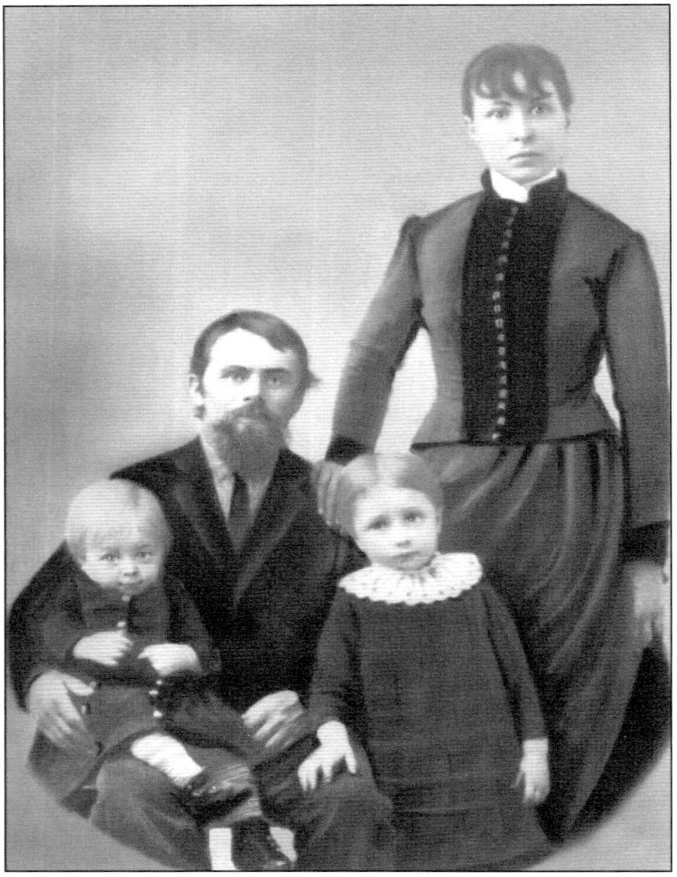

Edson Sr. and Harriet Whipple came to Arizona in 1880, locating in Show Low at a place later known as "the Whipple." It included a block house for defense against the Apache and later was known as Whipple Hall. As was common of many early settlers, they moved on to Mexico and later the Gila Valley. However, several of their sons stayed in northeastern Arizona. At left is a photograph of Edson Jr. with his wife, Rowena, son Joseph (left), and daughter Lucy about 1889. Uncle Ned and Aunt Rene, as they were known, had a large family and ran a boardinghouse. Pictured below are two sons, John (left) and William, who died as young men. William died during World War I; three other brothers also served but came home safely. (Left, SLHisSoc Museum; below, Sheila McCleve Stewart.)

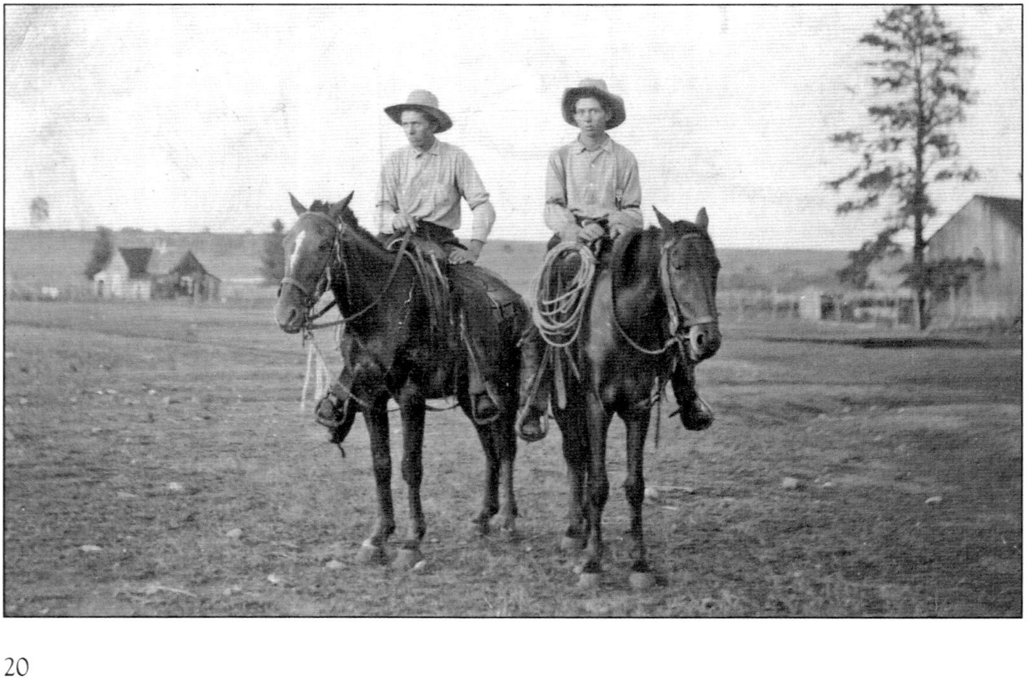

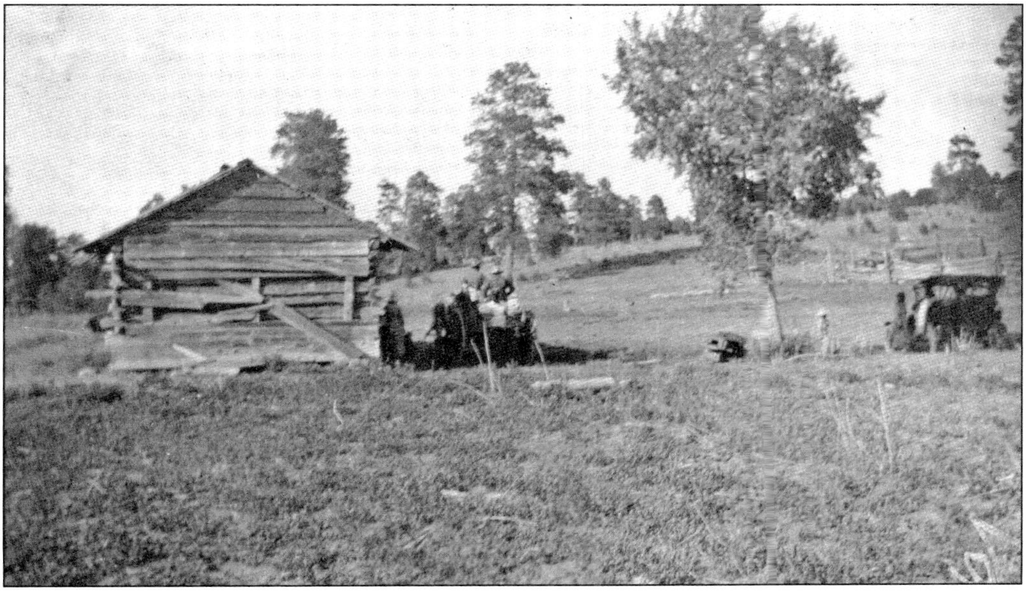

Another son of Edson Whipple Sr. was Willard, who married Emma Oliver in 1884 at the Whipple ranch at Adair (above). In 1886, Willard and Emma homesteaded a dry land farm, 1.75 miles from water, which meant that they hauled most of the water they used for many years. In the 1890s, they raised sheep. Hans Hansen first settled at Adair, and daughter Annie Hansen Whipple wrote, "We raised mostly corn and sugar cane, squash, and some potatoes. It was all dry-farming. Sometimes we raised a garden and watered it with buckets of water from the well." At Show Low, settlers constructed ditches to water fields on both sides of the creek. Standing next to their corn in 1943 (below) are William Lewis (left), Larry Frost, and Nancy Lewis. (Both, Sheila McCleve Stewart.)

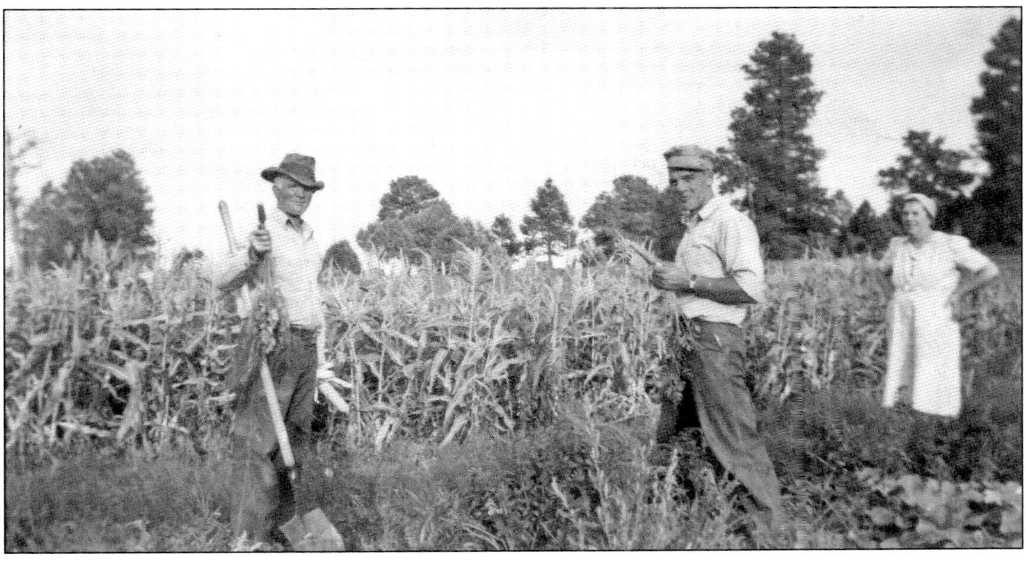

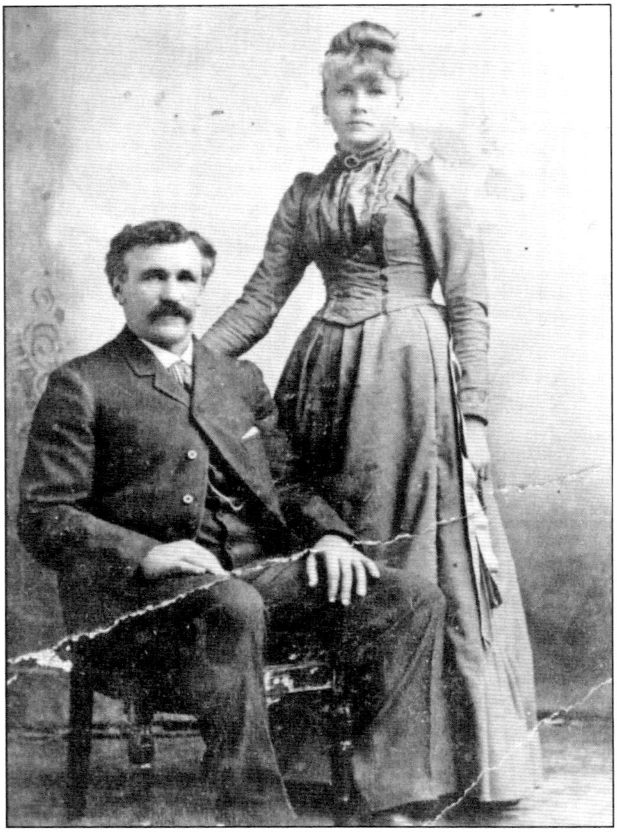

This wedding photograph of Joseph Sponseller and Martha Louise Adams was taken in 1890. Louise was the daughter of George and Martha Adams. Their wedding was celebrated with a dance at the old fort. Sponseller was a sheep rancher whose range was on Silver Creek east of Show Low, near Vernon. Today there is a Sponsellor Lake at the foot of Porter Mountain (west of the dipping vat). Robert and James Scott and William Morgan also ran sheep in the White Mountains. Victor Adams had sheep in 1922. Sponsellor and his family lived at Show Low, Shumway, and Taylor until about 1920. Below is a photograph of the extended George M. Adams family in front of the original Huning home. (Left, Navajo County Historical Society; below, Helen Adams Capps.)

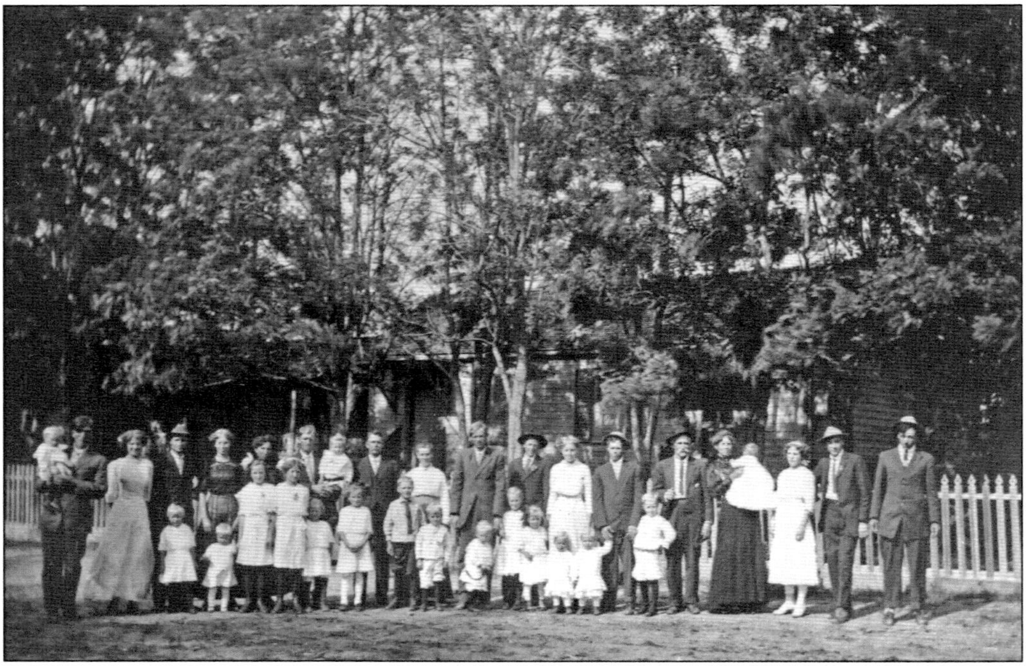

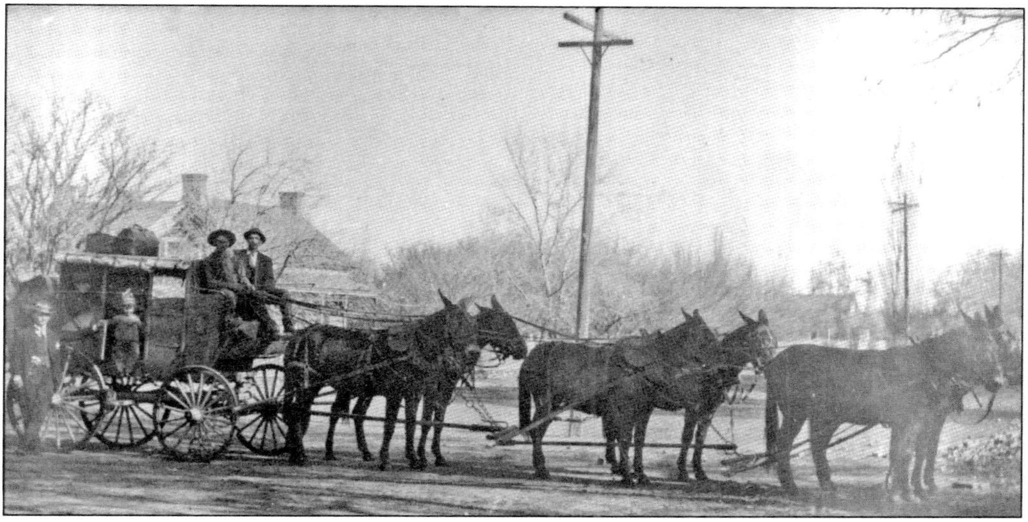

The army ambulance (above) was the fastest means of conveyance from Fort Apache to Holbrook. About 1885, John Addison Hunt rode across a swollen Silver Creek at Snowflake 18 times while a Captain Beck looked for a place to cross. Finally, straps were attached to the lead mules, and Hunt entered the water. He said, "The canyon boxed about 200 or 300 feet below us, and if that government officer, his driver, ambulance, and six mules had not had a half grown boy and a big horse weighing about 1600 pounds in front of them, they would have gone with the current into that box and would have been lost forever." (Louise Levine.)

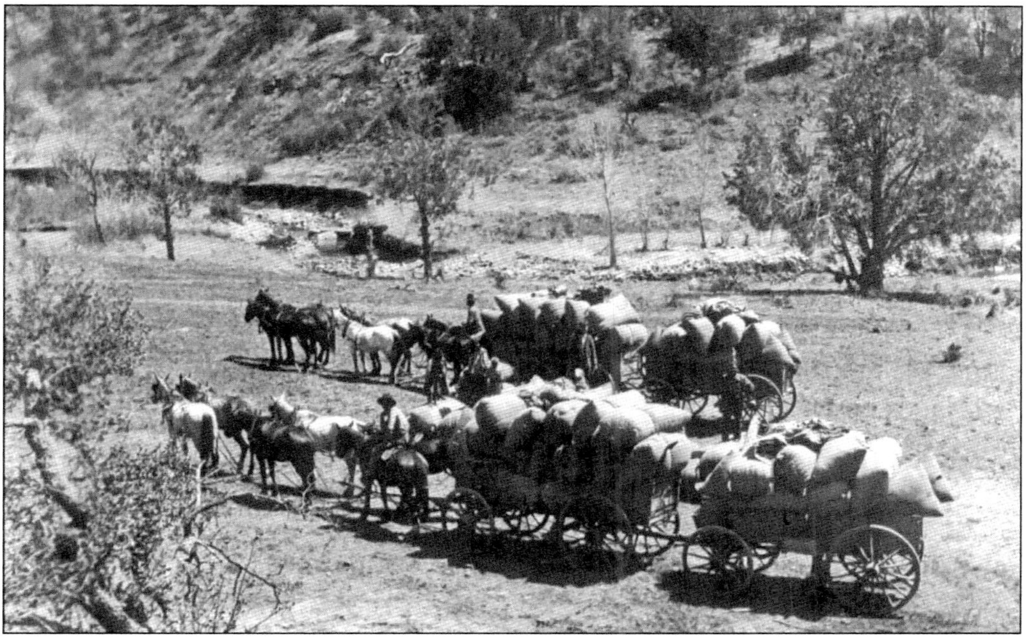

Hunt, and his brother Lewis, also hauled freight to Fort Apache (above near Cibecue). About 1918, Col. H. B. Wharfield watched Sgt. Charles "Peasoup" Larzelere trying to move one wagon with four teams: "He was plastered with mud from head to foot, and so were the animals. Up and down the line of mules he waded." When Peasoup got the wagon on hard road, Wharfield wisely suggested the men receive their pay "on the spot." (Louise Levine.)

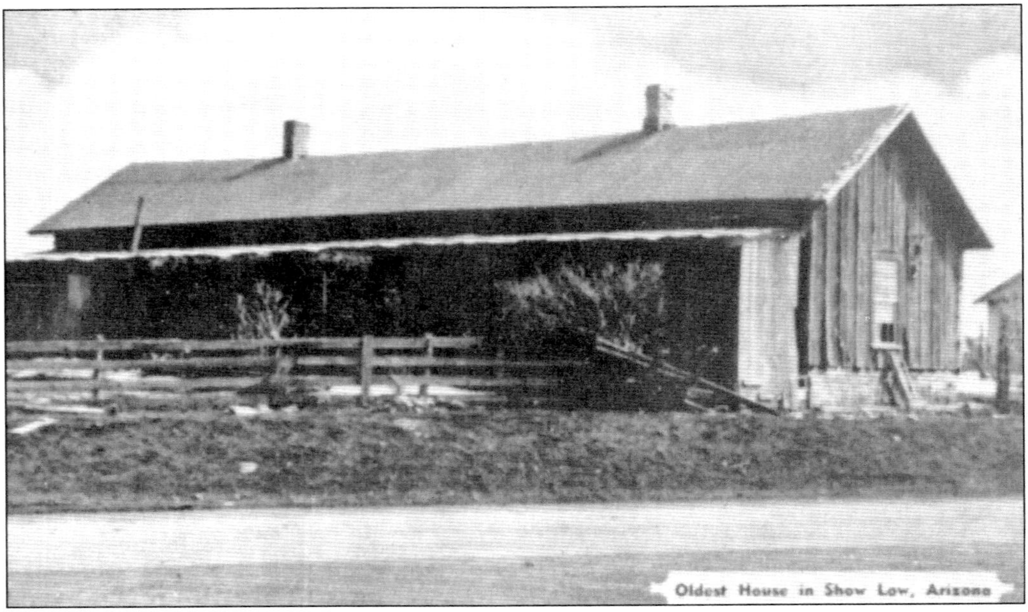

Huning employed many people to manage his empire. Ed Beelar, Marion Clark, and Tom Pressly were range and ranch foremen, and Ernest Ellsworth worked as coachman. By 1899, Huning sold his cattle and bought sheep (with William Morgan), wintering them (all 23,000) in Phoenix. In the 1940s, this men's bunkhouse built by Huning was listed as the "oldest house in Show Low." (Mary Sexton.)

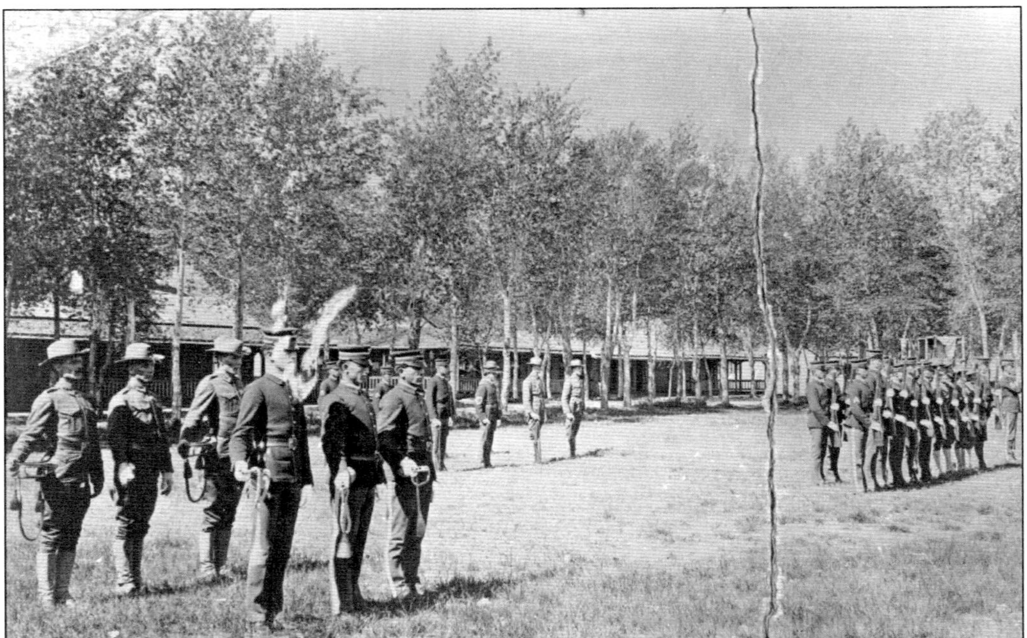

Men stationed at Fort Apache sometimes married local girls and remained in the area. William W. Franklin, second from left, was assigned to Fort Apache and married Katie Sponsellor in 1908 at the fort. Later he worked as a barber in Holbrook. (Navajo County Historical Society.)

Alchesay (right) was one of the great leaders of the White Mountain Apaches. He served as one of General Crook's Apache scouts and received the Congressional Medal of Honor. Later when Crook encouraged the Apache to raise cattle and horses, Alchesay became a prominent stockman. Joseph Pearce remembered, "Chief Alchesay would invite me to his wickiup and there in the presence of his family would sit and discuss the American way of running cattle [and] tilling the soil. . . . Alchesay was a big cattle and horse owner [with] his two sons Baha [born in 1872] and Willie. . . . Baha [also known as Dahlson] became chief after the death of his father." Pete Ellsworth remembers Baha coming into Show Low to trade goods. Below, Bill Sexton photographed Apache cowboys branding and dehorning cattle in the 1970s. (Right, photograph by Edward Curtis, Library of Congress; below, Mary Sexton.)

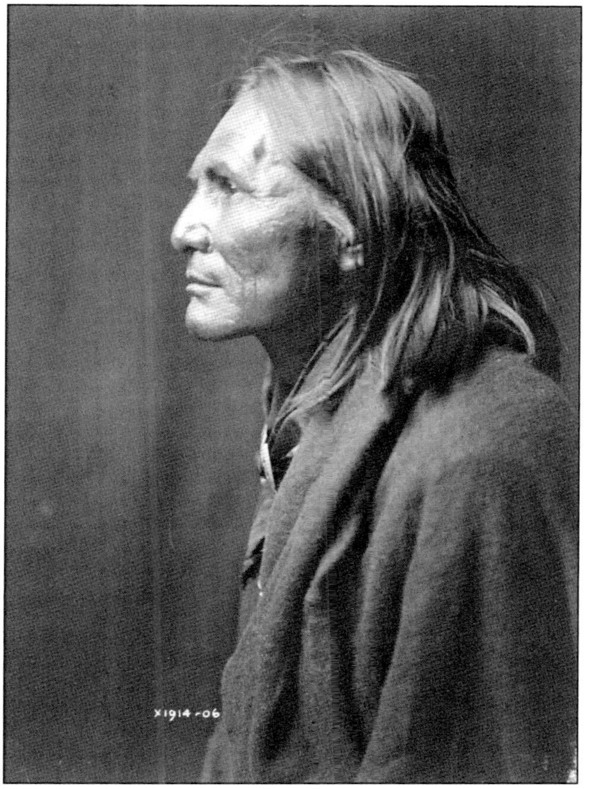

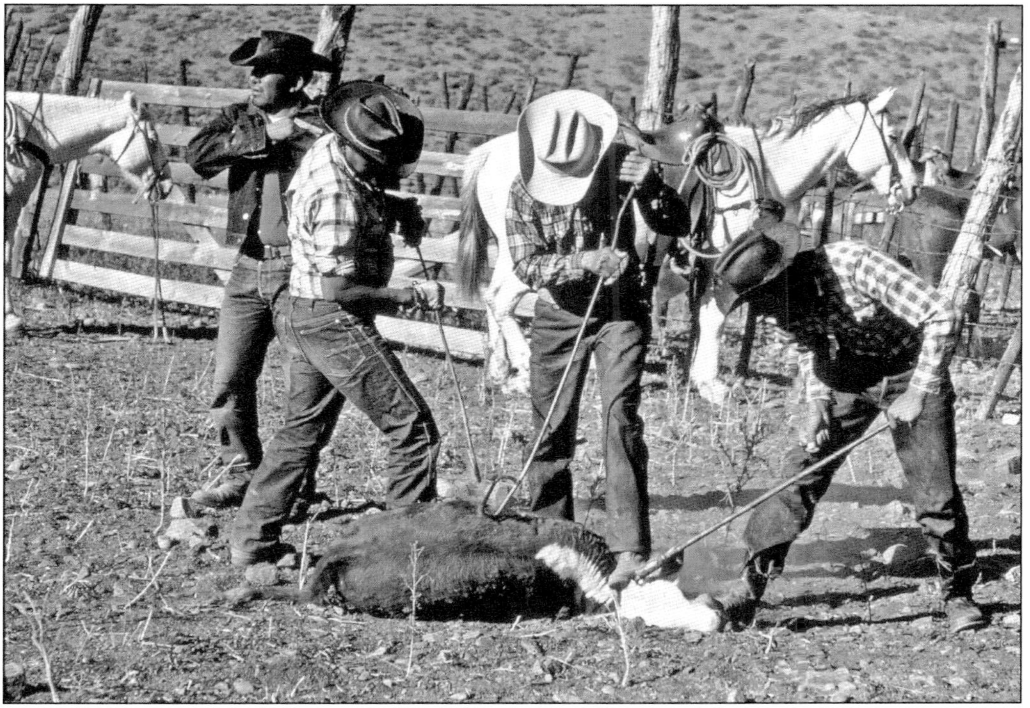

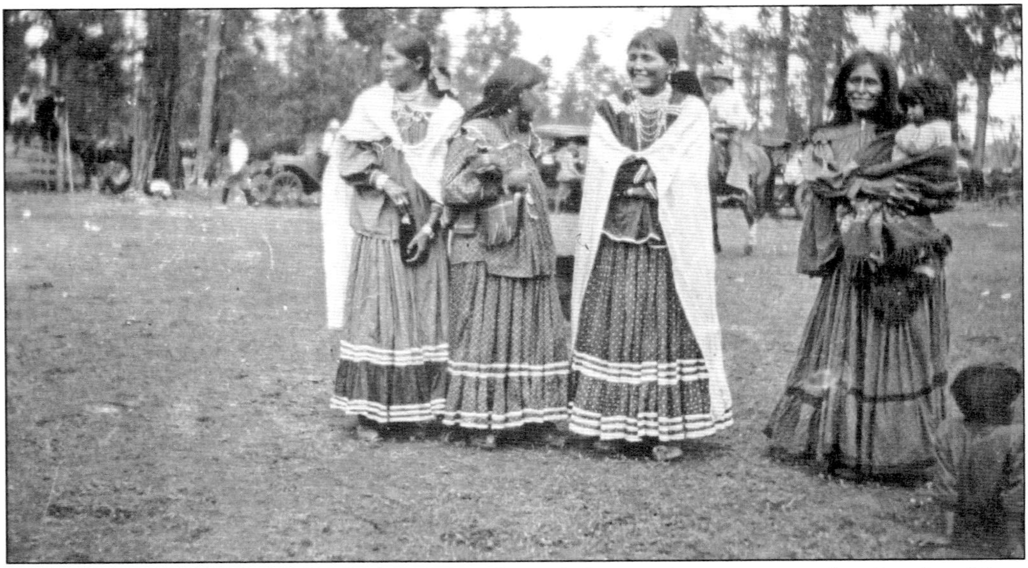

In the early years, both Anglos and Apaches depended upon the assistance of each other. Mary Ann McNeil described sewing skirts for Apache women, with each skirt using 10 yards of material (as illustrated in these Apache women, possibly in Lakeside). Shawls were often worn by the women. (Karen Schuck LaDuke.)

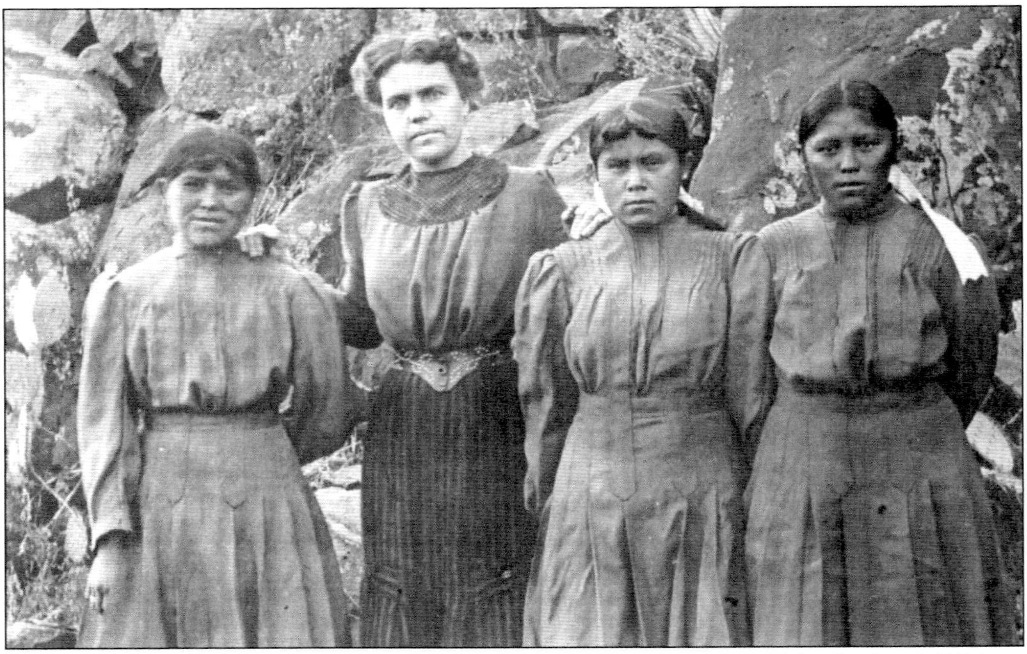

Maybelle "Aunt Belle" Stock Seymore was widowed at age 21 when, in 1905, her husband, William Alma, went to Ely, Nevada, to work in the mines. The mining company was drilling test holes, and Seymore was in a 30-40-foot hole sending debris up in a bucket. He complained of "bad air" and was brought up but then passed out, falling backward into the hole. Aunt Belle then began her life raising her two boys, Roy and Harl "Hod." She worked at Fort Apache supervising Apache girls who worked as domestics. (Beatrice Jarvis.)

Two

Mormon Settlers

In 1880, Emma Oliver came to Arizona from Utah with her parents. After a three-month trip (because they were driving about 300 head of cattle) and after spending a few months working on the railroad at Holbrook, the family settled at Adair. They "built houses, from logs cut from the timber," wrote Emma's brother William, "got range for our stock, and prepared land for farming. It was very hard to get started in this new country. We had to take any kind of work we could get—driving mail, hauling freight, punching cows, or any other kind of work available. We all helped each other. We built the houses, made ditches, and fenced the land. It was very hard pickings until we got our first crop. After that we got along fine. . . . We exchanged things with one another. Some would have meat to exchange for flour or potatoes or molasses."

Mormons who settled this area were scattered from Adair to Fort Apache. Their ward (similar to a parish) had no central meeting place; the bishop lived in Fair View, with counselors in Ellsworth and Adair. Then in 1903, many moved into Show Low proper; Forestdale and Adair were abandoned.

In 1913, Thomas Riley Greer noted, in what he called "A Community Survey," 39 houses and 28 barns, with the post office in the center of town and the school on a hill. Four families got water from wells; the rest got water from the creek. Eleven families had comfortable homes, 18 families needed better homes, 9 houses needed repair, and one home was built that year. The town had one sawmill, two stores, and no bank. He calculated about 50 went to Sunday school and 38 to church each week, but about 200 people "seldom go to church." There were 1,100 acres of land under cultivation, mostly hay but two orchards. Five families owned sheep, 21 men worked with cattle, and 3 teachers were hired. "Indians live here," he said, and "it is about 2½ miles from one end of town to the other."

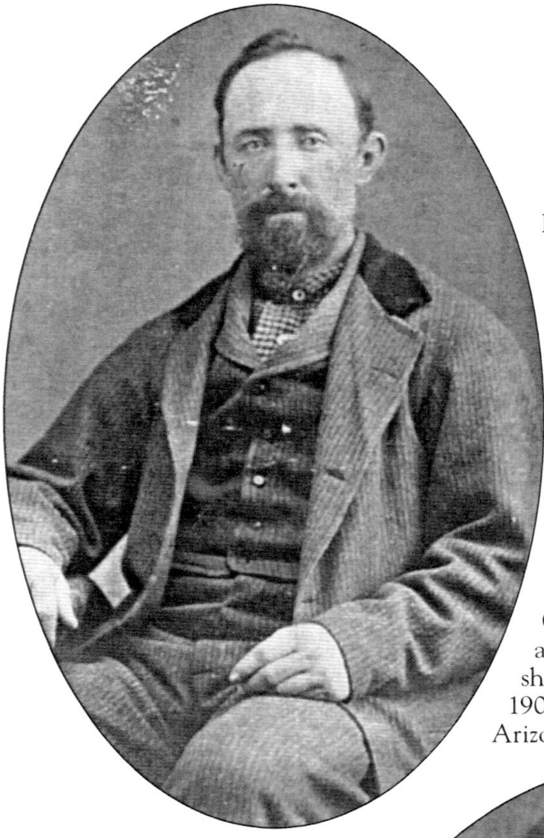

In early spring 1903, Huning wanted to sell all his Arizona property and move to California. William J. Flake (left) had the reputation and capital to make the purchase, which required borrowing some of the $13,500. Flake then divided the land with John H. Willis (below), Abner and Frank Ellsworth, James C. Owens, and Neils Hansen (half share). An epitaph that has been applied to Flake is, "He bought ranches; he made them towns." Show Low was the last property Flake bought for this purpose. Part of this purchase included a large number of wild horses east of Show Low. In July, Flake's sons Osmer and Joel sold 46 partly broken horses around Pleasant Valley. Additional horses were shipped by rail to Texas and Mississippi in 1905, 1906, and 1907. (Left, Beulah Stratton; below, Arizona State Archives 97-9573.)

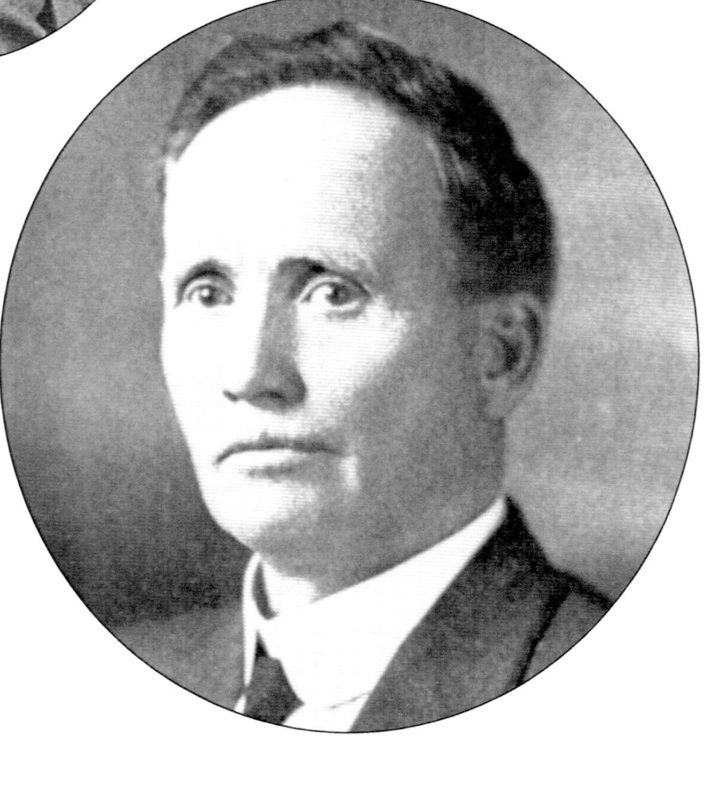

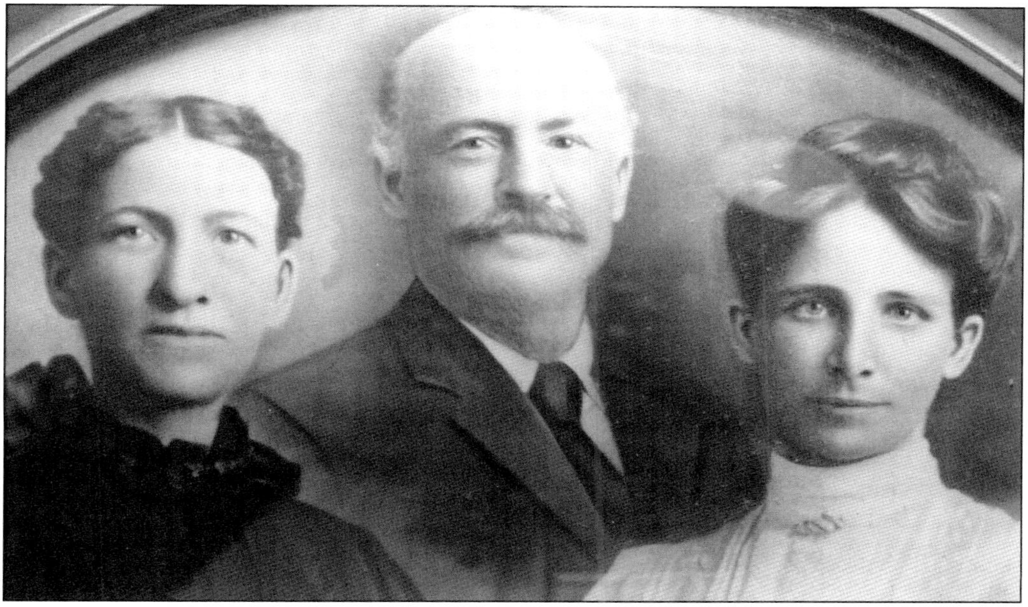

James C. Owens (above center) came with his family to Cooley's ranch in late fall 1878. Here he met and married Cecelia Cluff (above left). They lived in Woodruff much of their early married life, but the 1953 Show Low chapel dedication book states, "The moving of the family to Show Low in May [1903] was one of the happiest experiences that came into the lives of Clark and Cecelia as they loved the mountains and thrilled at the thought of building a town and new home in the little valley where they had first met." After Cecelia's death in 1907, Owens married Adah Porter (above right). Owens was bishop of the Show Low Ward from 1903 to 1919. His counselors were Frank Ellsworth (below with wife, Edna Merrell) and Willard Whipple. (Above, Elizabeth Nikolaus collection; below, Ardell Ellsworth.)

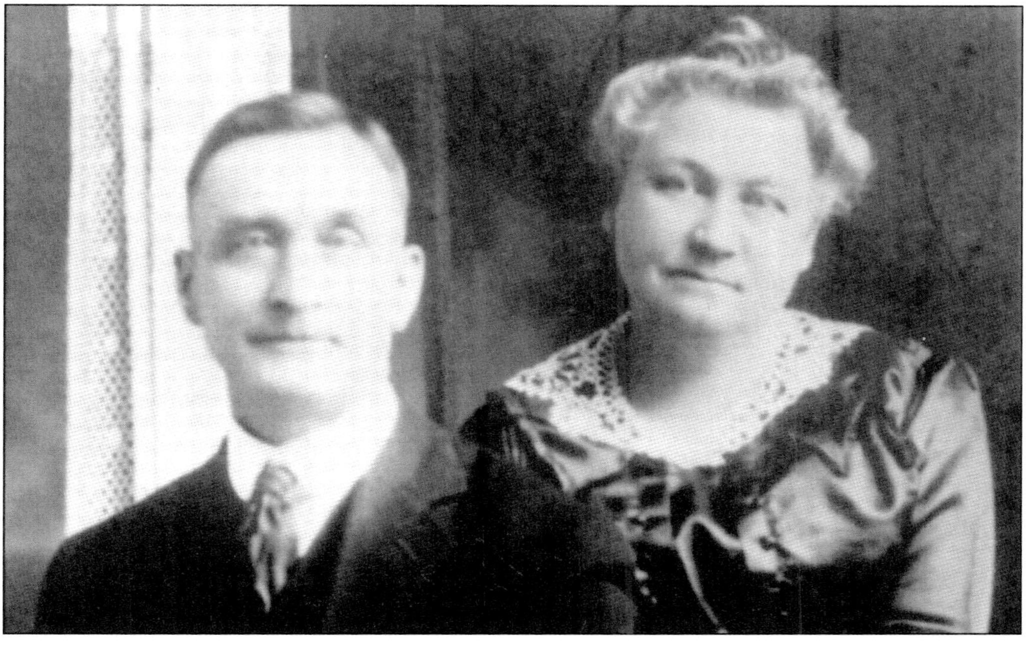

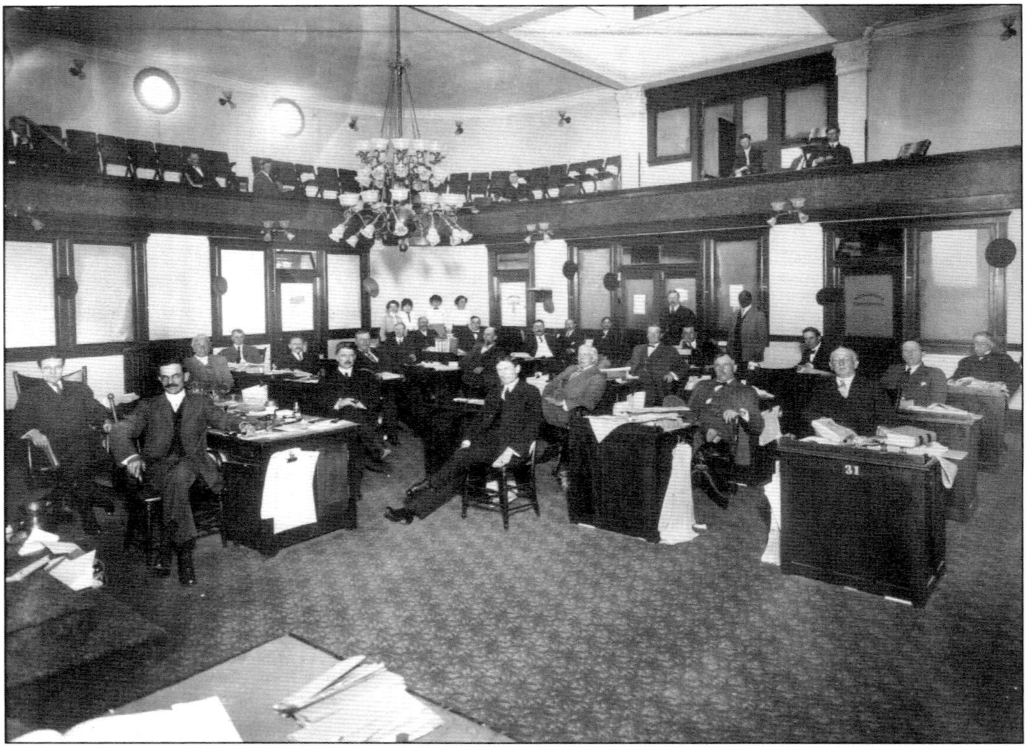

John Henry Willis held many civic offices. When Navajo County was formed, he was appointed a member of the Board of Supervisors and then reelected. He was a member of the Territorial Convention, drafting the Arizona constitution before Arizona was admitted as a state in 1912. He was then elected the first state senator of Navajo County (above, 1912–1913). (Arizona State Archives 99-1219.)

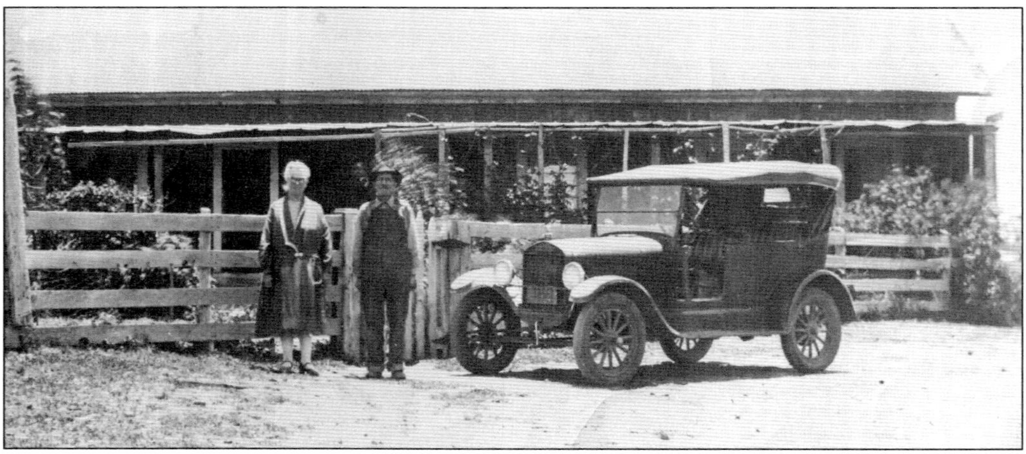

When the Huning purchase was complete, W. D. Rencher was hired to survey the town site. Fields and home sites were divided and lots drawn; then the trading began. William Flake lived in the Huning home, James Owens in the Cooley White House, and Willard Whipple lived in the Huning men's quarters (above with his wife, Emma). This is reputed to be the site of the legendary card game. (Beatrice Jarvis.)

Jens Peter Hansen came to America from Denmark in 1890 with his father. They settled about four miles south of Show Low and built a barn with a floor suitable for both dancing and threshing wheat. In 1900, he married Sofia Pederson, also from Denmark. The photograph at right was taken in 1913, when they took their children to the Salt Lake City Temple. The children are, from left to right, (first row) Alfred and Orson; (second row) Anna, Emma, and Christina. Sofia died in 1919, leaving seven children from age 2 to 15. Jens Peter did not marry again and raised the children by himself. Below, Ruby Brewer takes a dip with an unidentified little boy in the tank at their ranch. (Right, Lois Adams Lemons; below, Dixie Stock Gillespie.)

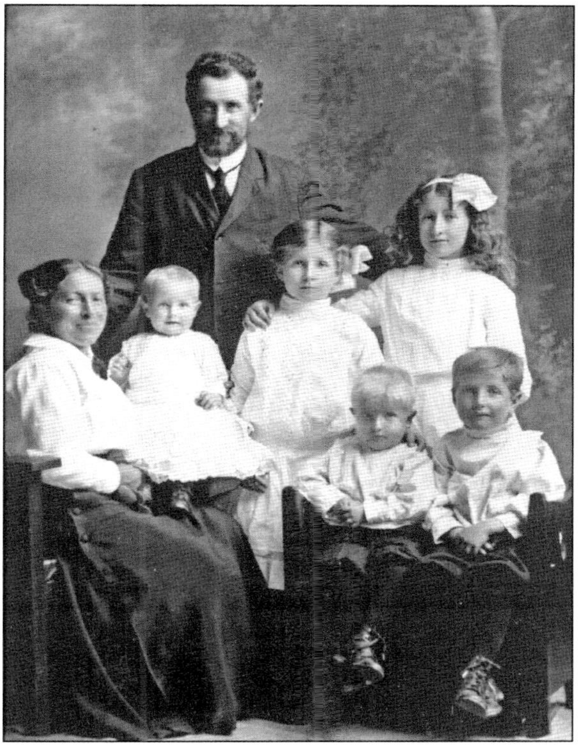

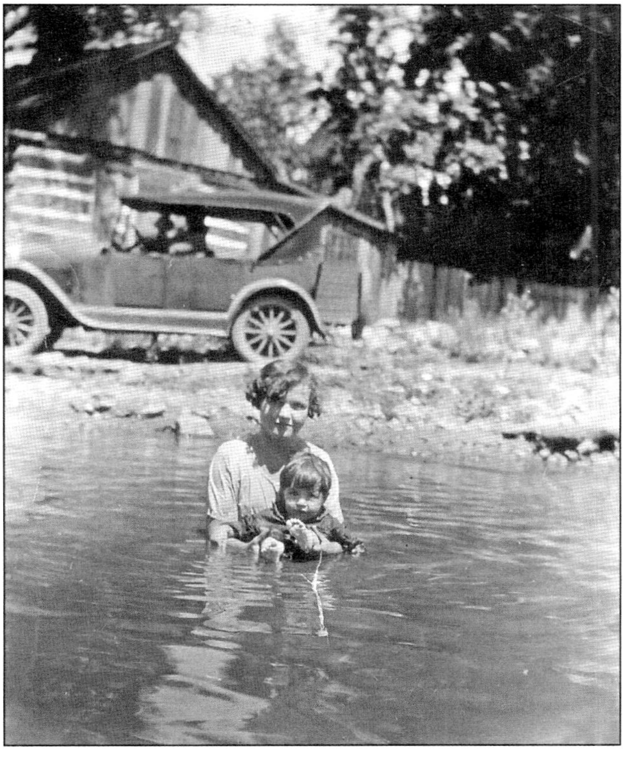

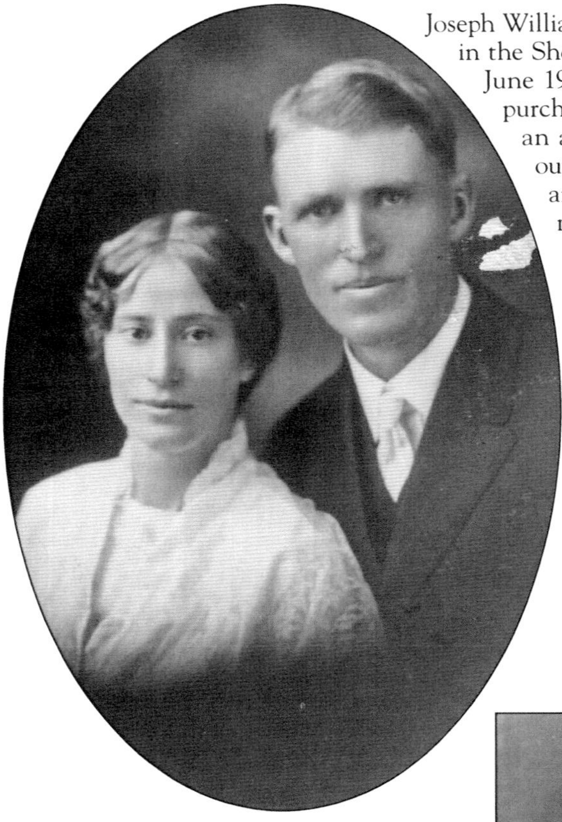

Joseph William "Bill" Nikolaus was the first man raised in the Show Low area to serve a foreign mission. In June 1913, he left for Holland. While there, he purchased a violin and took lessons, becoming an accomplished violinist. When war broke out in 1914, he returned to the United States and finished his mission in Pennsylvania. He married Maggie Mills (left), daughter of Dan and Sarah Mills. (Beatrice Jarvis.)

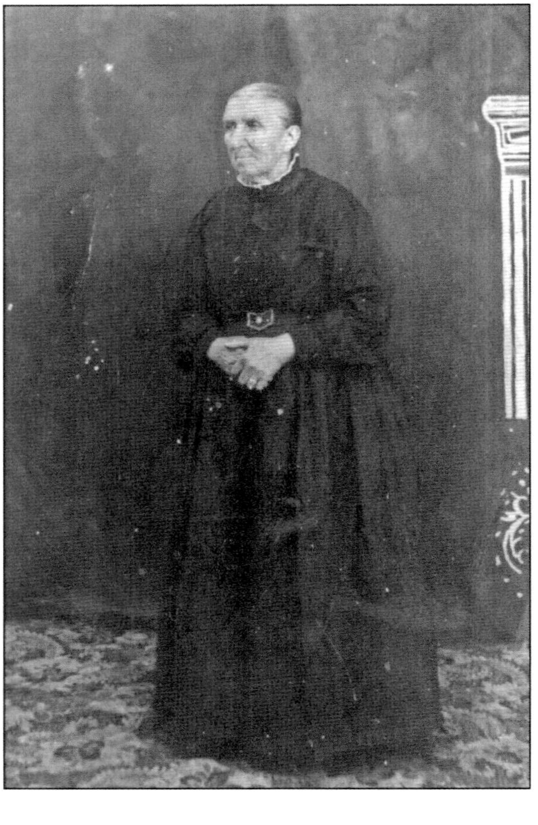

In 1953, many Show Low pioneers were memorialized in a poem, "Our Heritage." Adelaide Laxton (at right in 1898), a widow for 25 years, was remembered because "At a Fast Day Sunday meeting / Grandmother Laxton always rose and spoke. . . . / She made a picture in her quaint black cape and hat." Jens Niels Hansen was remembered because he always spoke in Danish: "Uncle bore a faithful testimony / though we couldn't understand him." (Elizabeth Nikolaus collection.)

Franz "Frank" Ludwig Nikolaus, born in Germany in 1856, immigrated to the United States at age 16 to escape military service. Coming west, he stayed with the Hancocks in Taylor and joined the LDS Church. He married Mary Laxton, and they had four children: Joseph, Mary Louise, Frank Jr. (right), and Henry. In 1910, Frank Jr. was killed crossing Show Low Creek when his horse slipped and fell on him. (Beatrice Jarvis.)

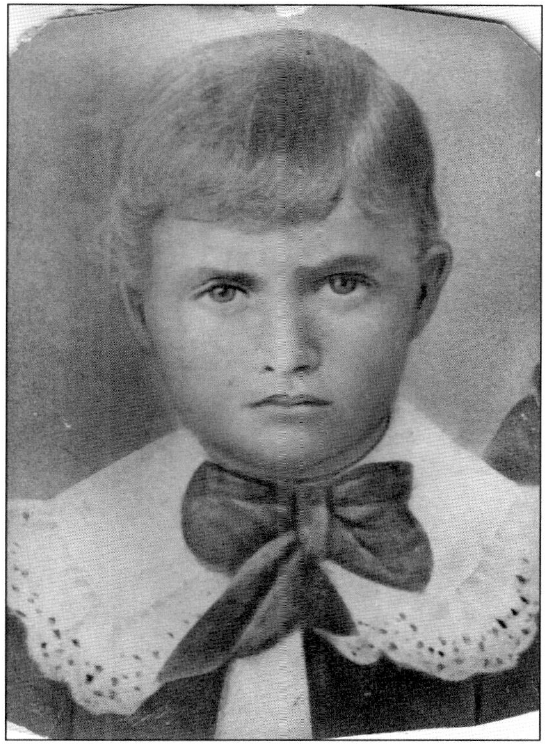

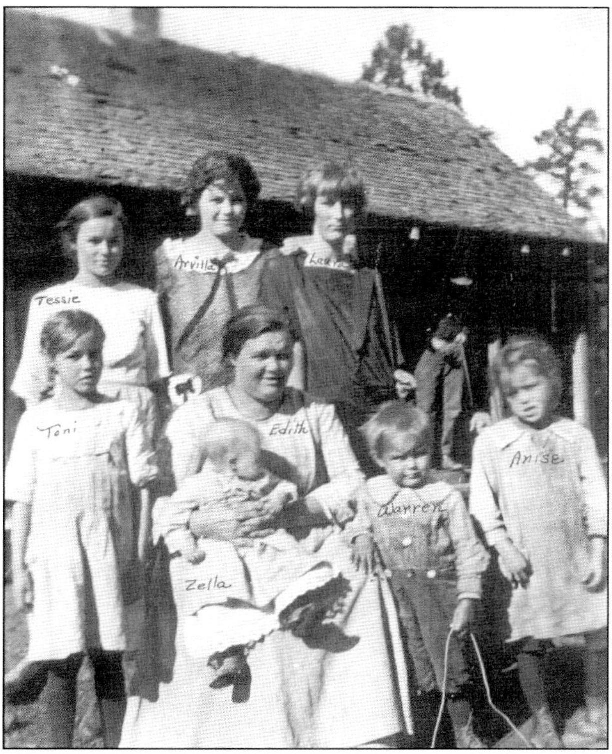

Many settlers homesteaded land, including Benjamin and Edith Peterson McNeil. Married in Luna, New Mexico, in 1900, they then traveled to Colonia Morales, Mexico, and returned in 1912 to homestead three miles west of Show Low. Their house was 37 by 17 feet (two rooms) and made of hand-adzed squared logs. Edith (center) is pictured at left with some of her younger children and Laura Stratton McNeil (back row, extreme right), who was married to Edith's son Jim. Ben (maybe camera shy) is standing on the porch. (Delores Perkins Padilla.)

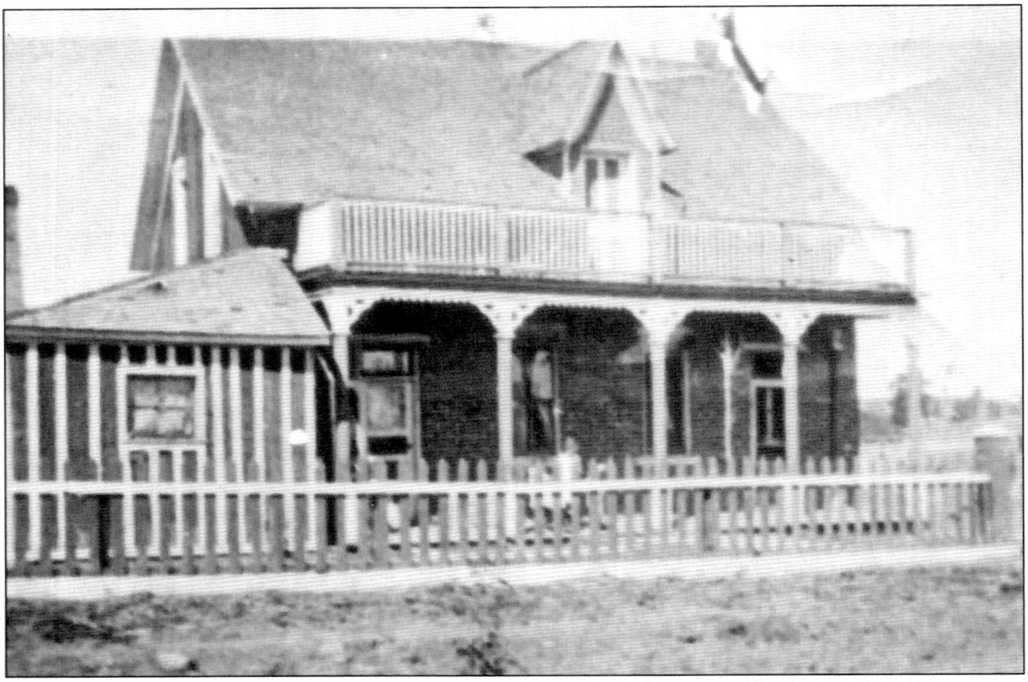

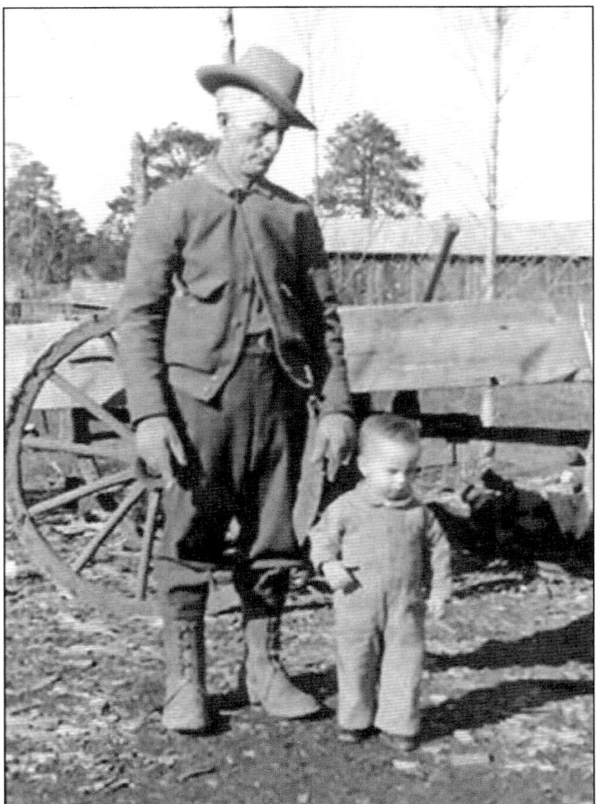

Clara Woolford moved to Show Low in 1905 after her husband, Joseph, a physician in St. Johns, died. Her sons built her a large home, and she provided meals and rooms for travelers. This home was later bought by Liona and Marcena Hansen Penrod (above). The Penrods added the front porch and the addition on the left. They continued to operate it as a hotel and had stables for horses of freighters and visitors to Fort Apache. At left is Liona Penrod with his grandson, James "Jimmy" Stock, about 1935. (Above, Kathy Mills Tippets; left, Lloyd Stock.)

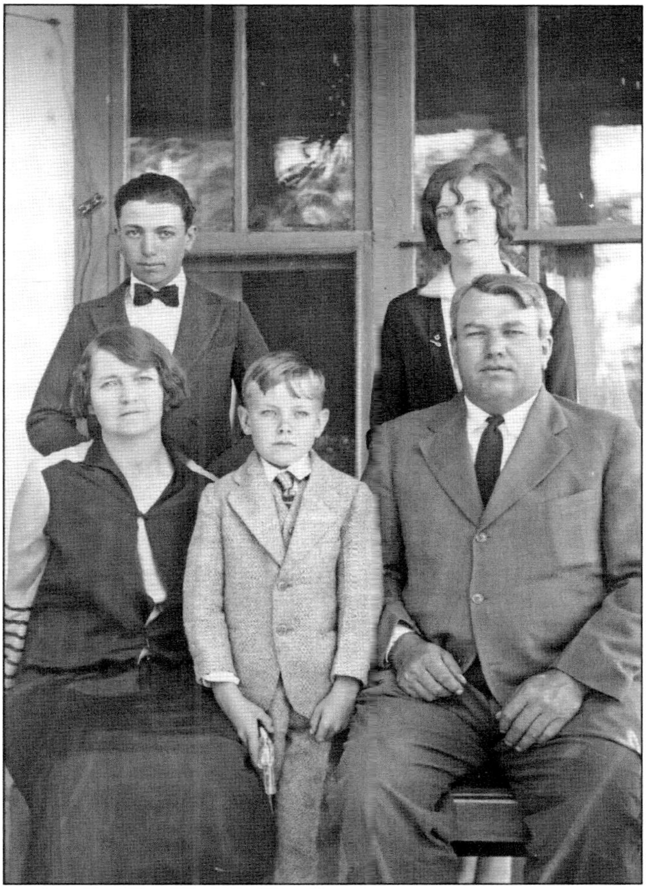

Pictured at right is Clara and Joseph Woolford's son, George, with his wife, Lillie Hall, and children George Jr. and Mildred, with Joseph ("Joe") between his parents. Note the toy glass gun filled with candy that Joe is holding. (Years later, Joe Woolford was a founder of the Show Low Historical Society.) Pictured below is the 2003 Woolford family entry for Show Low's parade. George Jr. (pictured below on the float with his wife, Nell Brimhall) originally built Woolford's Garage, and now the garage is operated by the second and third generations, Doug Woolford and son Jerry. (Both, SLHisSoc Museum.)

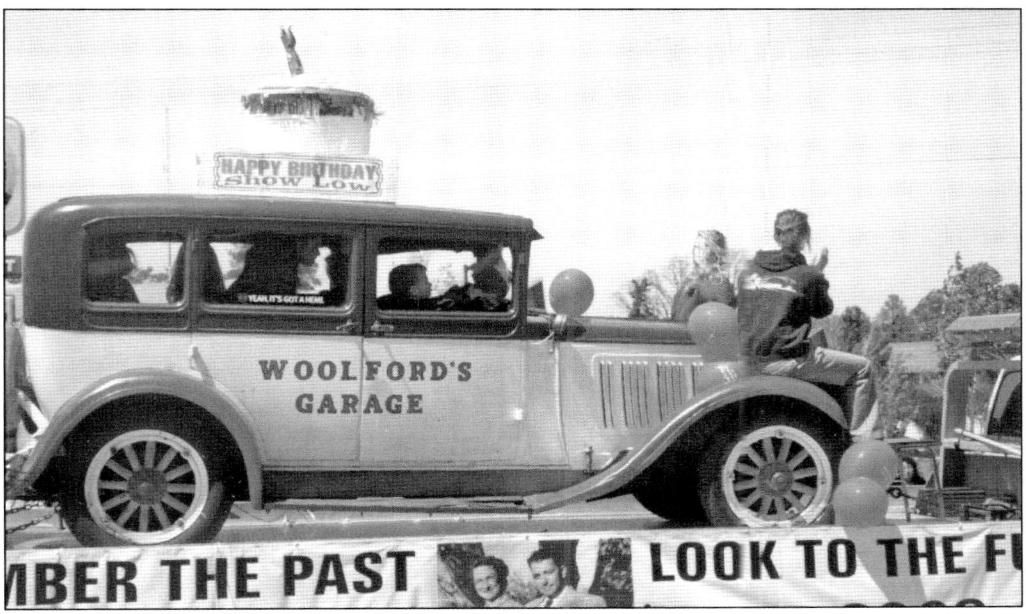

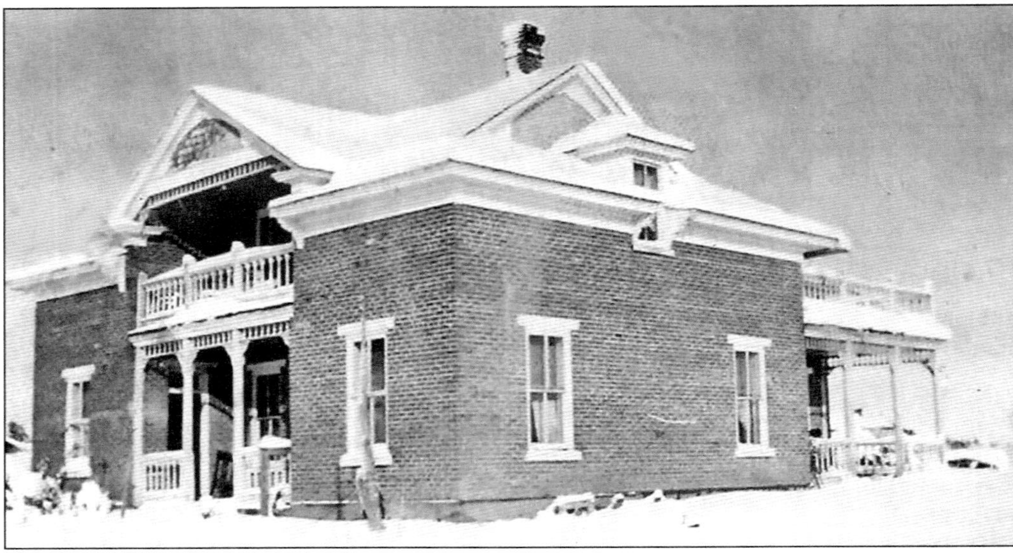

With the abundance of lumber surrounding the town, most homes in Show Low were frame houses. However, there were four brick homes: the Charles Savage home, the Abner and Betsey Ellsworth home (above), the James and Adah Owens home, and the Charles and Margaret Reidhead home. For about two years in the early 1910s, there was a brick kiln on the Ellsworth property. All of these homes were built in that era. Pictured below is the Abner and Betsy Ann Ellsworth family about 1919. (Both, Sylvia Ricks.)

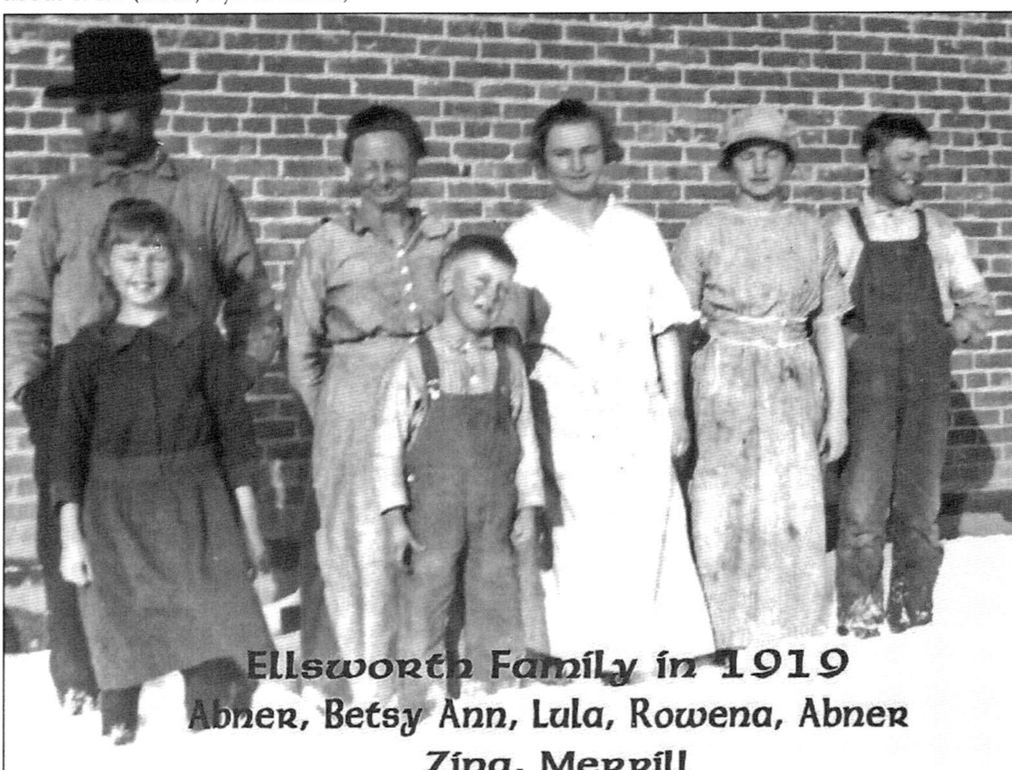

The Charles Savage home (right) was north of the downtown LDS Church. The Savage children included Lettie (married Sid Toliver), Ruby, Arthur (married Myrtle Gibson), and Russell (married Rose Ramsay). When Arthur and Myrtle married, their home on the north side of Main Street was also referred to as the "Savage home." This house burned in the 1940s, and components were later used in Fred and Emma Hansen Adams's home. (Hilda Frost.)

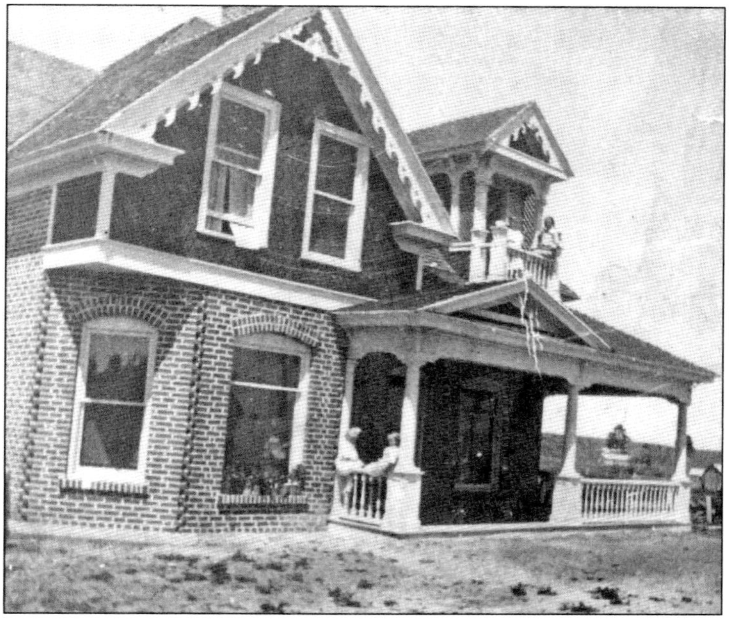

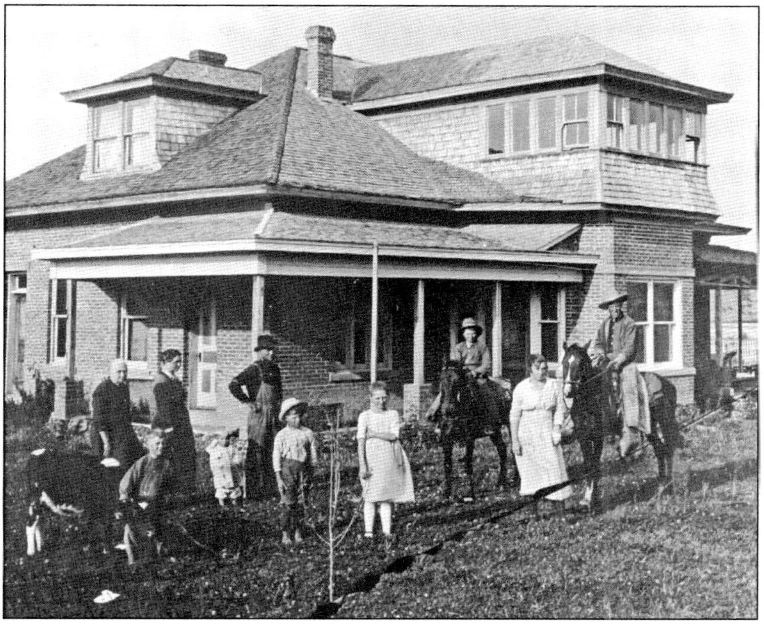

The Reidhead home is the only early brick home now livable. Pictured here are members of the Reidhead family about 1917: from left to right, grandmother Lucinda Reidhead, Karl, mother Margaret, Guy, father Charles, Joseph, Lavonne, Ralph, Loa, and Roy. (Beatrice Jarvis.)

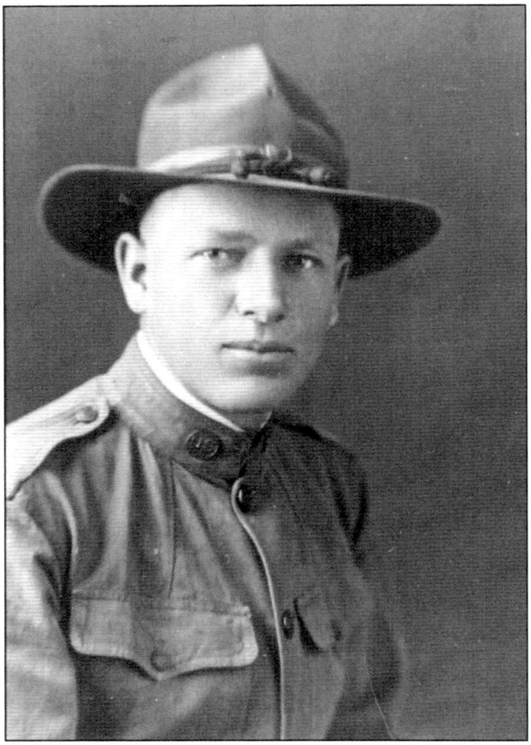

Two of the times when young men left the area were for the military and to serve a mission for the LDS Church. Pictured at left is Fred Adams, who served in the military from September 1917 to March 1919. Pictured below is Adams as a missionary in Michigan (from January 1920 to January 1922). Adams married Emma Hansen and lived in Show Low until 1960. (Both, Helen Adams Capps.)

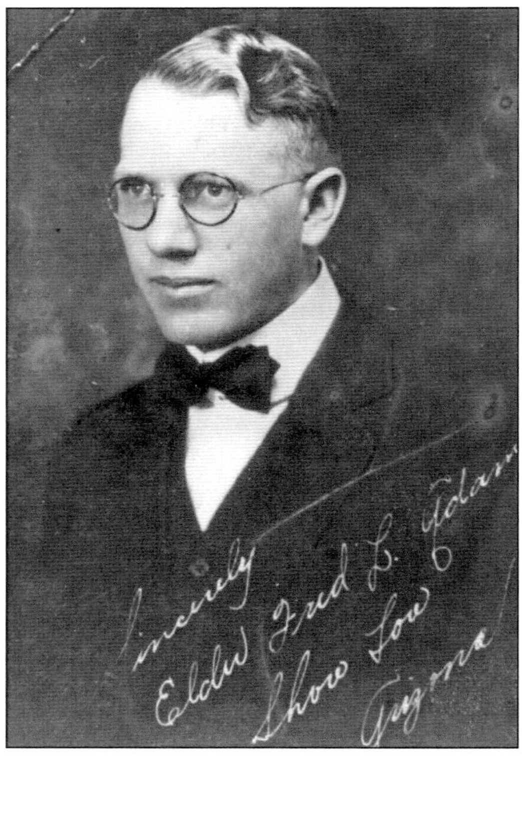

Brothers Clyde (left) and Marion "Trix" Merrell both were in France during World War I. Others who served from Show Low included Jesse Brady, William Brady, Roy Chlarson, LeRoy Ellsworth, Daniel McNeil, Don Carlos McNeil, Fred McNeil, George Reidhead, Columbus Whipple, John Whipple, Joseph Whipple, and Hosea Wheat. Later Clyde Merrell kept bees and never got stung, even though he would tend the bees without protective gear. (Idella Seymore.)

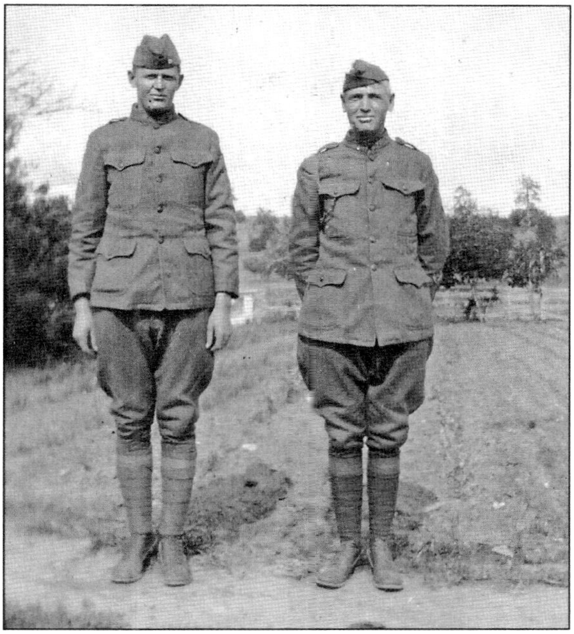

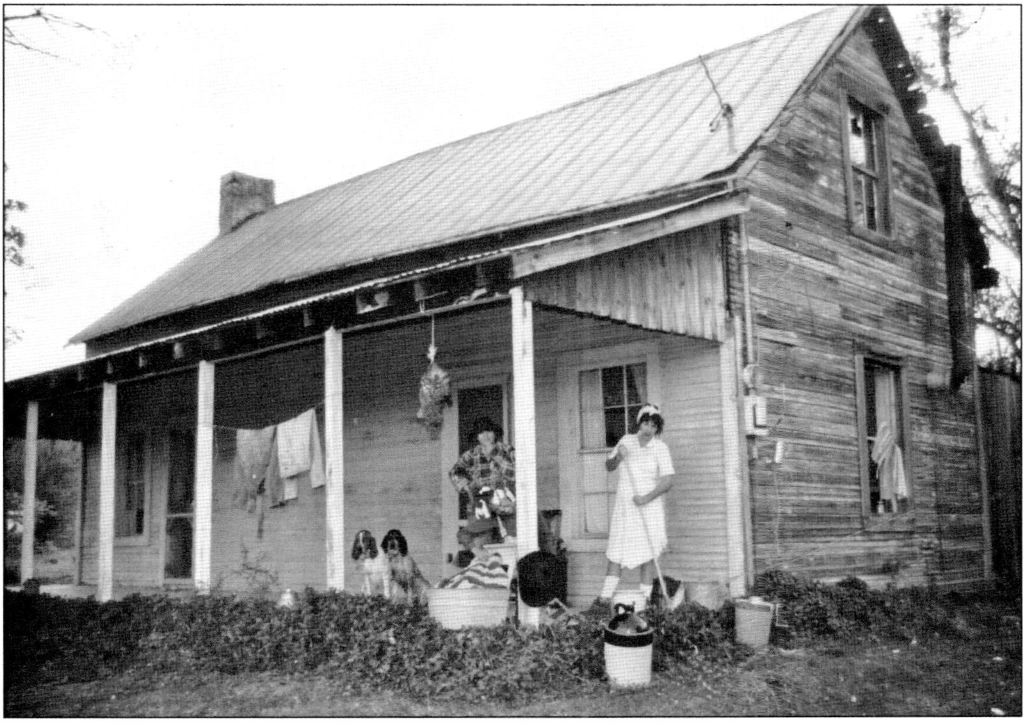

A few years ago, when looking for a picture to advertise her cleaning business, Deborah Austin borrowed two hound dogs, added some artifacts, included two employees, and photographed Clyde and Trix Merrell's abandoned home on South White Mountain Road. This is a self-portrait (her tripod is out of sight on the right). Daryl Seymore said that his great-uncles' home was taken down piece by piece, with the buyers planning to reassemble it. (Photograph by Deborah Austin.)

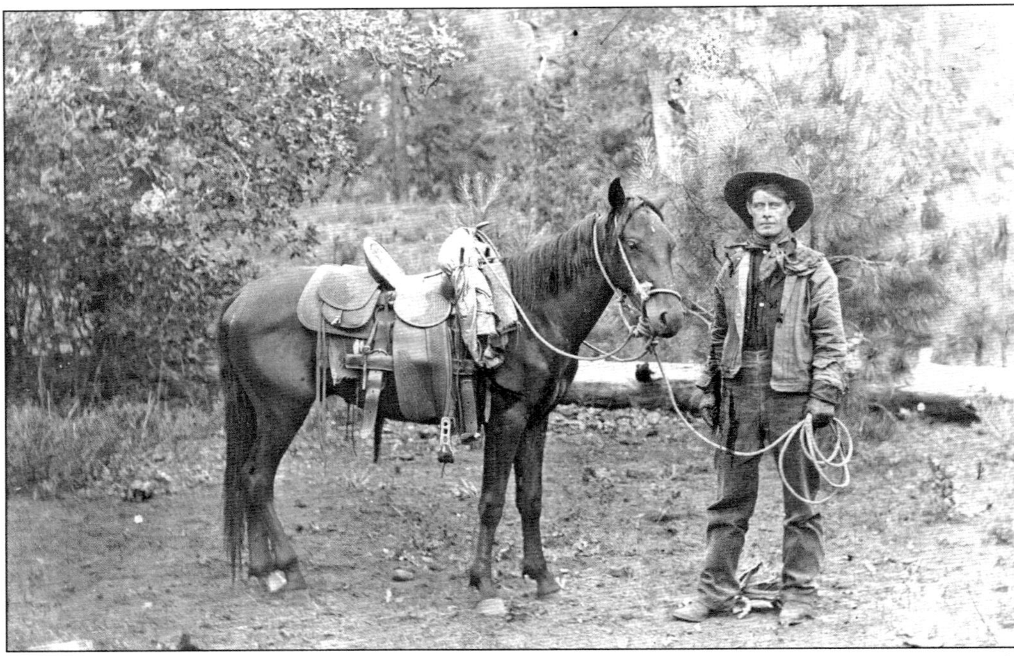

Estella Jacobson was born in Draper, Utah, in 1892 and married Ray Mills, son of Dan and Sarah, in 1914. In 1920, Ray died, and Estella's brother, Roy (above), came to live with her. Pictured below in the mid-1920s are, most likely from left to right, Ray and Estella's three girls: Marge, Myrtle, and Virginia (with the Relief Society building, left, and church in the background). After Estella died in 1929, Roy continued parenting the girls, even though he never married. According to Debbie West Wood, Myrtle's granddaughter, the three girls loved Roy very much. Roy died in 1934 when the girls were reaching adulthood. (Above, Ray West; below, Shirley Reidhead.)

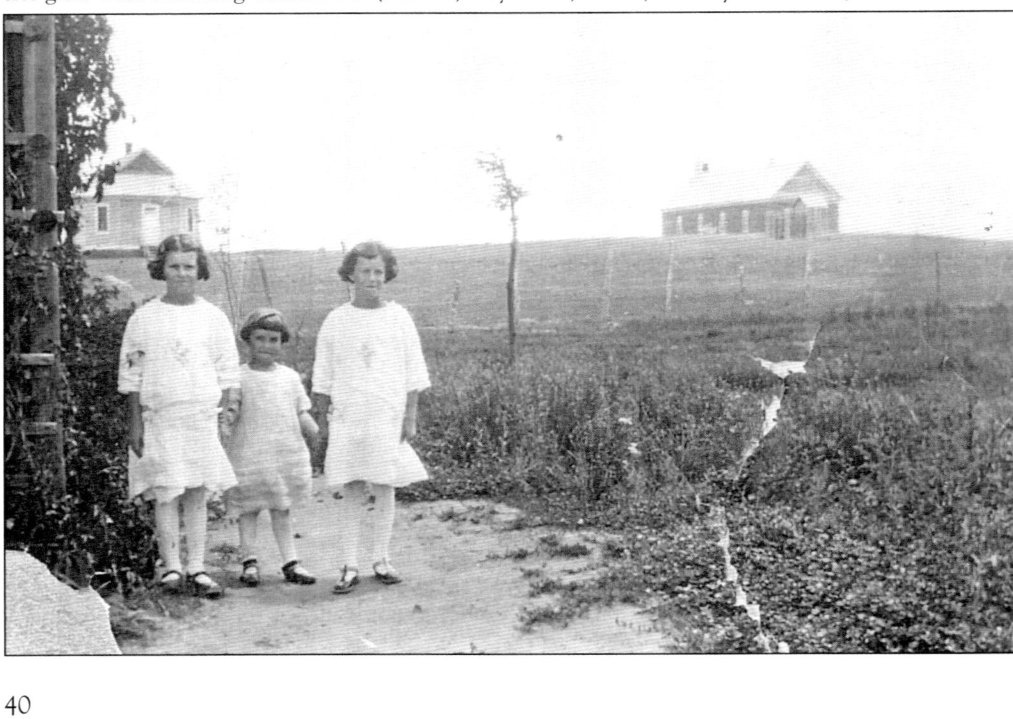

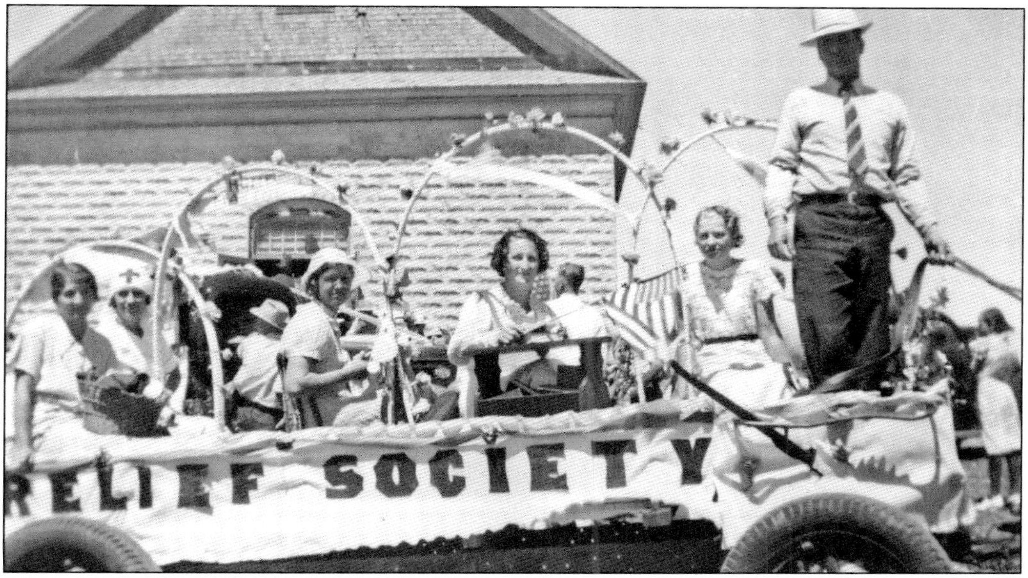

The Fourth of July celebration of 1933 featured this Relief Society float, presumably representing various charitable acts of women in the town. The ladies above include, from left to right, Emma Adams (with a basket of sewing), Nellie P. Mills (nursing), Annie Seymore, Anna H. Gardner (teaching), and Elaine Gardner. The float is in front of the original gray cement-block church; Bishop John L. Willis is standing, holding the reins of the horses pulling the wagon. Others dressed in costume that same day were (right), from left to right, Lavenia Ellsworth, James A. Stratton as Uncle Sam, and Geraldine Savage as Lady Liberty. (Both, Elizabeth Nikolaus collection.)

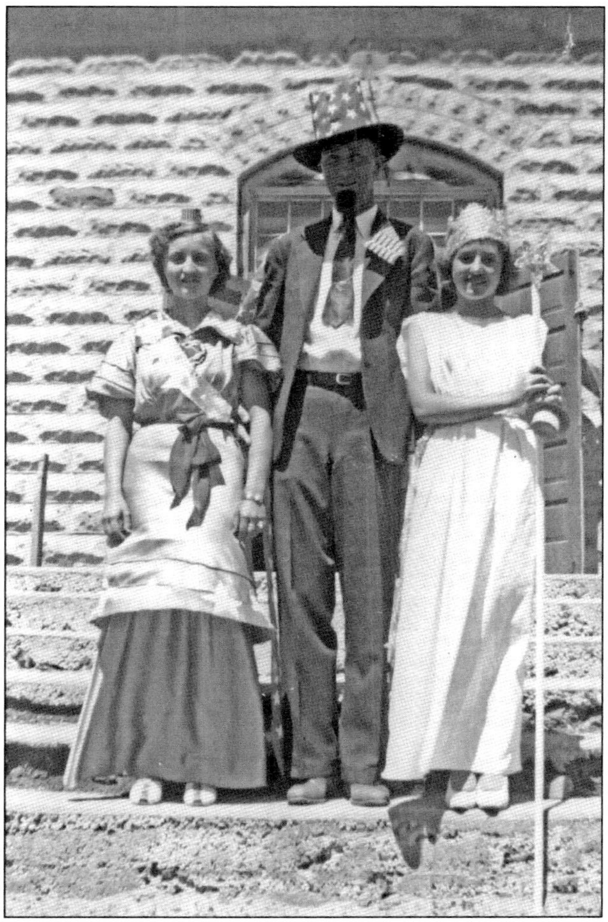

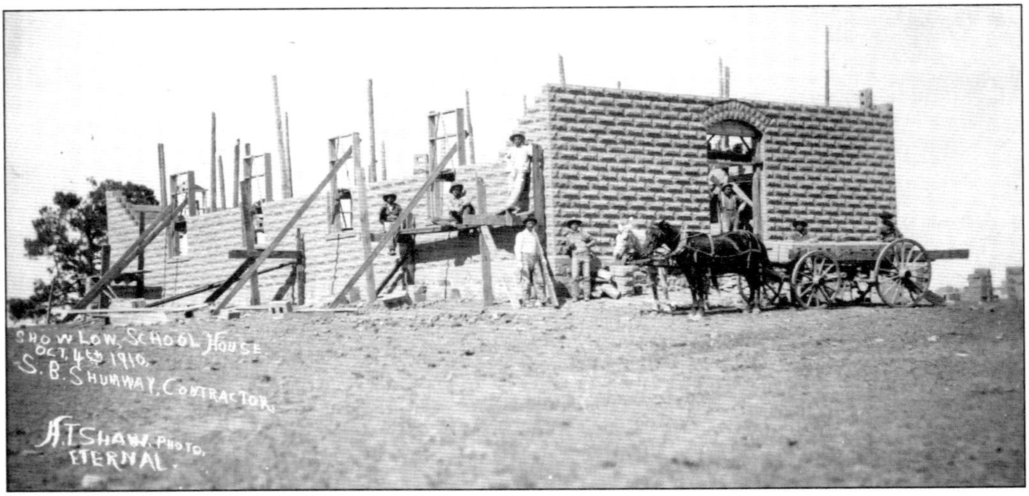

This photograph is labeled "Show Low School House, October 4, 1910," but it is really the LDS Church under construction. With large families and a church that emphasized education, school was held here from 1911–1912 to 1919, when a four-room schoolhouse was completed. Three teachers were assigned rooms, and the fourth room was used for music. (SLHisSoc Museum.)

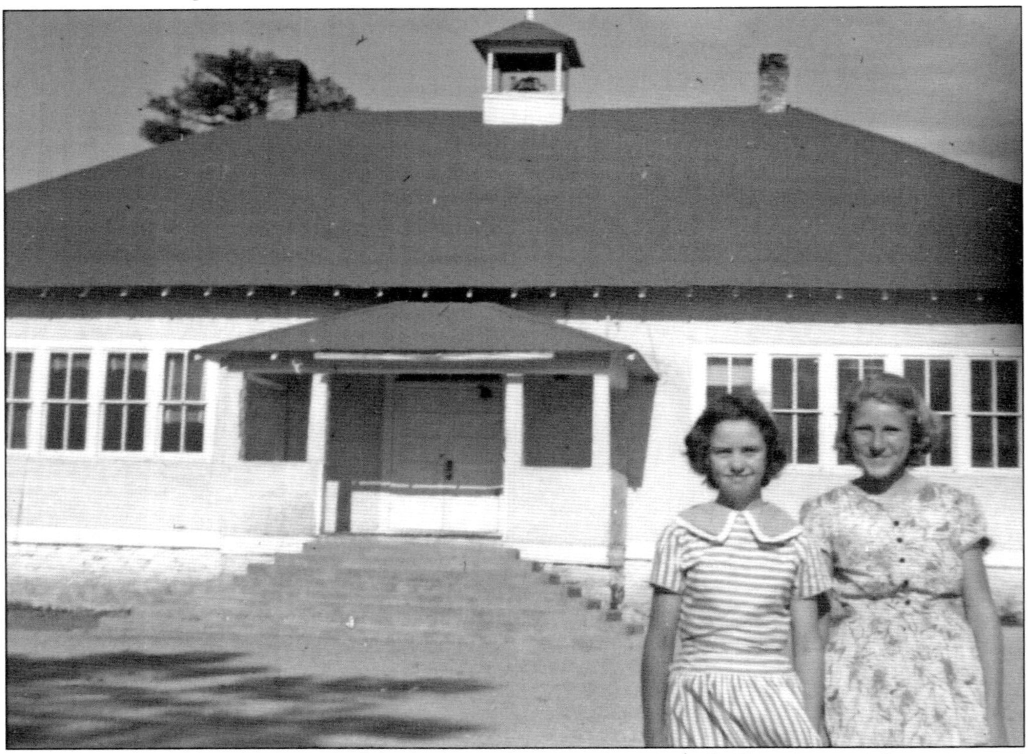

The schoolhouse was used from 1919 to 1974, with Nora McCleve (left) and Lois Adams pictured here in the 1950s. Myrna Tanner described school in the 1940s as "four teachers, each teaching two grades." She said, "I thought then we had the best teachers anywhere, and in retrospect I feel I was not far wrong. Phosia Smith, Ella Chlarson, Leora Kartchner, Ina Ellsworth, and Charles Whipple were exceptional teachers." (Sheila McCleve Stewart.)

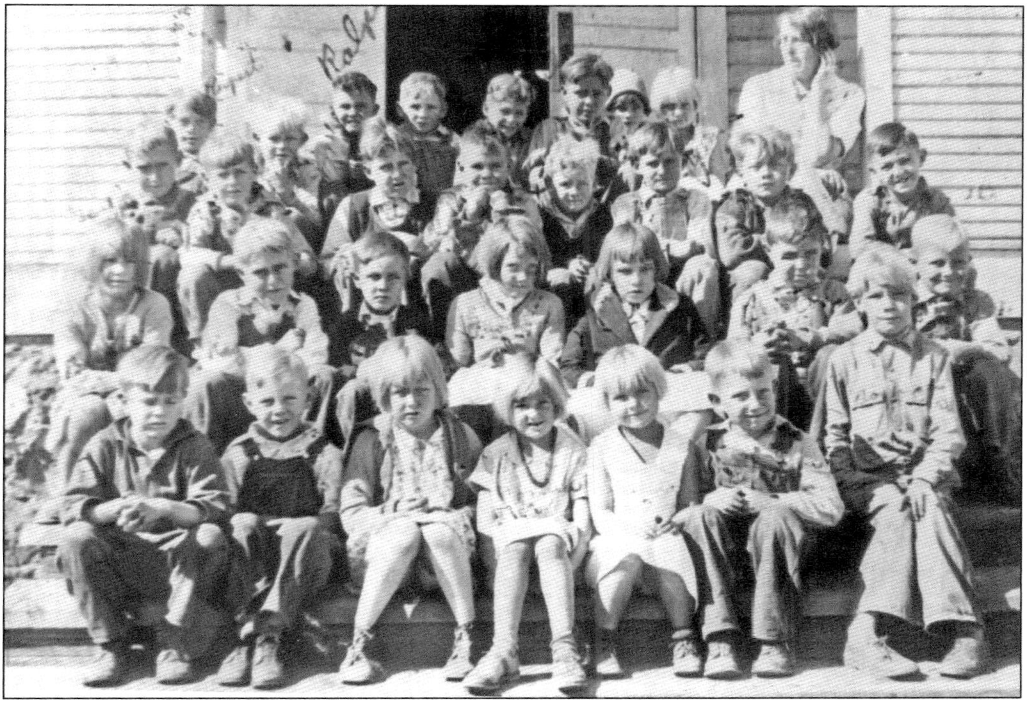

This group of first- and second-grade children (in about 1932) included, from left to right, (first row) Donnie Stock, Phillip Merrell, Maurice Mills, Norma Savage, Norma Owens, Norman Adams, and Norman Burke; (second row) Bessie Adams, Kay Reidhead, Boyd Woolford, Thorella Adams, Naomi Penrod, Benton Adair, and Duane Owens; (third row) Garth Nikolaus, Ronald Mills, Chester Adams, Clarence Taylor, Kenneth Campbell, Jack Reidhead, Ned Whipple, and Otto Mills; (fourth row) Rupert Stock, Dell McNeil, Ralph Taylor, Hal Butler, Derrel Woolford, Charles Adair, Roxie Nikolaus, June Penrod, and teacher Lavenia Peterson. Longtime teacher and principal Charles Whipple is pictured to the right with a new school and his old truck. (Above, Helen Adams Capps; right, Sheila McCleve Stewart.)

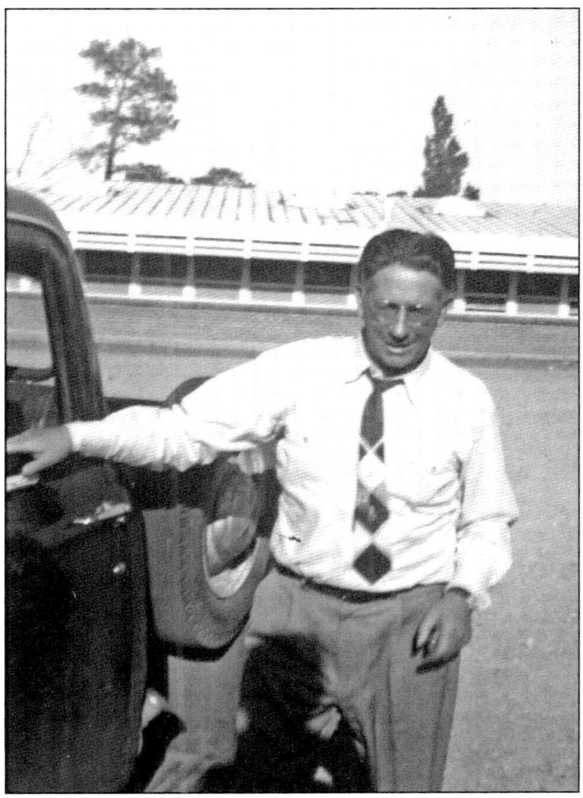

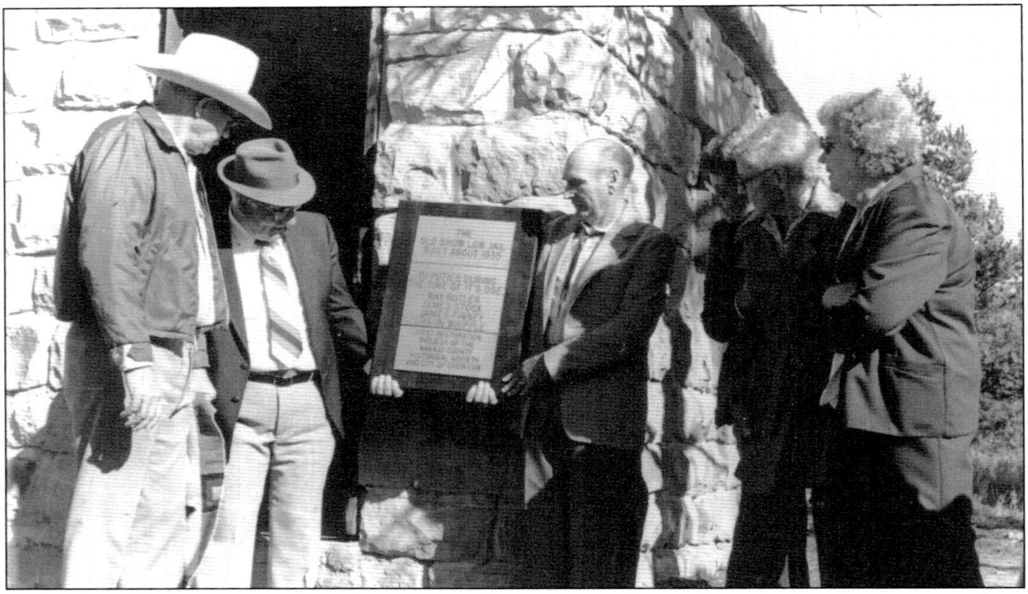

Ray Butler, deputy sheriff, built this jail in the 1930s so he would "no longer have to rope members of a certain family to trees." Attending a restoration celebration in the 1980s are, from left to right, Jim Stock, longtime deputy sheriff; Claude and Hal Butler, sons of Ray Butler; JoAnn Hatch and Leola Finney, daughter and wife of law enforcement officer Jim Finney; and Hilda Frost, daughter of justice of the peace William Henry Lewis. (Hilda Frost.)

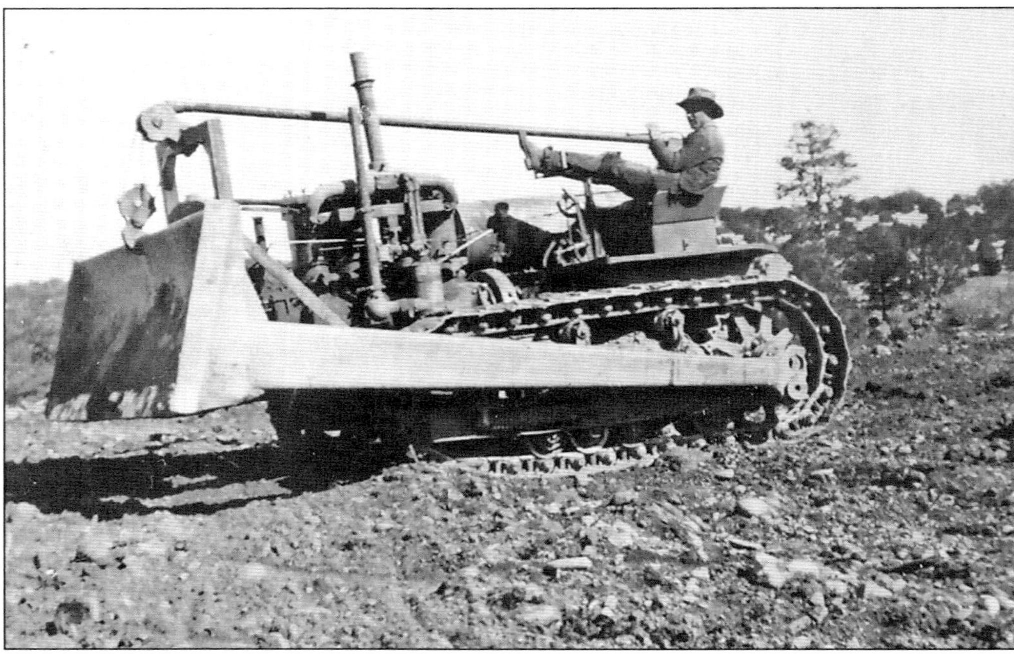

Settlers downriver were always in competition with settlers upriver for precious water to irrigate crops. In 1934, the downriver towns of Snowflake and Taylor received a WPA loan/grant of $148,000 and approved a bond for construction of Lone Pine Dam. Construction began in September 1935, with Leo Frost supervising. Pictured here is Walter Goodman operating a crawler. (Larry Frost.)

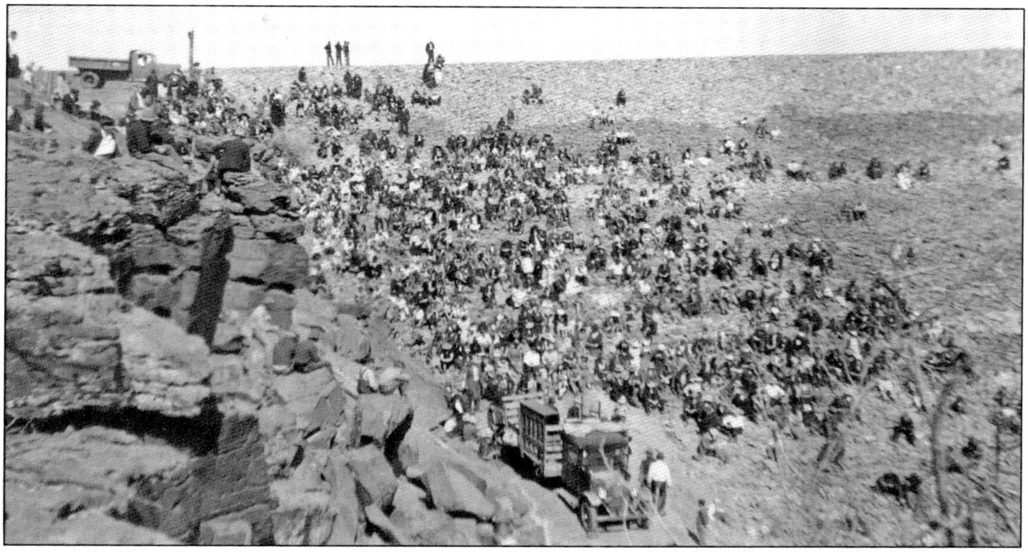

State engineer James B. Girand thought the soil at Lone Pine would hold water and a reservoir could be built to provide reliable irrigation. Leo Frost brought three bulldozers (a 60 Best, an AC Crawler, and a Caterpillar), two dump trucks, a shovel, and teams of horses. An additional dozer was rented from Harry Hagen but had to be returned when construction began on Hagen Hill. Quill Hatch; Lynn Rogers and his brother; Newt Kay; Larry and Joe Frost; and Bill and Mert Richards all worked at the site. "Red" Hutchinson operated the shovel. These photographs show the dam dedication, March 7, 1936. Almost immediately, seep holes formed in the limestone, which the irrigation district tried to seal with clay. An adequate solution was never found. (Both, Hilda Frost.)

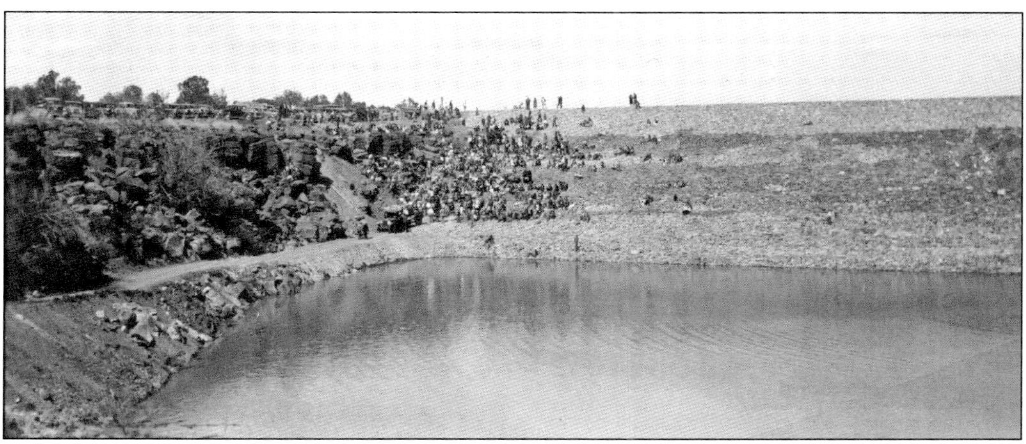

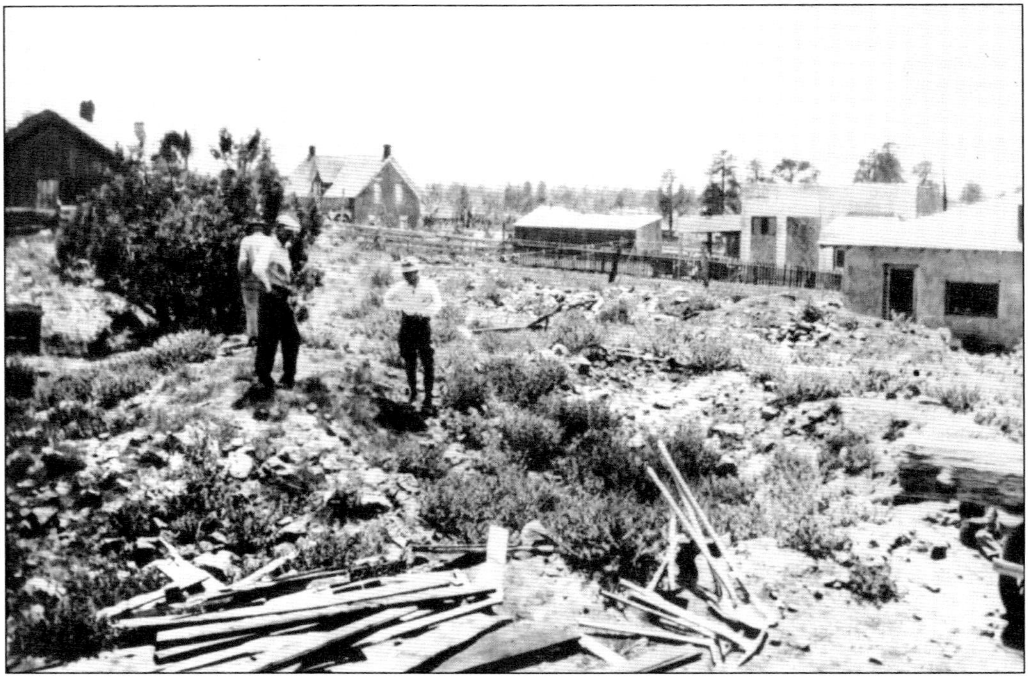

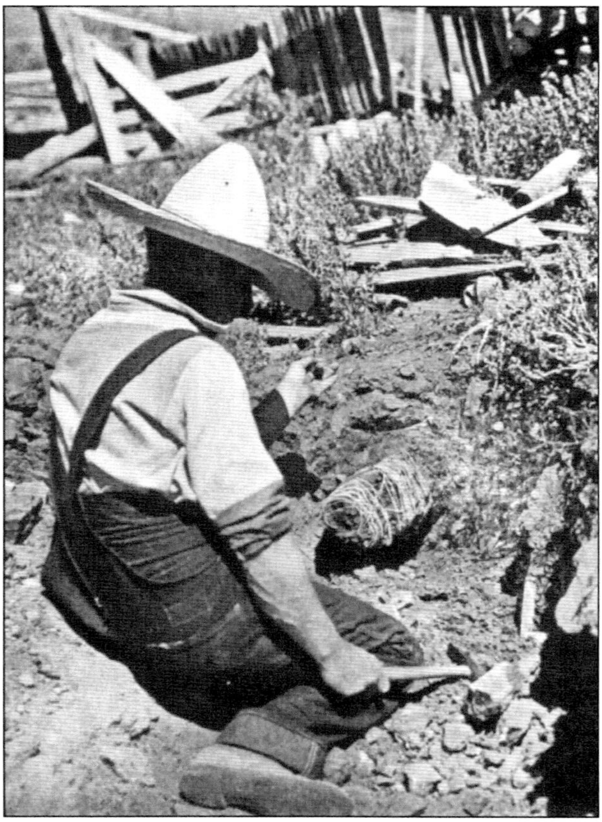

Andrew Ellicott Douglass, a University of Arizona astronomer interested in sunspots, noted that wide and narrow bands in pine trees around Flagstaff corresponded with rainfall. He received a National Geographic Society grant to study beams in both archeological digs and Pueblo homes and kivas currently in use. He then constructed two time lines, one ancient and one recent. In the summer of 1929, Douglass, Emil Haury, and Lyndon Hargrave were excavating in Show Low (above, on Edson Whipple's property). Haury wrote that on June 22, "Reed Whipple . . . exposed a good-sized timber near the surface." Twine was wrapped around the charred log so it could be removed intact; this log became the missing link between the two time lines and was labeled HH-39. Information from the Show Low dig also identified the Great Drought of 1276–1299 AD. (Above, AHS/Tucson 43,294; left, National Geographic.)

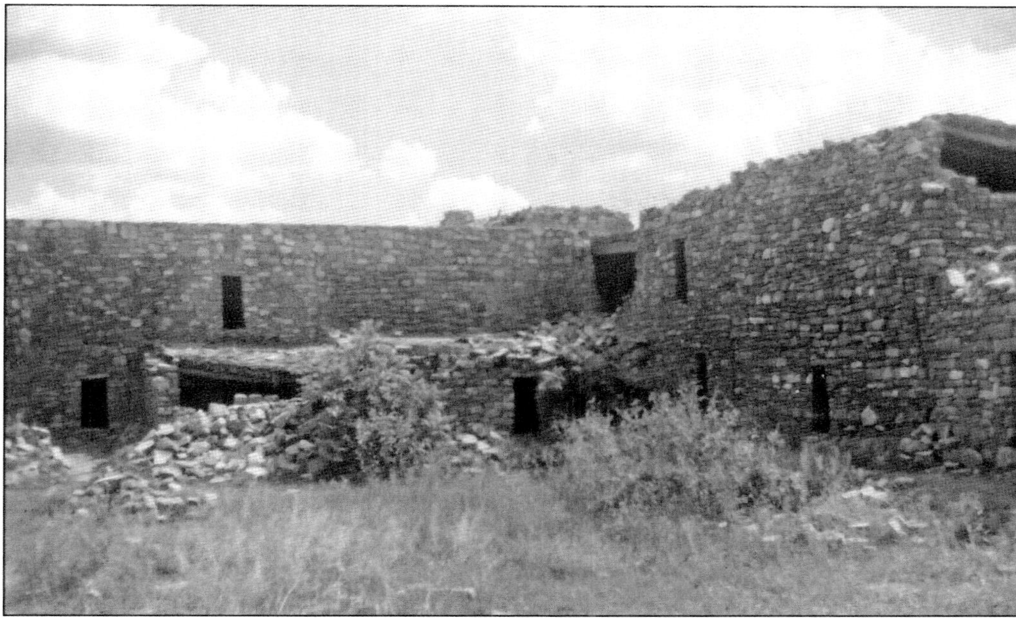

Another important archeologist working in the White Mountains was Byron Cummings, also from the University of Arizona. He brought student workers to the Kinishba site for nine years, starting June 1931. This 1965 photograph shows Cumming's reconstruction of the pueblo, but it was beginning to fall into disrepair again. (Earlene Jarvis Rhoton.)

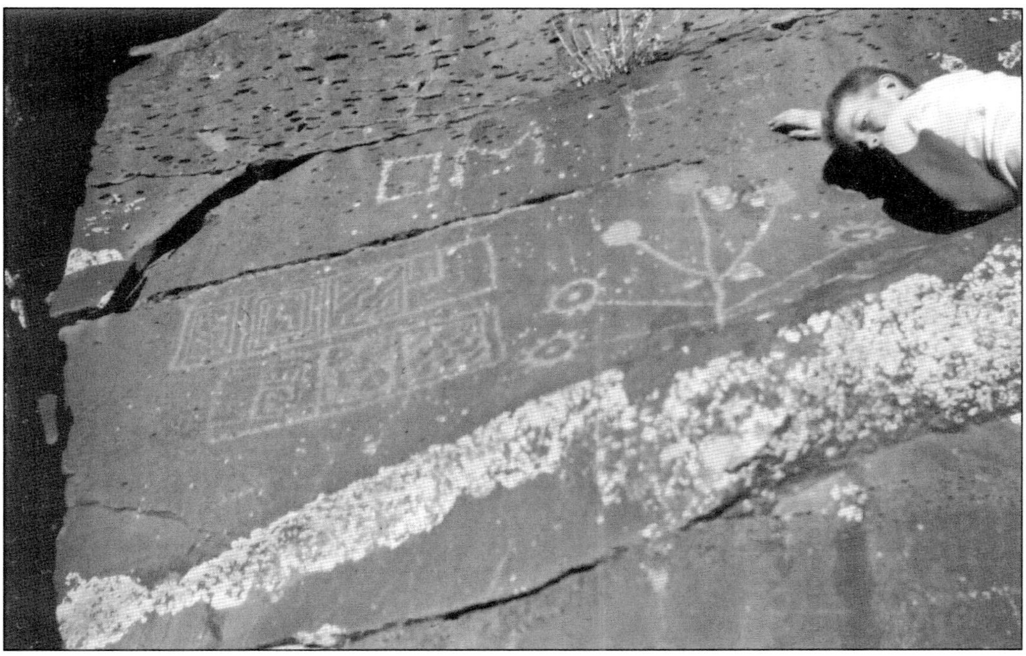

Navajo County is well known for its extensive ancient petroglyphs. This one on north Show Low Creek has been called "The Tree of Life" and has been a popular hiking location for both teenagers and adults. Pictured here is Veldon Seymore, about 1949, during a hike with Mike Huso. (Huso collection.)

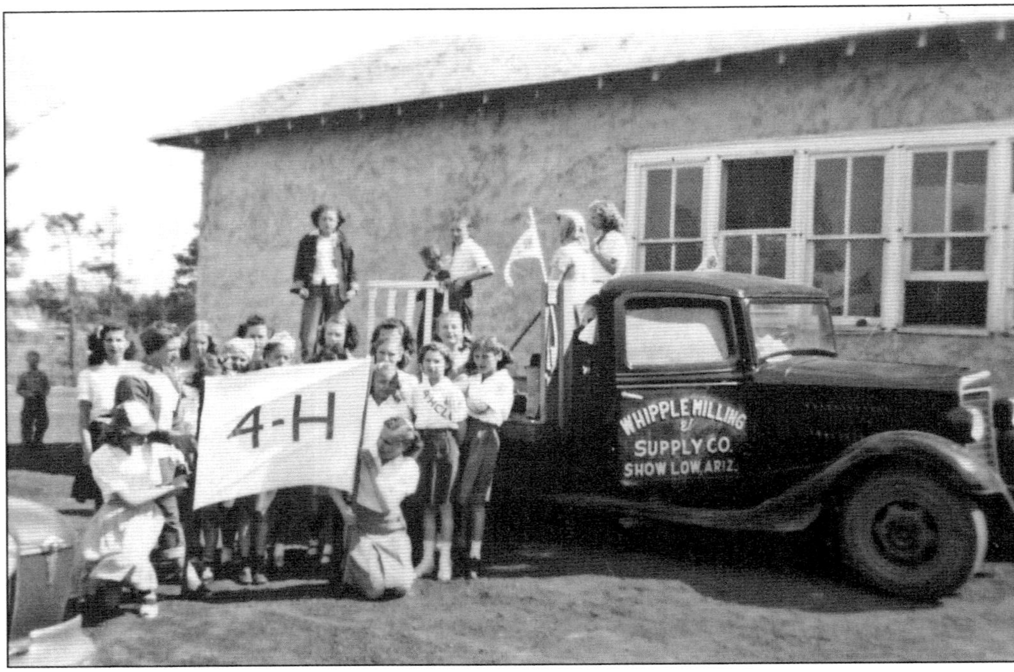

In 1948, the town of Show Low began a "Let's Beautify Show Low" campaign. Everyone worked to clean up the community. This also became the theme of the Fourth of July parade that year. Above, 4-H youth get ready to use the Whipple Milling truck for their transportation down the town's then-unnamed main street. Sarah Mills Willis was an early and dependable 4-H leader. Below, a piano has been loaded into the back of a pickup truck to accompany smaller children singing as they march in the parade. (Both, SLHisSoc Museum.)

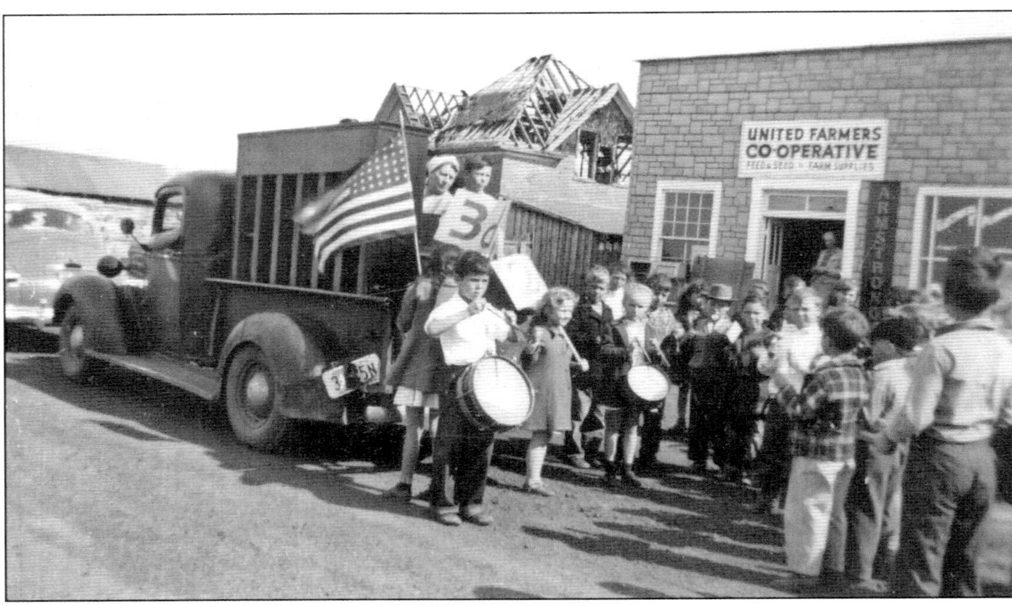

Three

Logging, Ranching, and Rodeos

The ponderosa pine forest around Show Low provided both a beautiful setting for the town and a livelihood for the men. C. E. Cooley and Henry Huning installed a small sawmill (probably from Fort Apache) near Show Low Creek and hired Henry Mitchell to operate it. In 1876, Warren R. Tenney, head sawyer, brought the Mount Trumbull mill, which had supplied lumber for the St. George Temple, to Arizona. It was installed at Pinedale in 1882 (and in 1890 moved to Pinetop). Clara Stratton Merrell wrote, "My earliest memories are of our homes at sawmills. I believe my father [Calvin Stratton] was among the first sawmill owners in this country. His first was on the Peterson Wash, south of Pinedale, Arizona, about 1890."

By 1952, two mills were operating in Show Low, the E. I. Reidhead mill and the Chlarson mill. These mills processed logs from both the Fort Apache Indian Reservation and the Sitgreaves National Forest. Clear scrap from these mills went to two moulding mills operated by Cliff Burrows and Hugh Whipple. Most of the lumber and moulding was marketed in Tucson and Phoenix. Other big mills included Southwest Lumber at McNary and Overgaard, Whiting Brothers at Pinedale, and Southwestern Sash and Door at Forestdale.

The forest also provided good summer grazing for cattle and sheep. Because much of this pasture was on U.S. Forest Service lease lands, it was forest supervisor T. C. Hoyt who helped organize a Stockgrowers Association in Show Low on March 11, 1921. The *Snowflake Herald* reported, "A number of representative cowmen were out to the meeting and the following officers [were] elected for the ensuing year: President, Joseph E. Stock. Vice President, Elwin Ellsworth. Secretary-Treasurer, J. W. Nikolaus. The above, with Chas. T. Savage and Earl Stock, compose the Advisory Board." On March 25, a stock growers association was organized in Lakeside. The outgrowth of these ranching operations was the Show Low rodeo, originally sponsored by the LDS Church to raise money for a new building.

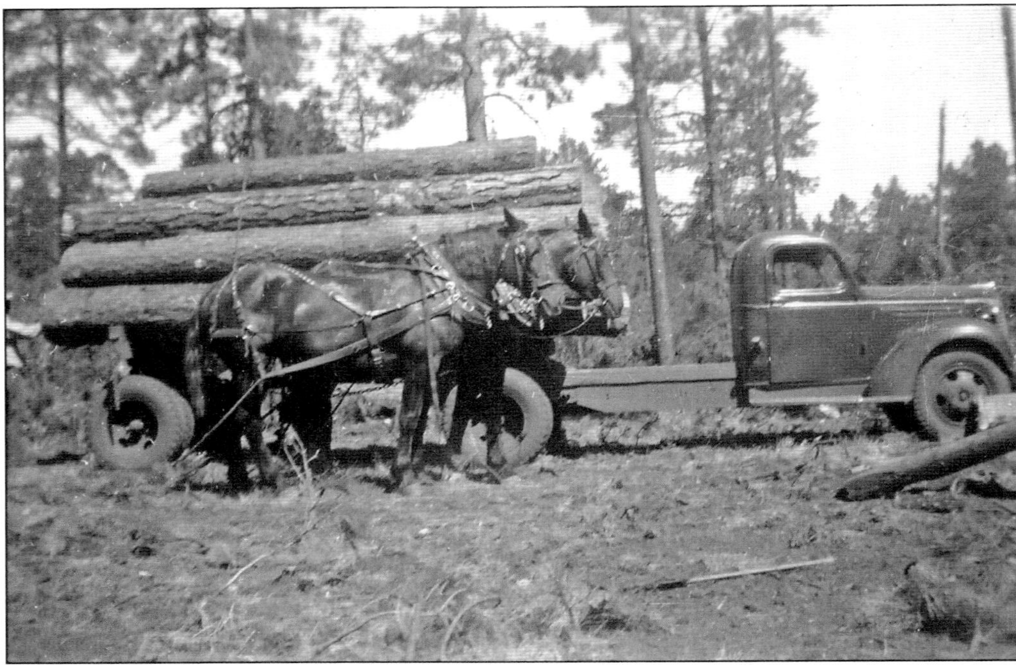

Hod Seymore and his sons logged for Hyrum Chlarson, whose mill was on the northwest side of Show Low. Seymore used both horses and trucks in his logging operation (above). His sons, Paul and Dean, missed the first and last months of school each year so they could work in the woods with their father. Below, Hod stands on a log suspended from a hoist he is using to load the trucks. Apparently the pickup motor was used to power the hoist. (Both, Idella Seymore.)

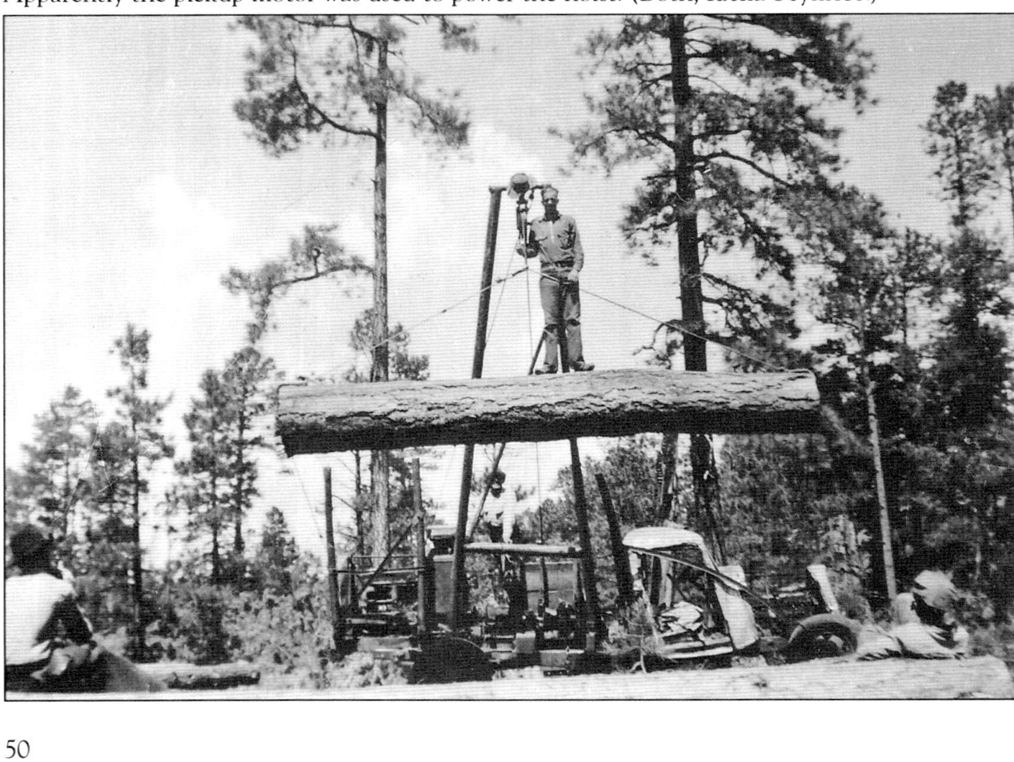

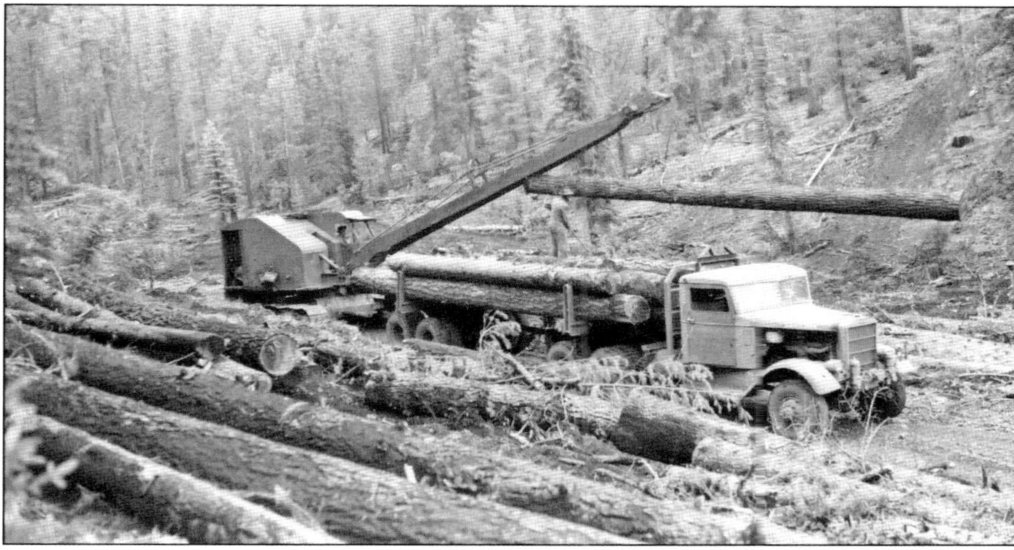

By 1950, cranes were used to load the trucks. This photograph shows a crane and truck belonging to Southwest Lumber and logging on the Apache National Forest. Men in the crane seldom met with accidents, but men on the ground were often not so lucky. (Photograph by Wayland G. Koogler, Ellis collection.)

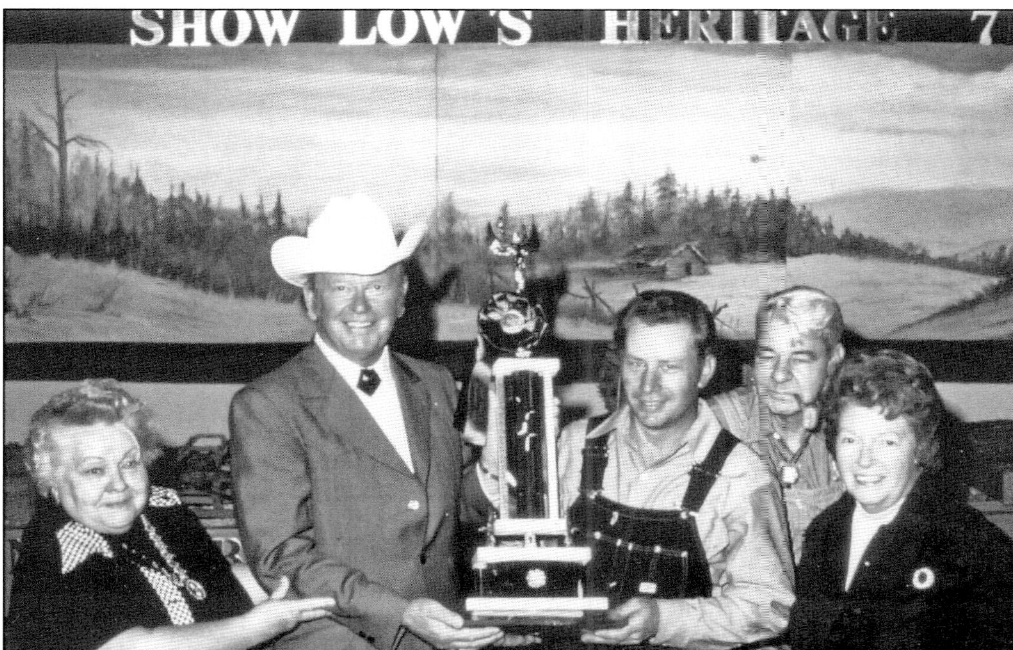

Rex Allen, actor and "Arizona's Singing Cowboy" from Willcox, here presents Meb Webb with the first-place ribbon and trophy for Show Low's booth entry in the 1974 Arizona State Fair. From left to right are Eleanor Vaughan, Allen, Webb, Harold Vaughan, and Dorothy Williams, Show Low Chamber of Commerce manager. The booth included a miniature sawmill, which actually cut tree branches into blocks of wood that were given to fairgoers. (Vaughan collection.)

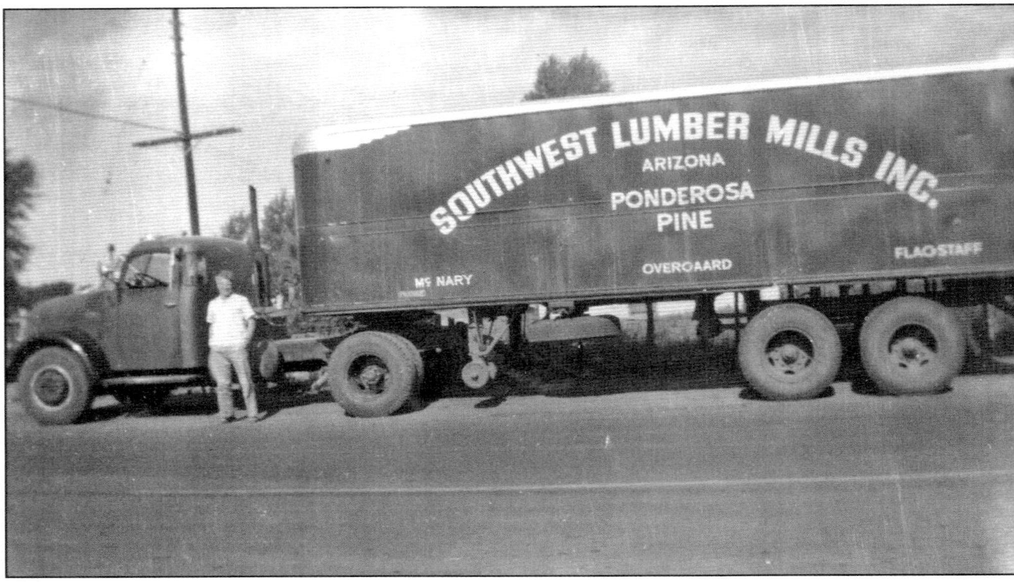

Pictured above is Arthur "Whitey" Adams hauling finished lumber for Southwest in the 1950s. Fred Adams and sons hauled and sold coal from Gallup, local juniper wood for stoves, and lumber from Lakeside to Mesa for Fish Lumber Company. In the early 1950s, they hauled the shake shingles for the new LDS Church from Holbrook. Once a truck they called "Little Susie" was loaded with 400 sacks of cement; it lost gears in Salt River Canyon and couldn't make one of the U-turns. Fortunately, the driver was unhurt. They also cut evergreens to sell in the Salt River Valley. Pictured below is the Adamses' truck about 1952 with Jim Adams standing on the running board. Jim died the next year in an automobile accident. (Both, Lois Adams Lemons.)

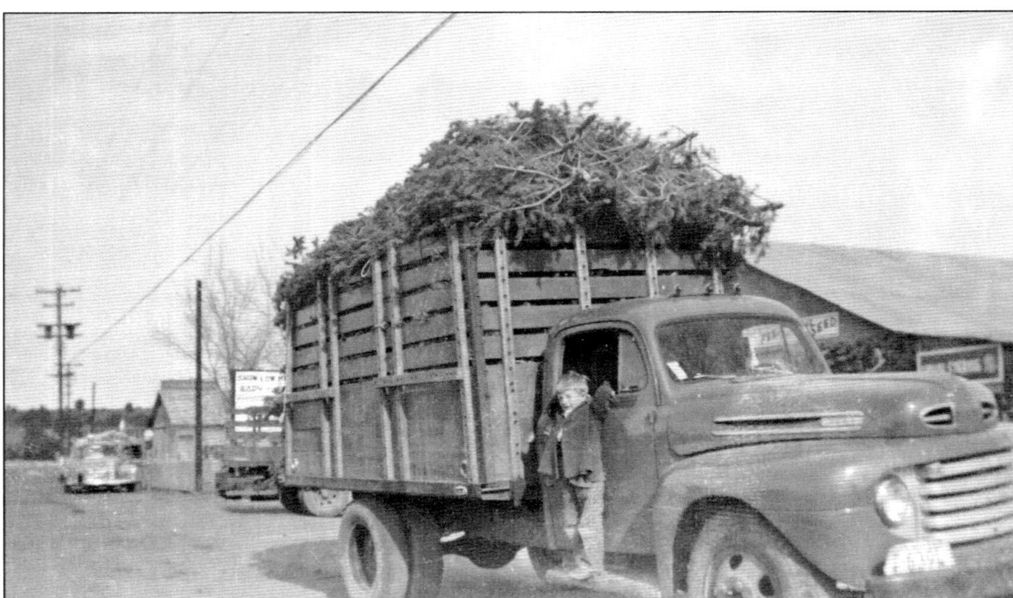

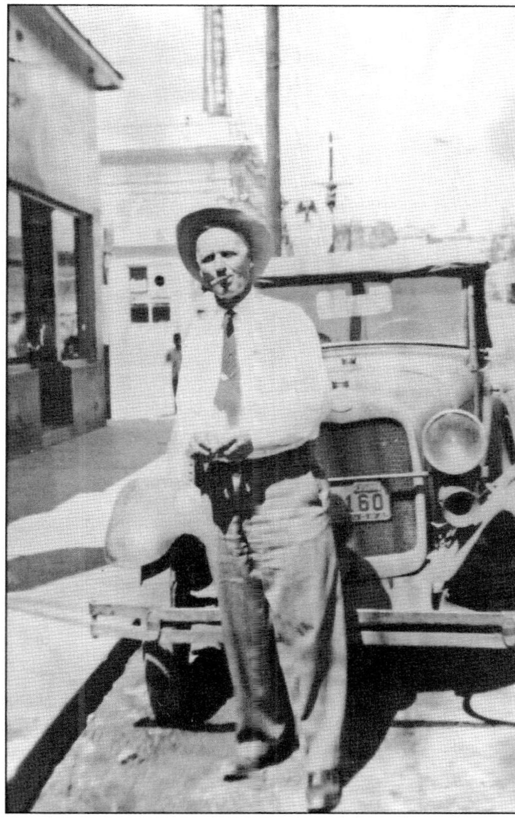

In Show Low, Edwin "Ed" Reidhead is remembered for his ever-present cigar and Stetson hat. He is pictured at right in 1929 in Globe at the Ford dealership with his new 1928 Ford. Below is an early Reidhead truck. Reidhead purchased several old army trucks and had them retrofitted to haul logs. Val Reidhead estimated that the three logs on this truck weighed about 10 tons. At Ed's wife Cora's funeral, many Apaches came to pay tribute for her friendship and the clothes and food she provided so their children could attend school. (Both, Val Reidhead.)

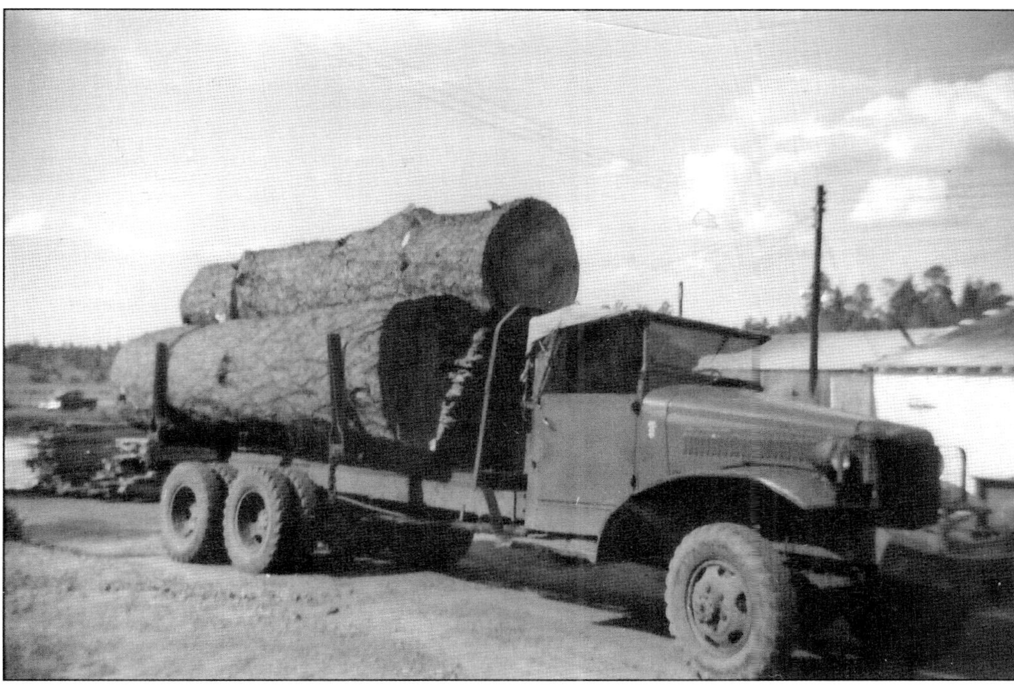

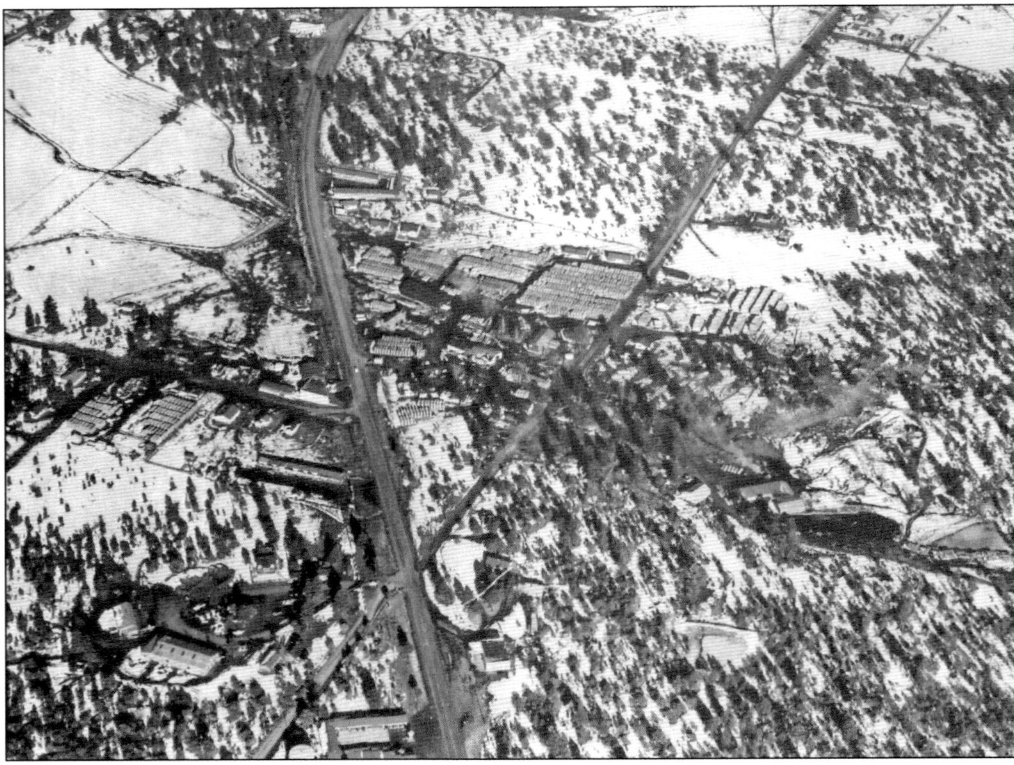

Above is an aerial view of Reidhead Lumber Mill west of Show Low about 1956. Note the lumber stacked ready for sale on both sides of the highway. Ed Reidhead first established a sawmill near Linden in 1913, then built another at Coal Canyon south of Clay Springs, and finally the mills at Show Low and Nutrioso. In the 1950s, he operated a mill at Carrizo with his brother Bruce. Reidhead Lumber advertised itself as "manufacturers and wholesalers of kiln and air dried ponderosa pine and Douglas fir." Below, Show Low's lumbering history is showcased in a parade following a Shetland pony ridden by Abner Owens leading a cow. (The boy is unidentified.) It is believed that this is a Reidhead truck. (Above, photograph by Bob Markow, McCarty collection; below, Vaughan collection.)

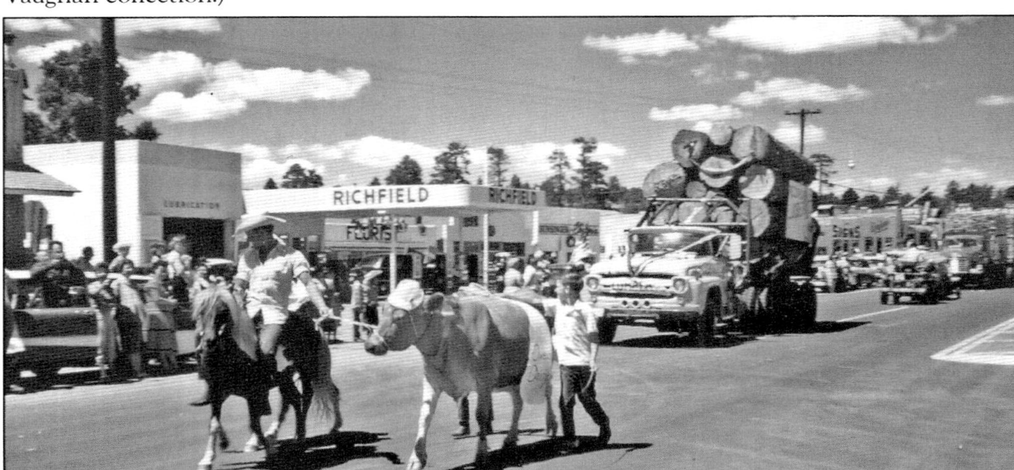

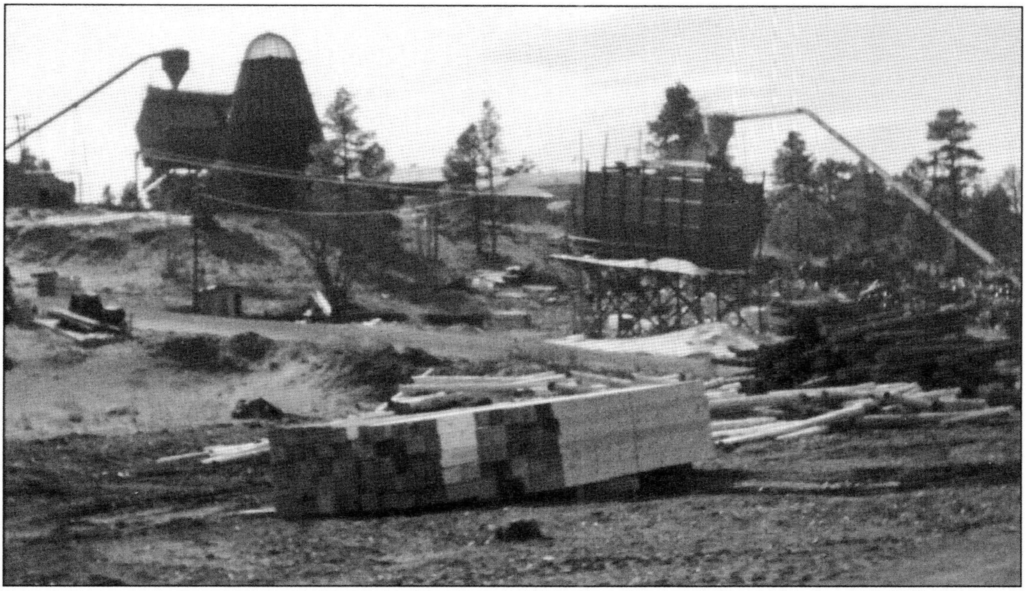

Pictured here is the burner of the Reidhead mill. When the Kiva Motel was first built, some in town tried to get the Reidhead mill moved farther away because of the smoke from the burner. Others thought the employees did not spend their money in the community. To prove his case, Ed Reidhead went to the bank in Holbrook accompanied by highway patrolman John Consoni, got his entire payroll in silver dollars, and then let the businesses observe just how much his employees spent. The Reidhead mill went out of business after 50 years because of the lack of good timber, pressure from environmentalists, and a sluggish economy. Jerry Reidhead stated, "Most of the timber available was so inferior it should be sold as pulp." The business was sold to Porter's Precision Pine and Timber, a Heber sawmill operation. (Both, Beatrice Jarvis.)

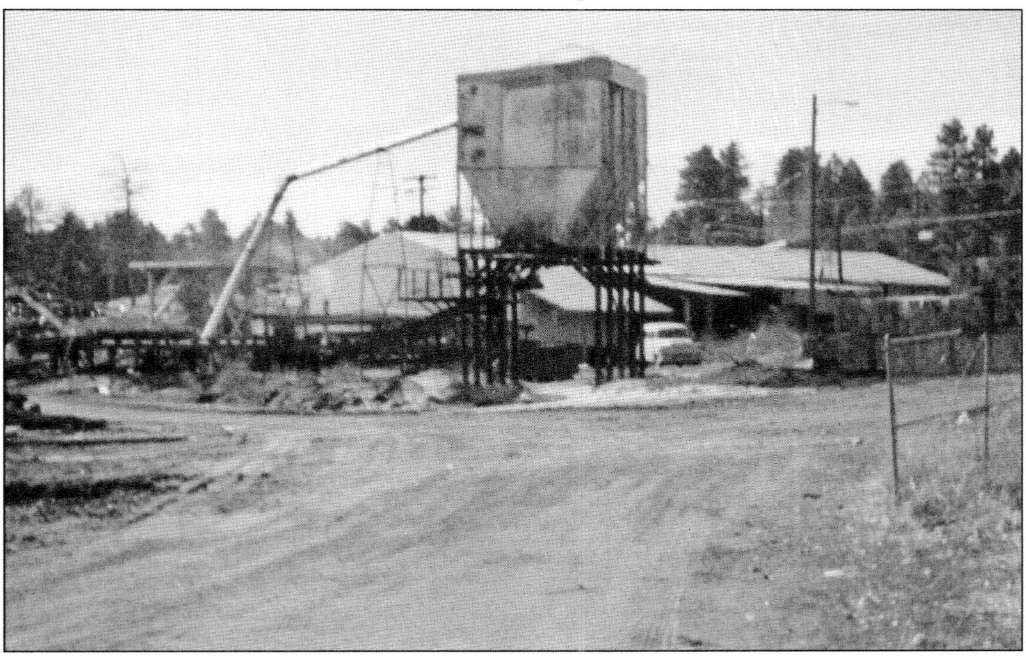

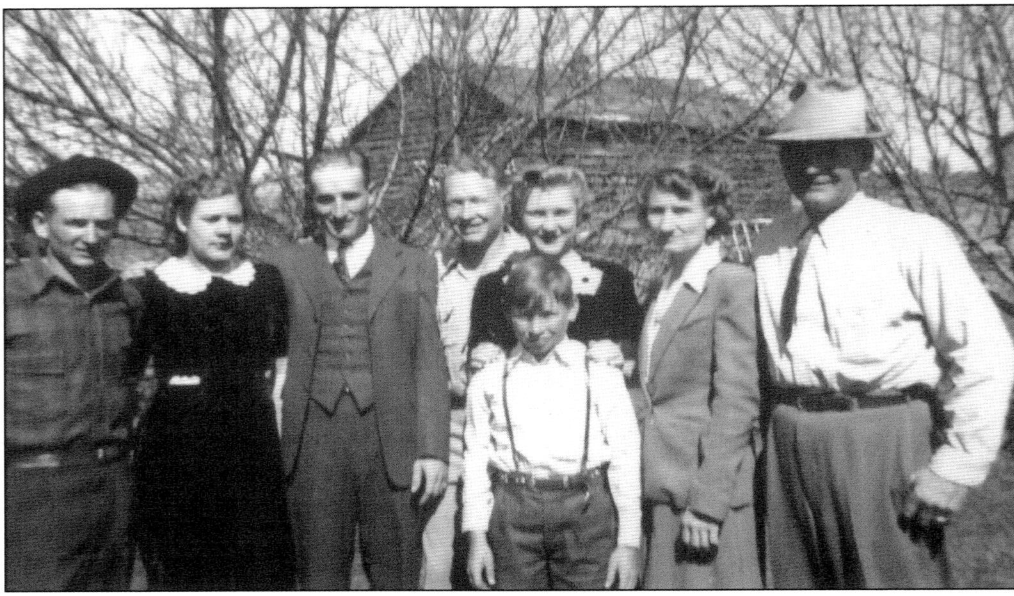

Pictured above are members of the Ray Butler family, including, from left to right, Hal, Olga Gardner Butler (Claude's wife), Claude, Bob, Valoe, May, and Ray with Wade in front. Hal Butler first worked for Reidhead Lumber mills and then, with his brother Claude, purchased his own trucks. Hal Butler and Bruce Reidhead started the Show Low Lumber Company by hauling from the O'Malley mill in Vernon, the Chlarson mill in Show Low, and FALCO (Fort Apache Lumber Company) in Whiteriver. They finished and planed the lumber before trucking it to the Salt River Valley. In 1964, Butler went to Whiteriver to build the first FATCO (Fort Apache Timber Company) sawmill (below). He and son Greg stayed on to run it for the tribe. Butler worked in the lumber industry for decades. (Above, Keith Butler; below, Hal Butler.)

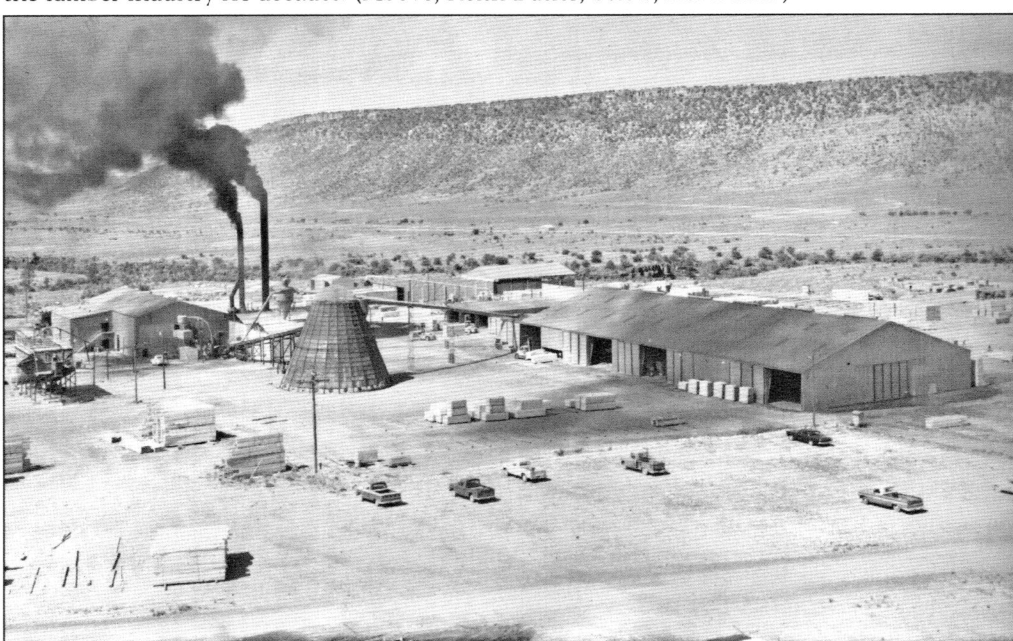

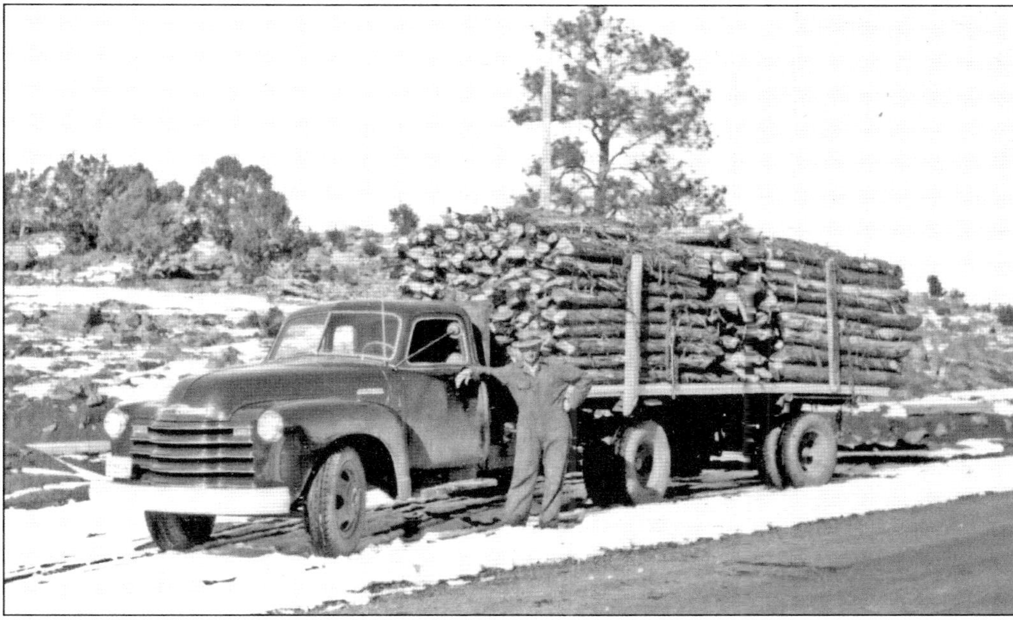

The trucks Hal and Claude Butler originally purchased were 2-ton diesel Chevrolets, locally called three-bangers (three cylinders). Later the Butlers upgraded to four-bangers and then to six-bangers. In 1954, they were primarily hauling cedar posts to the Salt River and Gila Valleys, selling to farmers and ranchers for fencing. Above, Claude is standing beside his loaded truck. Below is the Claude Butler family in 1958. From left to right are Claude, Shirl (standing), Barbara Ann, Olga, Donna Faye (standing), and Keith. Note the flagstone fireplace built by Gary Hatch. (Above, Keith Butler; below, Elizabeth Nikolaus collection.)

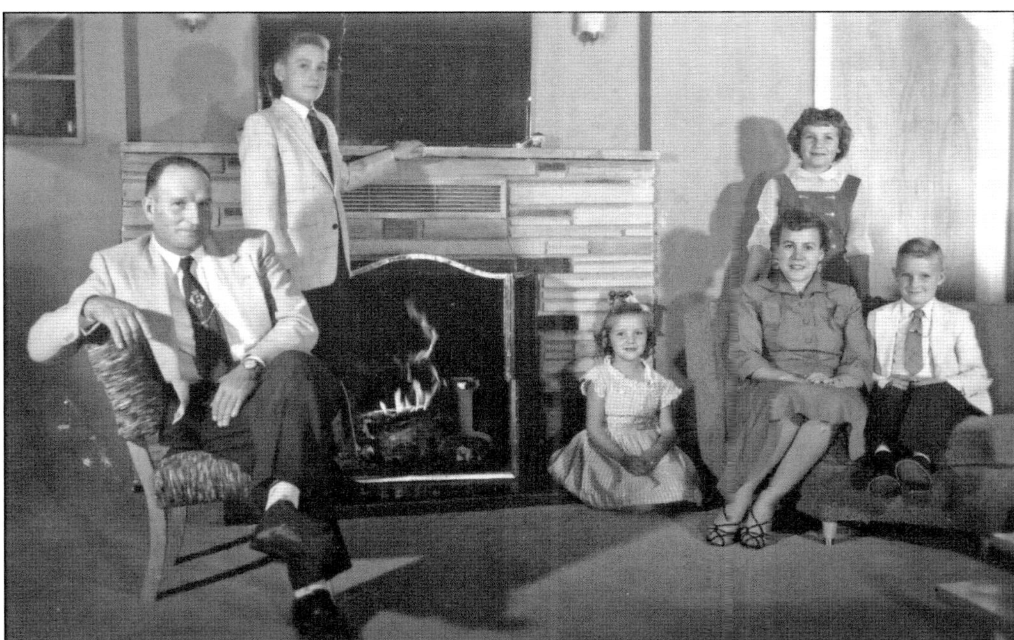

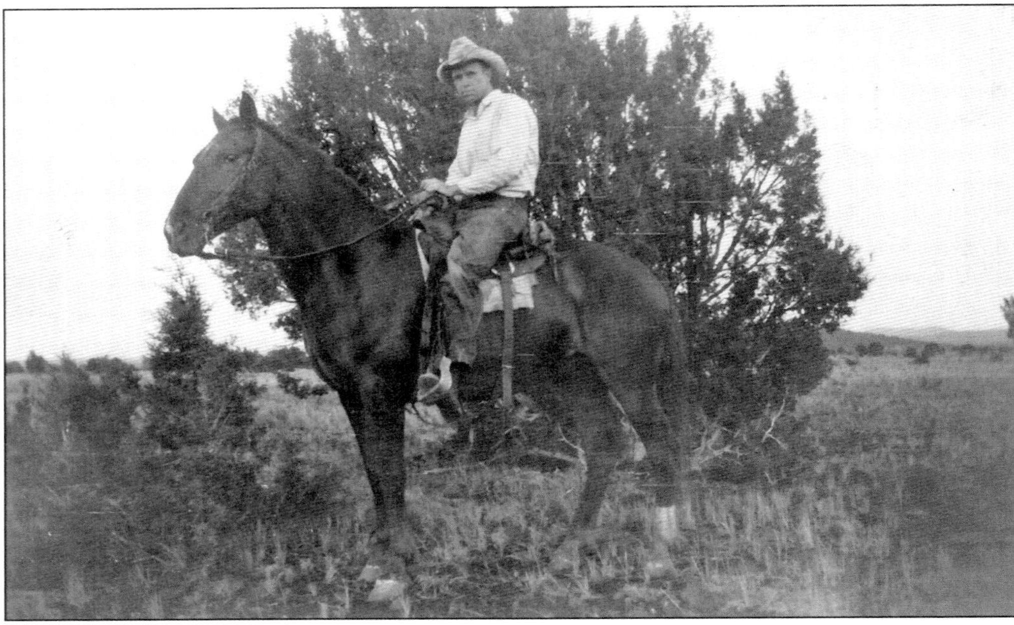

The ponderosa forest was also used for cattle. At first, areas were homesteaded, but later the U.S. Forest Service began issuing grazing permits to the ranchers. Above is Ray Merrell, brother-in-law of Hod Seymore, saddled up and ready to gather cattle. Grazing permits for local ranchers encompassed the area from just north of Lakeside almost to Taylor and out to First and Second Knoll. Normally Joe Stock, Pete Ellsworth, and Larry Whipple would work together gathering cattle like the unidentified men pictured below. (Above, Idella Seymore; below, Pete and Betty Jo Ellsworth.)

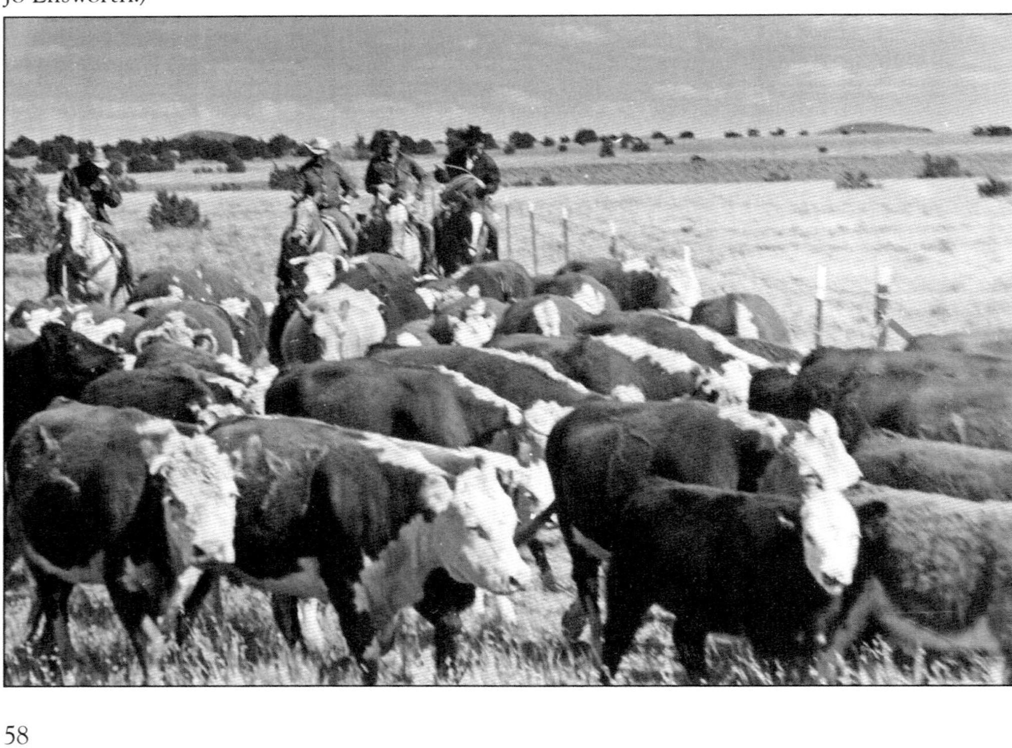

With open ranges and cattle rustling, branding is imperative to indicate ownership of animals. At right, the smoke curls as Chet Adams singes the hair of a bawling calf with a branding iron at the LDS Church ranch. Beef raised on the ranch is canned and used to feed the poor. All labor at the ranch is voluntary. Below, Greg Stock brands a calf as a mother cow keeps an eye on him. Stock, a hospital administrator, loved getting back to his parents' ranch to hone his cowboy skills. (Right, photograph by Deborah Austin; below, Dixie Stock Gillespie.)

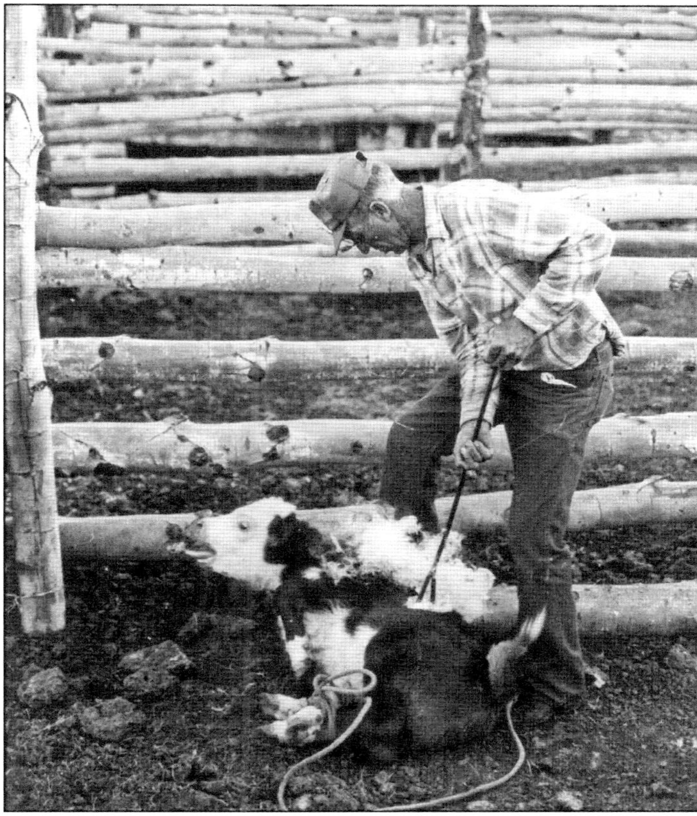

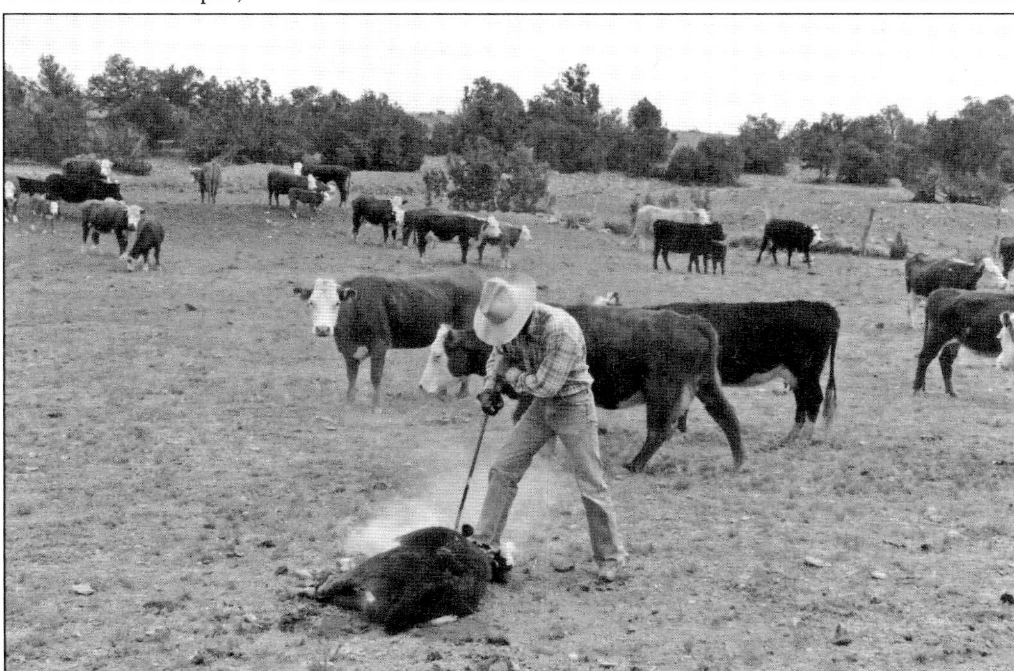

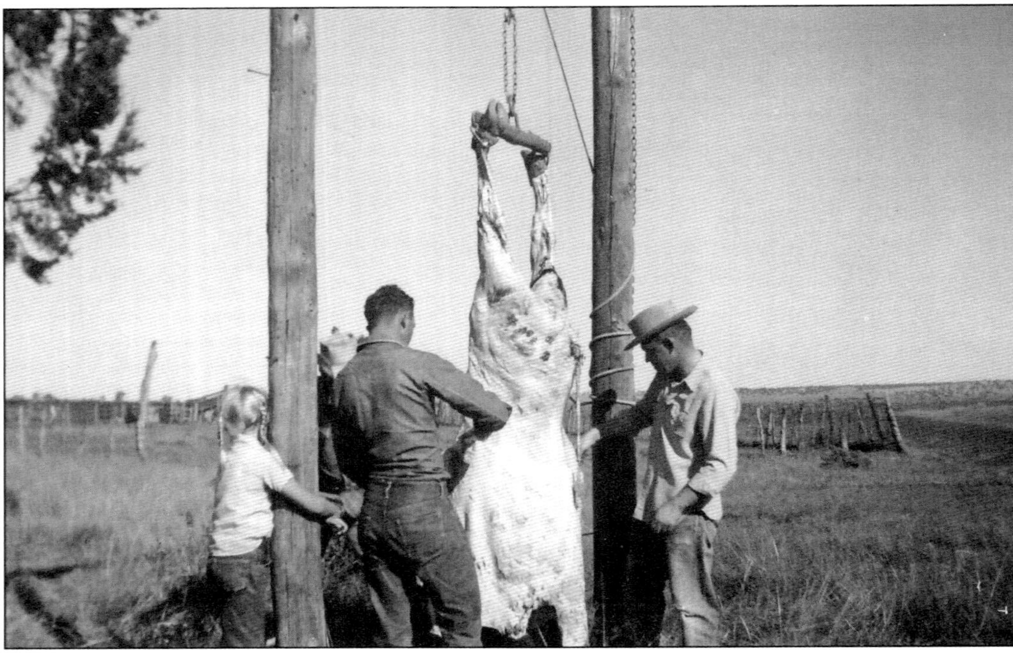

Paul (left) and Dean Seymore butcher a beef cow on their parents' ranch in the 1950s. Dean's daughter, Linda, is an occasional onlooker. In 1958, Paul Seymore, Jim Bryant, Dallas Stock, Pete Ellsworth, and Pete and John Reidhead (from Shumway) started a roping club and practiced at the LDS rodeo arena. Most became successful rodeo contestants. (Idella Seymore.)

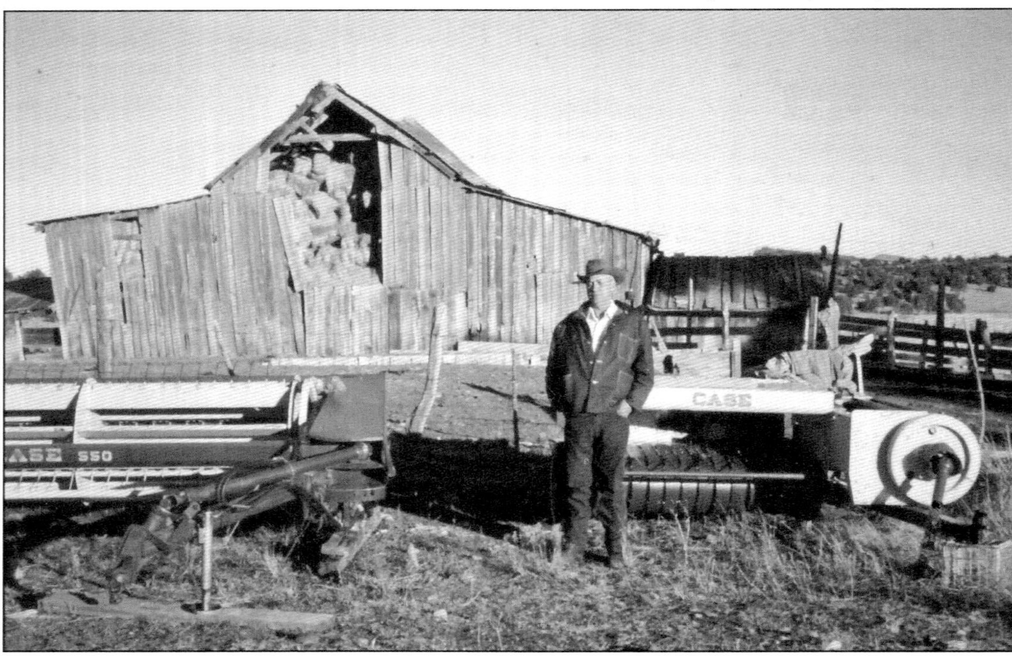

Here Joe Stock stands in front of his farm equipment and picturesque barn brimming with hay. The barn, on Stock's ranch in northwest Show Low, burned not long after this picture was taken. (Dixie Stock Gillespie.)

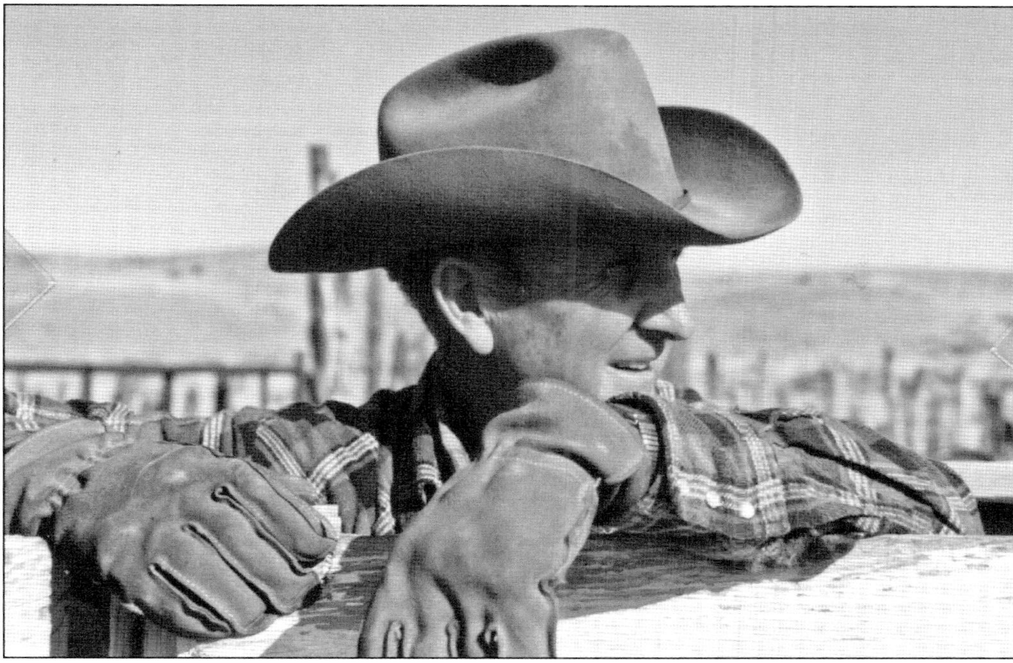

Wendell "Winkie" Whipple (above) was a Show Low native who worked in road construction and maintenance with Navajo County and the City of Show Low. He was mayor of Show Low in the 1960s and, while on the city council, was in charge of eight departments, including city park, animal control, cemetery, and library. The responsibility he liked least was animal control, especially the calls from irate women whose dogs were impounded. His wife, Babe, said, "Some men have a hobby of fishing or hunting. Wink's hobby was ranchin'. He would ranch for himself and family, for friends, and at the LDS Church ranch." The photograph below was taken on his last roundup. His casket was made of boards from his uncle Charlie Whipple's barn. It was branded by friends and family and had horseshoe handles. His son drove the casket from the church to the cemetery in Wink's old green-and-white Ford truck. (Above, photograph by Nancy Thornhill; below, Ione Pearce Whipple.)

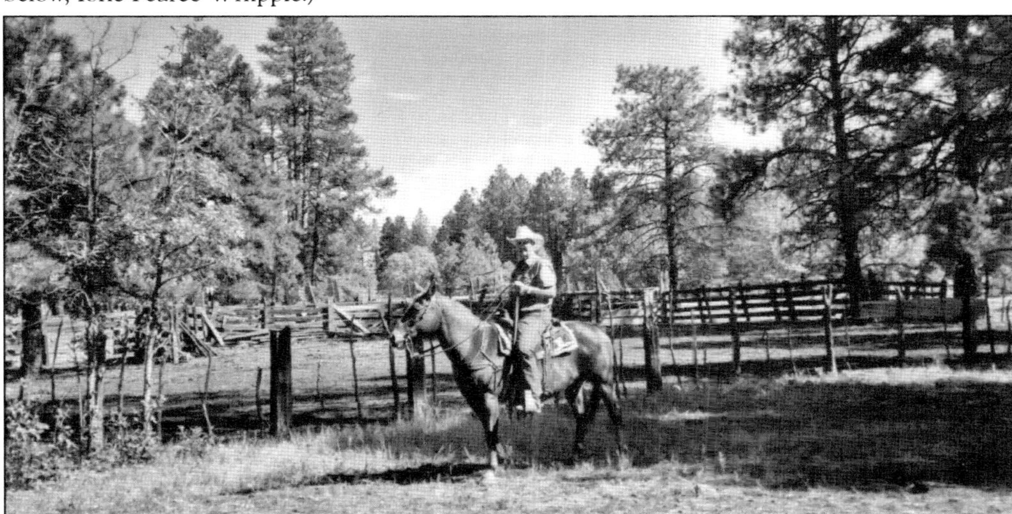

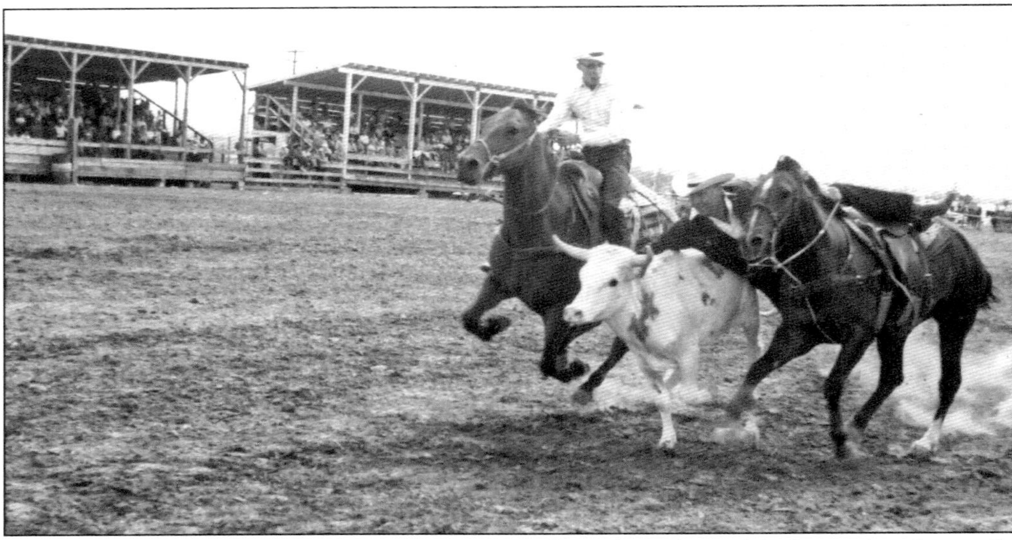

Show Low's rodeo grounds were on "The Bench" where the Industrial Park is today. Originally, people sat in or on their cars. Some backed up a pickup and sat on the tailgate or top of the cab, and some people were really organized with chairs or a bench in the pickup. The first wooden, covered bleachers were on the south; later ones (without a roof) were on the north, with the announcer's stand and bucking chutes adjacent. Above, Pete Ellsworth makes a successful bulldogging run. This was after a second set of bleachers on the south were completed. In 1959, Ellsworth won both the bulldogging and the bull riding (below) championships of the Arizona Rodeo Association. (Both, Pete and Betty Jo Ellsworth.)

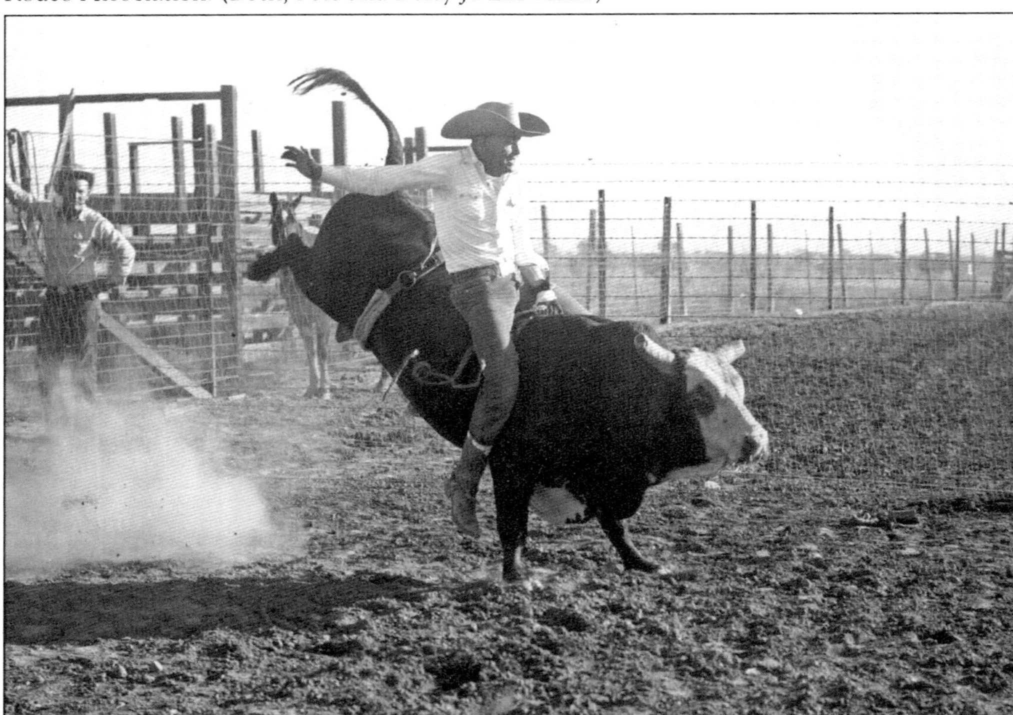

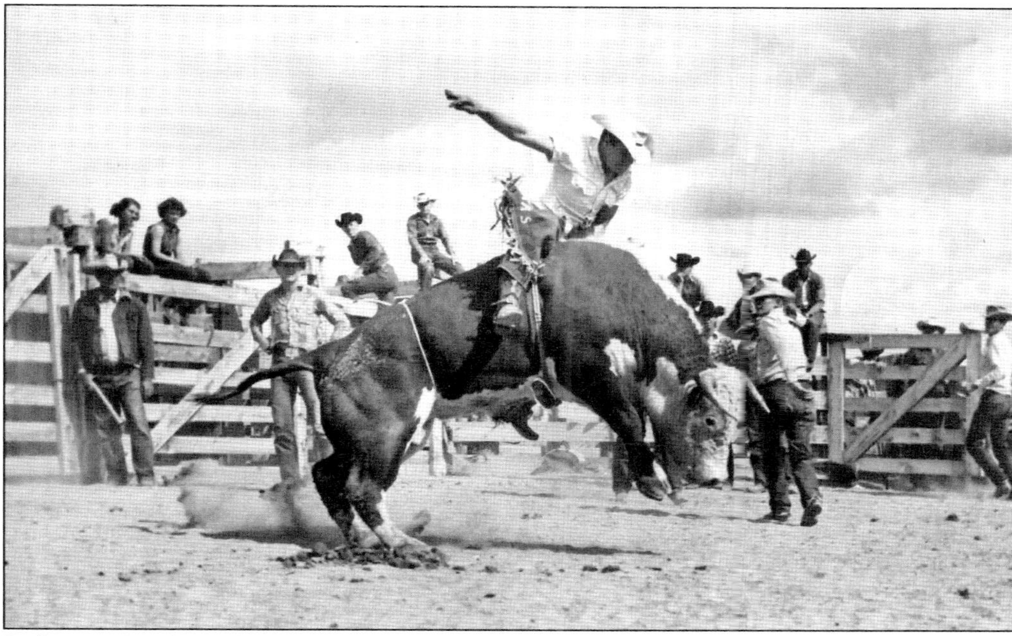

Dallas Stock is shown here riding a bull at Quemado, New Mexico. In 1959, he and Pete Ellsworth went to a "bull buck-out" in Dallas, Texas. Out of 80 bull riders, these two Show Low men were the only two cowboys to ride all three bulls. Stock won first place, and Ellsworth won second. (Pete Ellsworth).

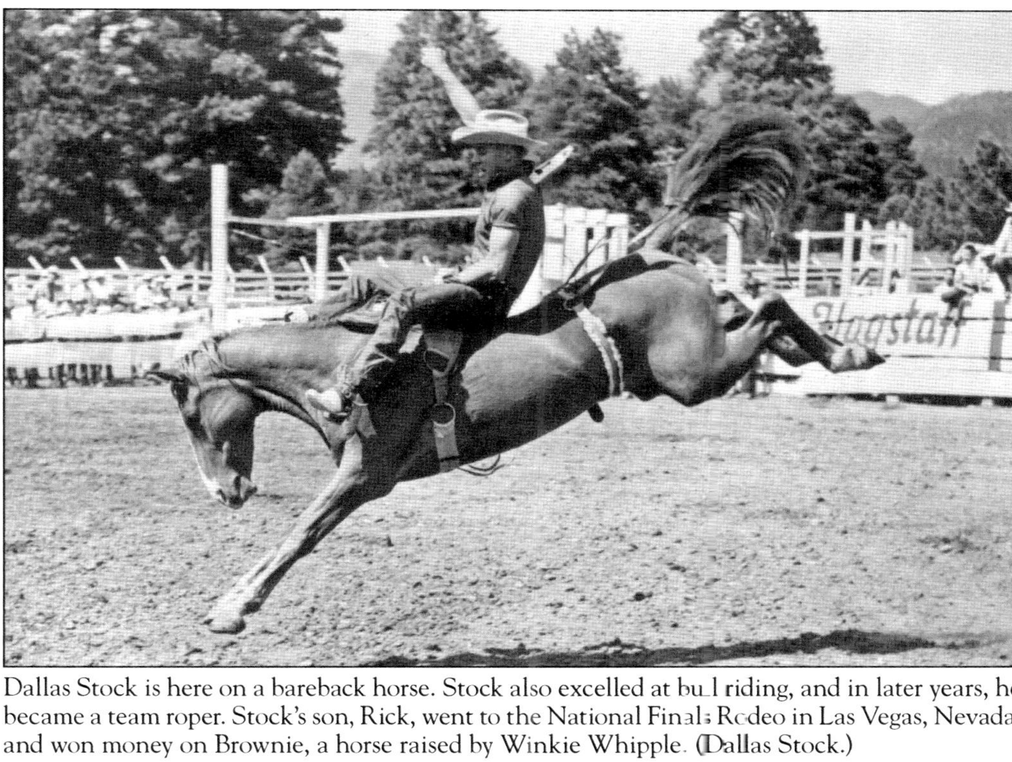

Dallas Stock is here on a bareback horse. Stock also excelled at bull riding, and in later years, he became a team roper. Stock's son, Rick, went to the National Finals Rodeo in Las Vegas, Nevada, and won money on Brownie, a horse raised by Winkie Whipple. (Dallas Stock.)

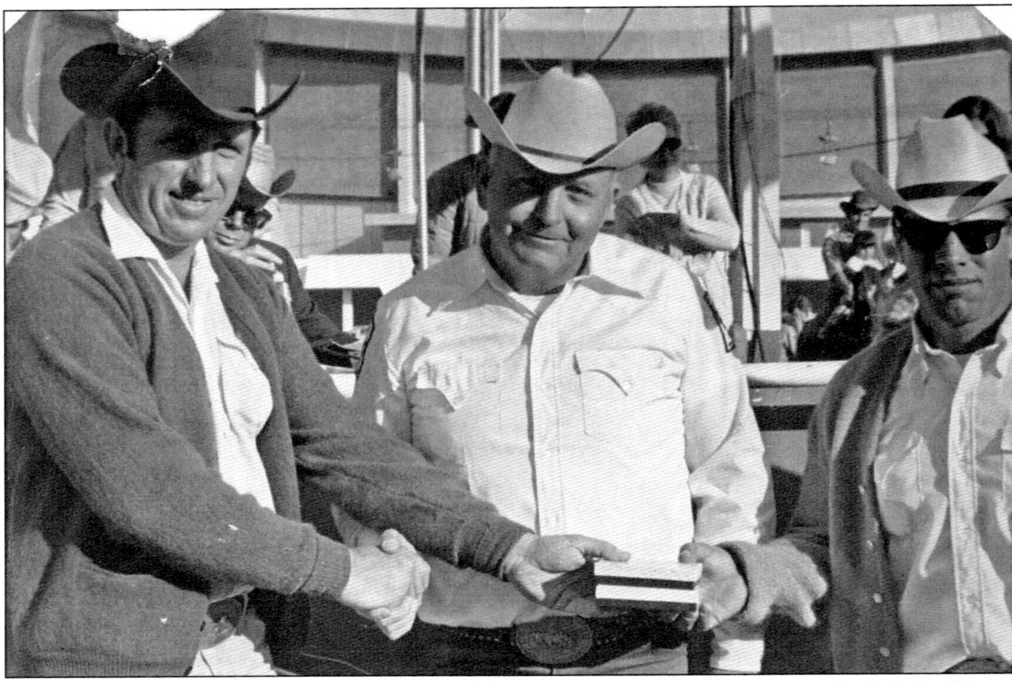

Mike Maddox (center) of the Arizona Sheriff's Posse Association presents trophy belt buckles to Pete Ellsworth (left) and Dallas Stock of Show Low in the late 1950s. (Dallas Stock.)

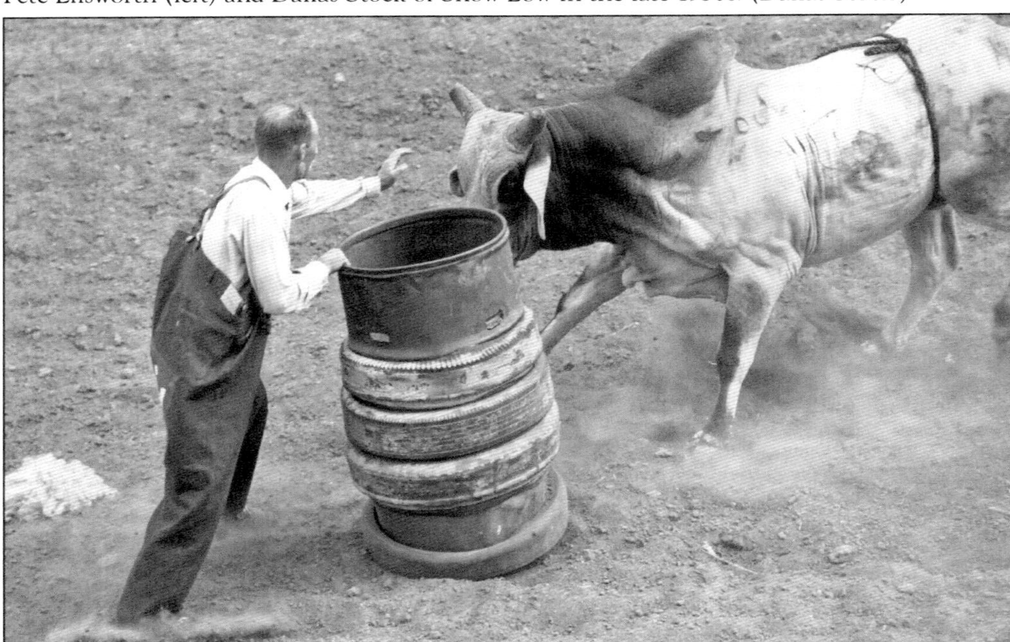

This photograph has been labeled "Bishop in the Barrel." Elizabeth Nikolaus wrote, "Eb Lewis always contributed to the spirit of the rodeo. Here you see him (or don't see him), but he is in the barrel during the clown act." Rodeo clowns work at keeping cowboys safe from rough stock in the arena. (Elizabeth Nikolaus collection.)

Four

Growth from Highway 60

In 1930, people living in Show Low wanting to travel to Phoenix either had to travel north to Holbrook, take the train west to Flagstaff, and then go by train or car south to Phoenix or they had to use the Black River road south of Fort Apache to Globe and then Phoenix. Neither route provided a way for growth of Show Low's commercial interests.

"Prior to the advent of National Highway 60 in the early 1930s," wrote Bill Huso, "Show Low was a small, quiet inland town with relatively few business establishments." As business owners across the nation wanted to promote automobile travel, they looked for a transcontinental road. Highway 60 became one such road, and one of the last sections to be completed was between Show Low and Globe, through the Salt River Canyon. Highway 60 stretched from Los Angeles to Virginia Beach, passing through Blythe, Socorro, Amarillo, Enid, Springfield, Louisville, Charleston, and Richmond. Huso continued, "But now [1954] tourist and vacation travel has transformed the main street [of Show Low] almost beyond recognition. [The town] can cater to almost any whim of a vacationist."

In 1947, Huso began promoting Highway 60 by participating in the U.S. Highway 60 Association, an organization of businessmen along the route. He served six years as national president. Don Dedera in the *Arizona Republic* reported that Huso "on the flimsiest excuse, . . . will fill your head with brags and cram your pockets with boastful literature about the transcontinental highway which divides America at the beltway." Dedera also observed that "Huso's shirt pocket looks like the headquarters office of the U.S. Highway 60 Association, which it is." Huso practiced his own sermon, making 103 Sunday radio broadcasts touting Highway 60. He also produced a brochure espousing the virtues of the road, and Show Low boosters contributed $1,000 toward its publication.

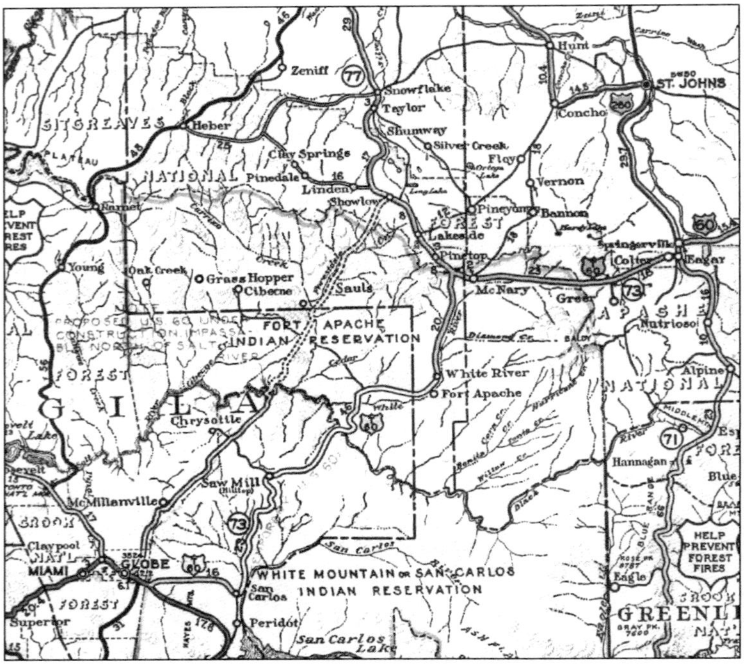

By 1930, the Arizona State Highway Department began planning a new route from Show Low to Phoenix, particularly one with lower elevations and therefore less winter snow. This is the current route through Salt River Canyon, which, upon completion, was designated U.S. Highway 60. (ASU Map Collection.)

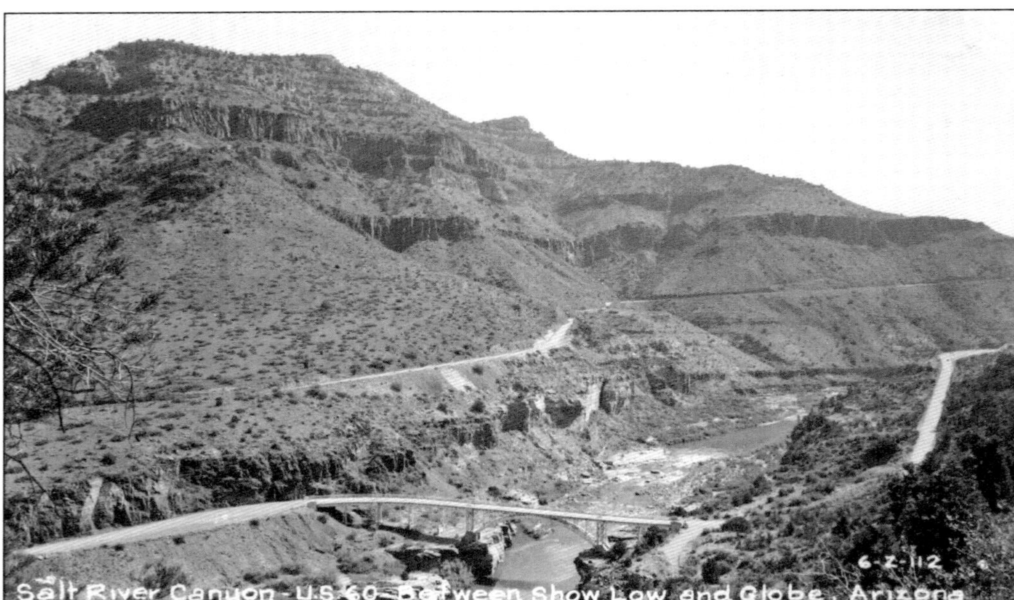

Construction on the new route began immediately. A bridge over Salt River was completed in 1934. It was a beautiful steel girder bridge with a traditional arch 186 feet long. The entire span was nearly 400 feet. (Ellis collection.)

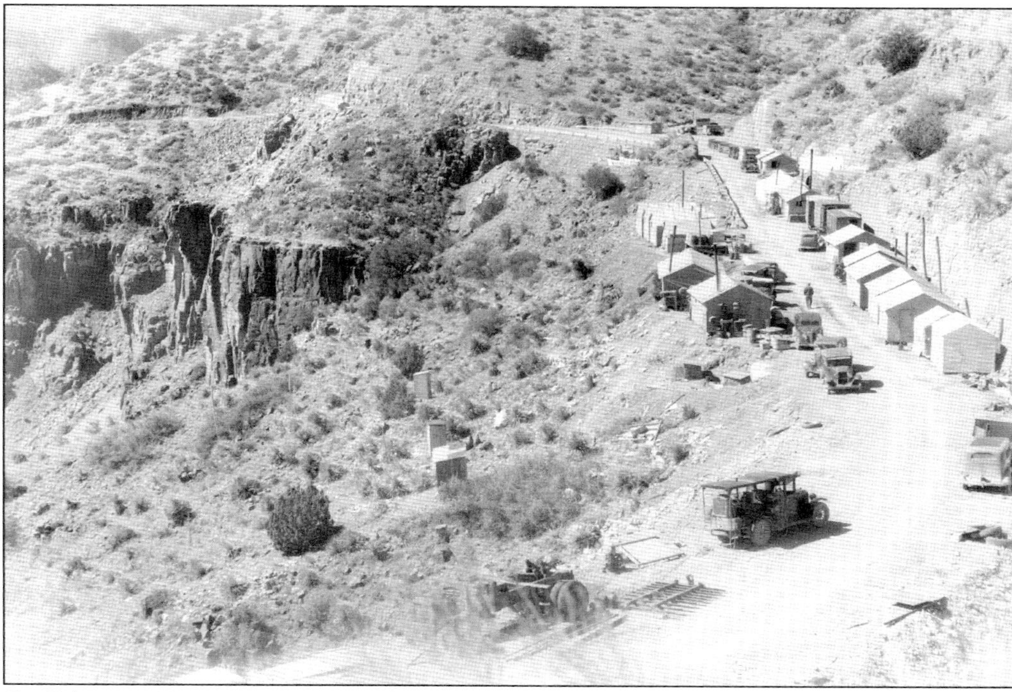

On February 25, 1935, Norman Wallace photographed the construction camp perched on the side of the canyon (above). Work was inherently dangerous. Even after the road was completed, travelers could usually look over the edge and see cars and trucks whose brakes had failed and had missed a curve. M. L. Curry, on his way to Casa Grande, sent the postcard below to his family in Plymouth, Indiana, in September 1951 and wrote, "I drove down & up this mt. It is 5 miles down & the same up. It was raining so hard the visibility was mighty bad." (Above, AHS/Tucson PC180/F26/74-2; below, Ellis collection.)

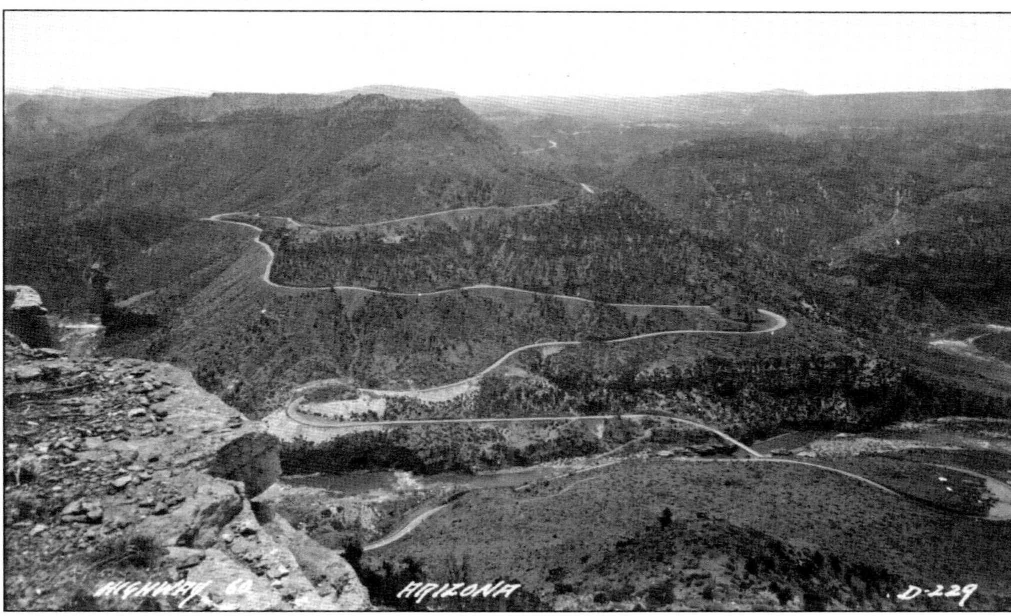

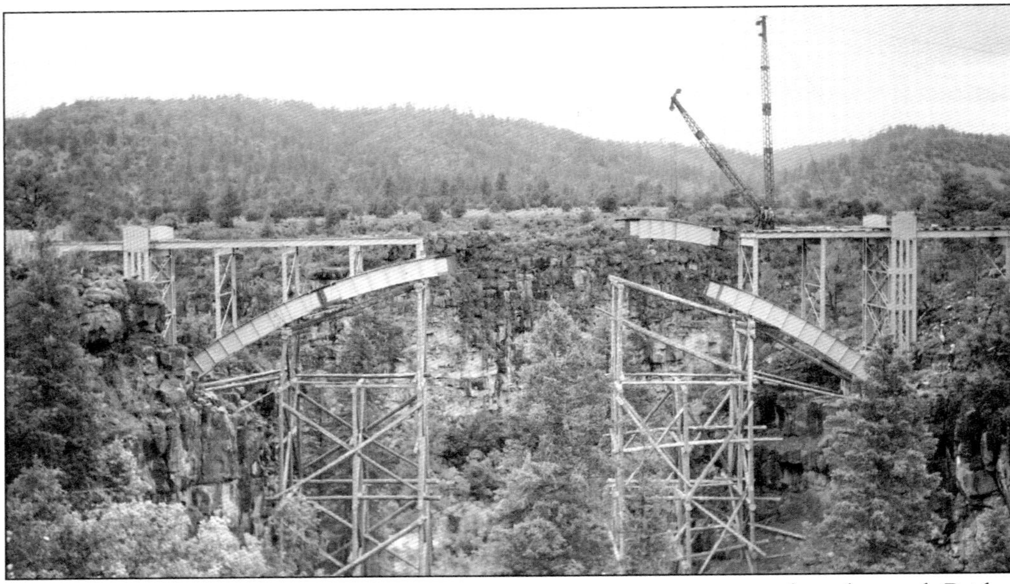

Other equally impressive construction projects were necessary to complete the road. Bridges over Cedar and Corduroy Canyons were completed from 1936 to 1938. Here Norman Wallace has photographed the lowering of a bridge section on May 28, 1937, at Cedar Canyon. Note the wooden scaffolding built from both ends providing support as the bridge is built over the 140-foot -deep chasm. (AHS/Tucson PC180/F25/537.)

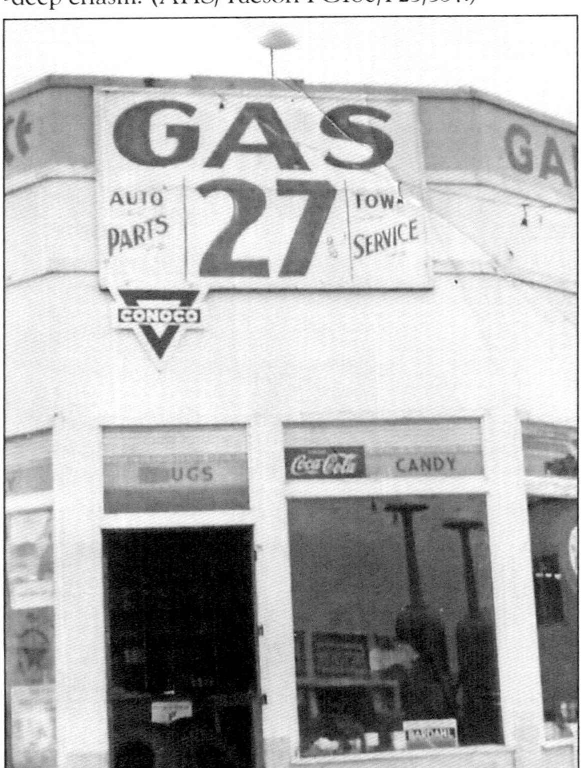

In the 1940s, gasoline was 27¢ a gallon at the Conoco station in the center of Show Low. One could also get a prescription filled and buy candy. This building housed several restaurants and a pharmacy successively before Jim Stock and his sons turned it into a full-fledged garage and gas station. (Lloyd Stock.)

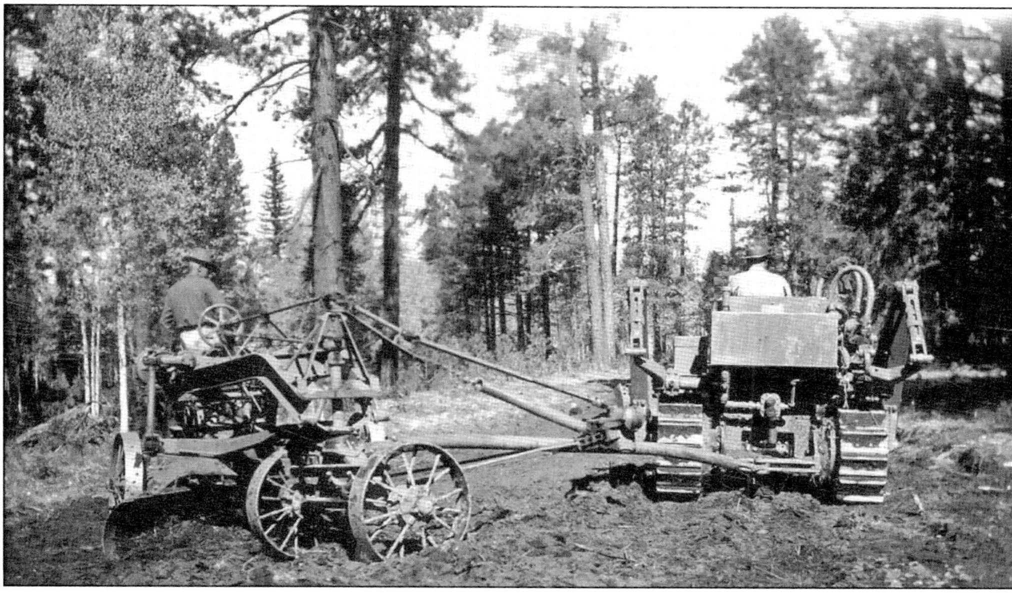

After completion of the bridges, construction of the road up Hagen Hill may have been the most difficult task for Highway 60 engineers. Harry Hagen of Globe was the contractor and hired several local men. Pictured above is a grader pulled by a crawler tractor, with Max Brewer on the tractor (right) and probably Jim McNeil on the grader. Below, Stanley Stephens is operating the bulldozer. Stephens, later known as "Pappy," sang on radio station KOOL in Phoenix. He also sang and played guitar, banjo, and fiddle at the Blue Moon in Show Low and the Ponderosa Club in Pinetop. (Both, Lloyd Stock.)

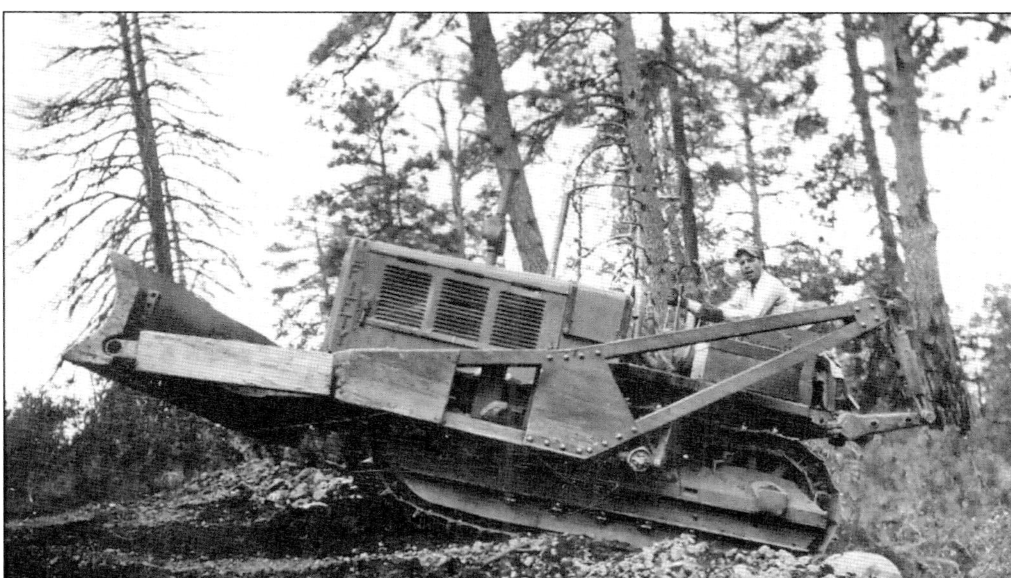

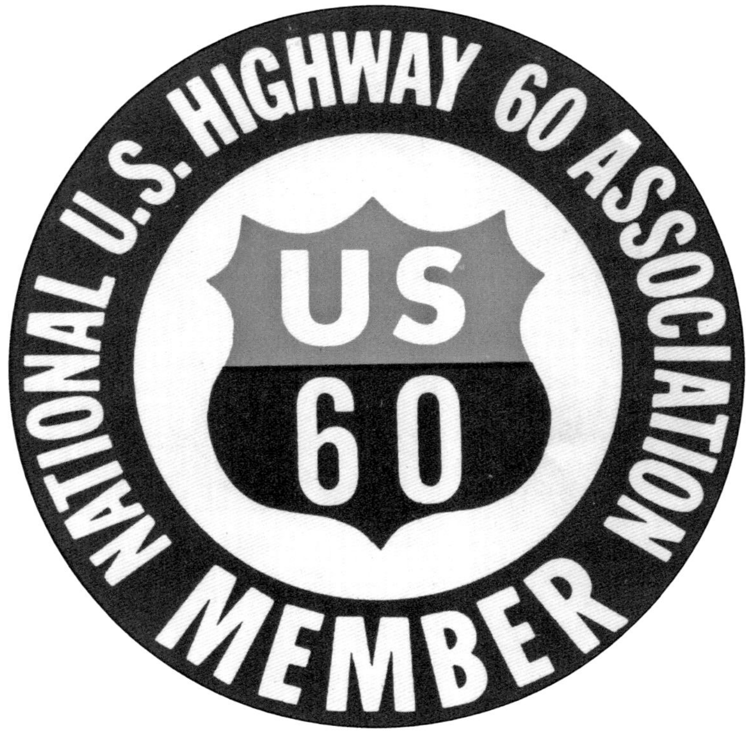

Once Highway 60 was complete, Show Low began to have a tourist season. The Highway 60 Association provided a seal (above) that could be displayed in business windows. They also sponsored annual conventions. In 1951, Eric Marks (back row, fourth from left) and Bill Huso (back row, 11th from left) traveled to Riverside, California, for the meetings. Of particular interest to the accompanying children were the elevators. The 38th convention was held in Springerville, April 17–20, 1968. Special events included tours of Mount Baldy/Big Lake and the Southwest Forest Industries sawmill, fishing in White Mountain creeks, a demonstration of dogs working cattle, a movie featuring Apache dances, and an address by Sen. Bill Huso. Springerville, "Gateway to the White Mountains," then invited everyone to return and enjoy four million acres "of year round pleasure." (Both, Huso collection.)

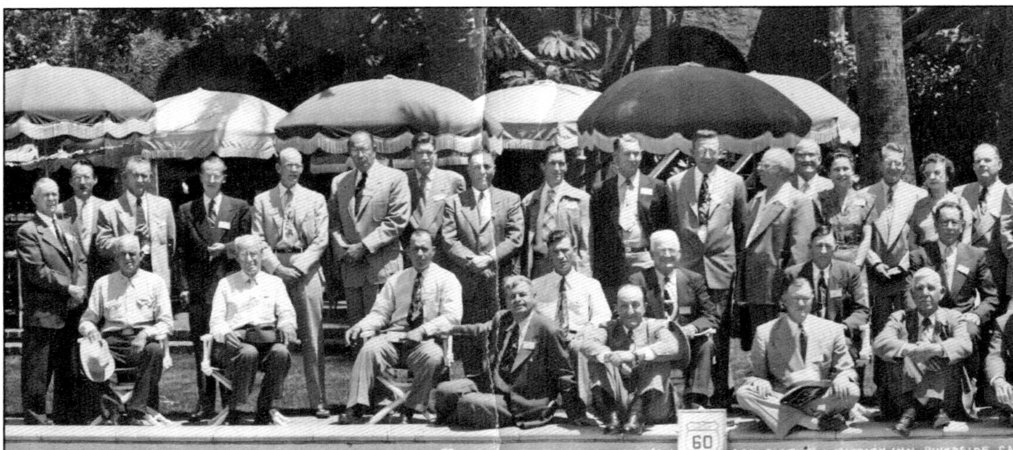

Show Low Highway 60 Association members hosted the 23rd Annual National Convention. Emma Adams (at right) wrote that the "meeting was held at Show Low in the Highway garage which was decorated beautifully, May 15, 1953. [After] an all day meeting, a big banquet was served that evening cooked by the LDS. Relief Society. The funds they cleared [were] used for furnishings for their Relief Society room." (Sheila McCleve Stewart.)

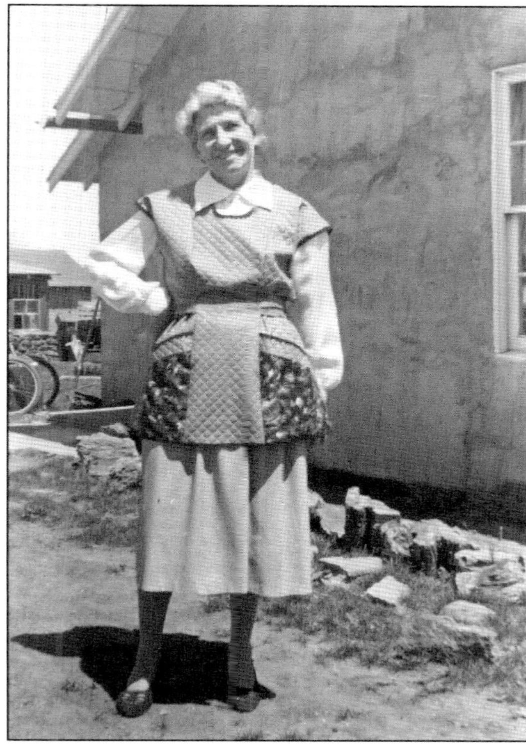

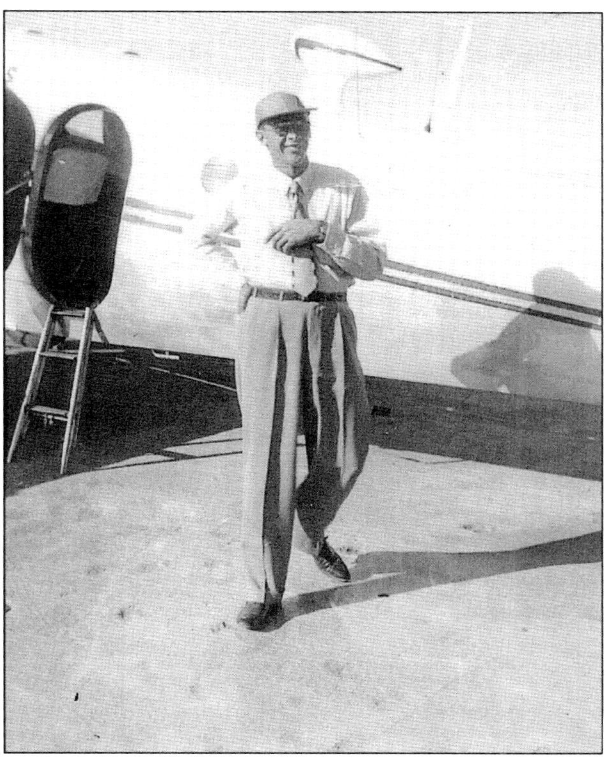

B. Y. "Flyin' Pete" Peterson was Southwest Lumber Mills' pilot for 35 years. Peterson ran the airport at Show Low, and his wife, Phoebe, was the "weather girl." He would call her to "get the wind to quit blowing so I can land," then local boys would bicycle to the airport to ride in the airplane as he taxied back to the hangar. Joe Baird took lessons from Peterson under the GI Bill. (Pete Peterson.)

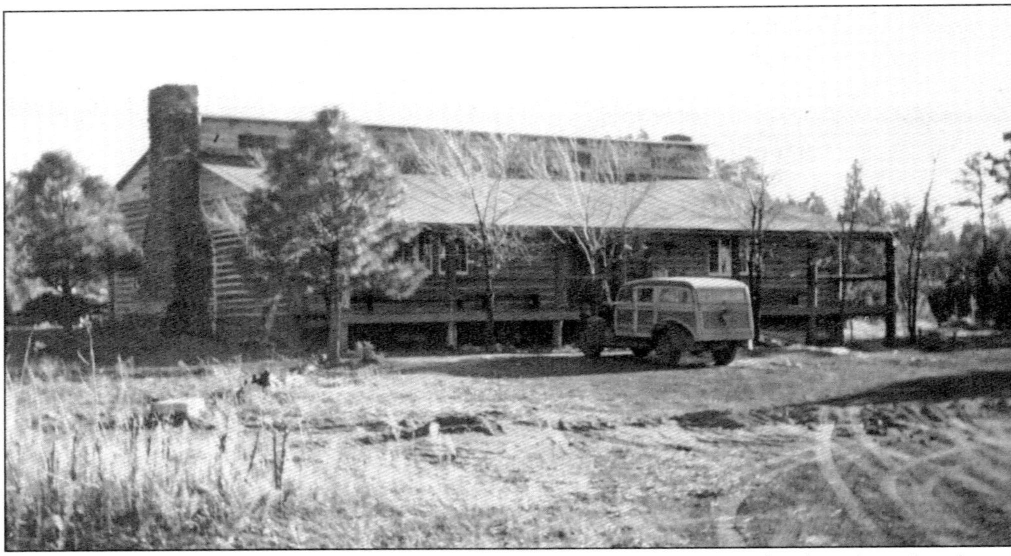

In 1947, Mary and Eric Marks purchased the Paint Pony Lodge (above). Their letterhead read, "We ain't got no pony—If'fen we did we wouldn't paint it—And this joint ain't no lodge! But isn't it a helluva purty name!?" A former member of the New York Stock Exchange, Eric still traded regularly and was the only man in town to subscribe to the *New York Times*. Eric worked to upgrade telephone service in Show Low; in the 1950s, it only operated eight hours a day. Mary, a former home economics radio show hostess in Los Angeles, was famous for her ginger cookies. The Markses (below) gave an annual Christmas party for local lads and lassies who were presented with gifts from the Markses' yearly trips to all corners of the world. (Both, SLHisSoc Museum.)

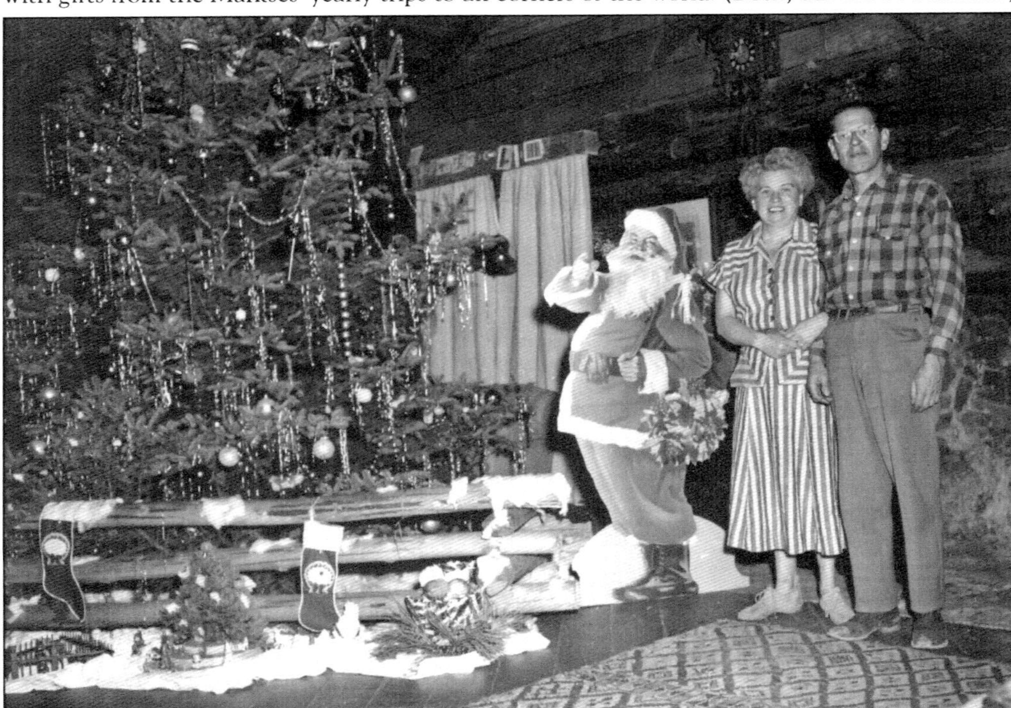

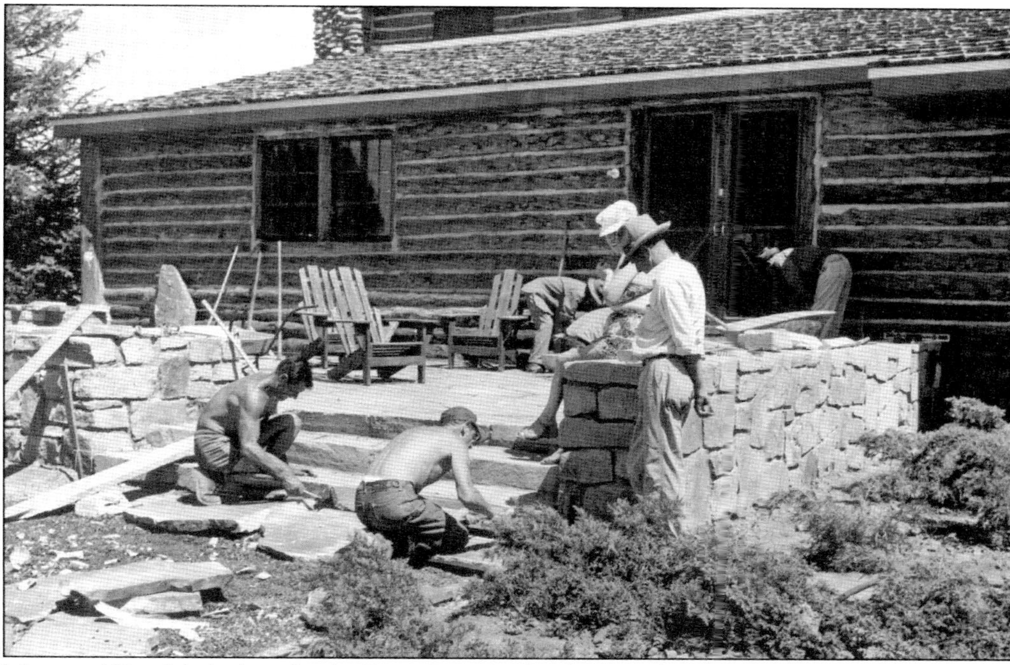

Mary and Eric Marks bought the Paint Pony Lodge from Walt and Esther "Dutch" Bassett, the third owners. It was originally built by Cmdr. Walter J. Willis in 1937, then sold to A. E. Dunn. The Markses made extensive renovations (above), both inside and out, getting it ready for guests. Guests often were dignitaries, artists, and Hollywood actors. Community members were invited to use the Paint Pony Lodge. Catholic mass was celebrated here; the cover of this book shows part of the eighth-grade graduating class in 1952. In the spring, pussy willows were always on display in the gathering room. The fireplace was made of three huge logs of petrified wood, and the cuckoo clock announced each hour (below). (Above, SLHisSoc Museum; below, Huso collection.)

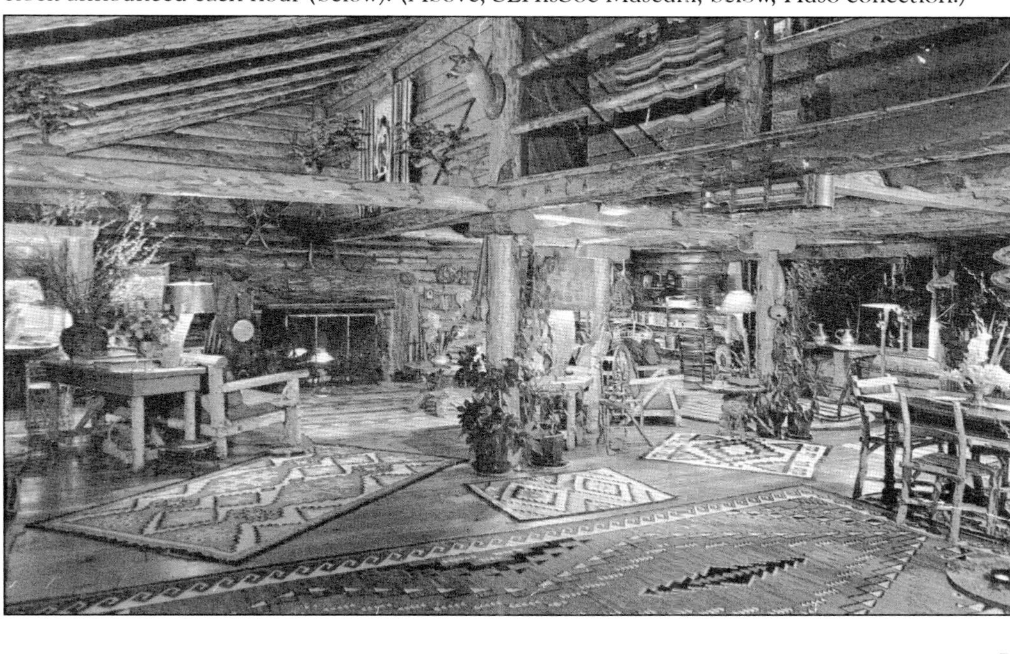

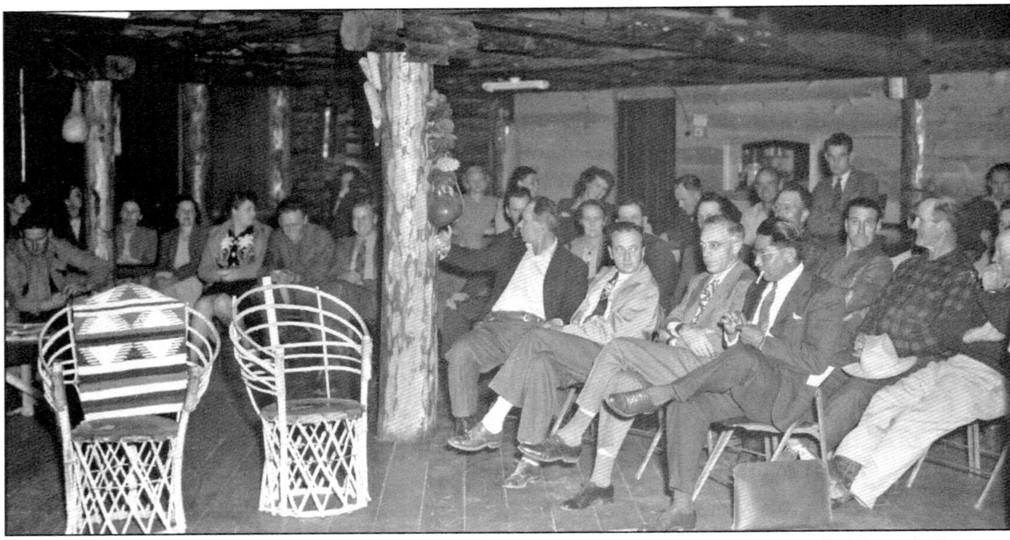

A district chamber of commerce meeting was held at the Paint Pony in 1947 (above). Some of the men include Ira McCleve, Ammon Hunt, Cliff Potts, Walt Mefford, Lester Oliver, Hugh Whipple, Arnold Kay, Clyde "Red" Rothlisberger, Devore Hudson, Ivan Larson, Ren Kay, and Lavon Turley. Pictured below are the women attending that meeting: from left to right, (first row) Neola Mills, unidentified, Irene Huso, Anne Scott, possibly Helen Rhoton, and Lavon Allen; (second row, leaning on couch) unidentified; (third row) Laura McNeil, Frances Rothlisberger, Kitty Kay, two unidentified, Dutch Bassett, Joy Chlarson, Esther Hall, Marzelle Higgins, and Dorothy Whipple. (Both, Huso collection.)

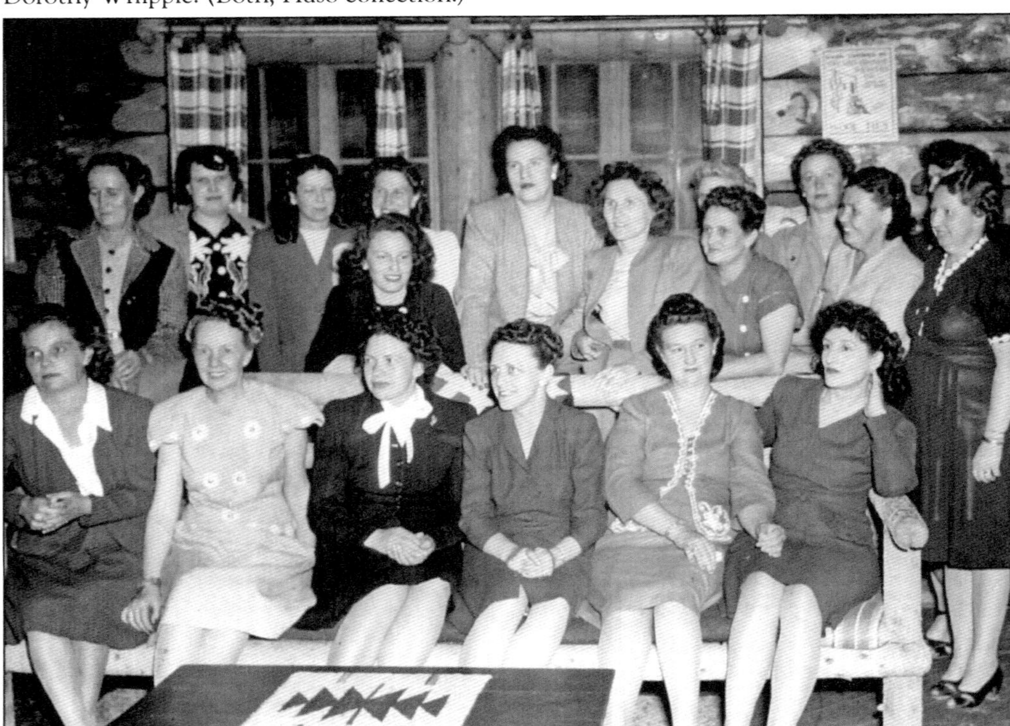

The Paint Pony Lodge (and other motels, bars, and restaurants) provided employment for many in the community. Often young girls worked as waitresses and housekeepers, especially during summer break from high school. Pictured here is Mildred Lewis, age 19 or 20, in front of the Paint Pony. Idella Penrod worked at the lodge for several years. (Sheila McCleve Stewart.)

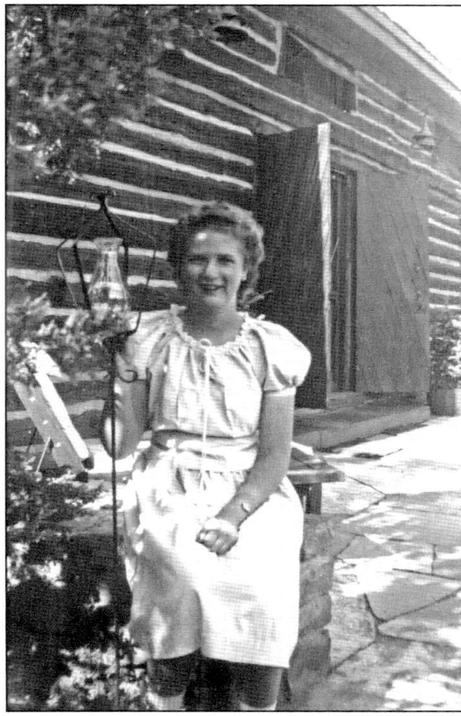

Nora Begay worked at the Paint Pony spinning wool and weaving Navajo rugs. Here she is in traditional dress with a Navajo upright loom. She spent two years weaving the long runner for the hall upstairs, and she made a large 9-by-12-foot rug for the main lodge. Mary and Eric Marks were godparents for her grandchildren. (SLHisSoc Museum.)

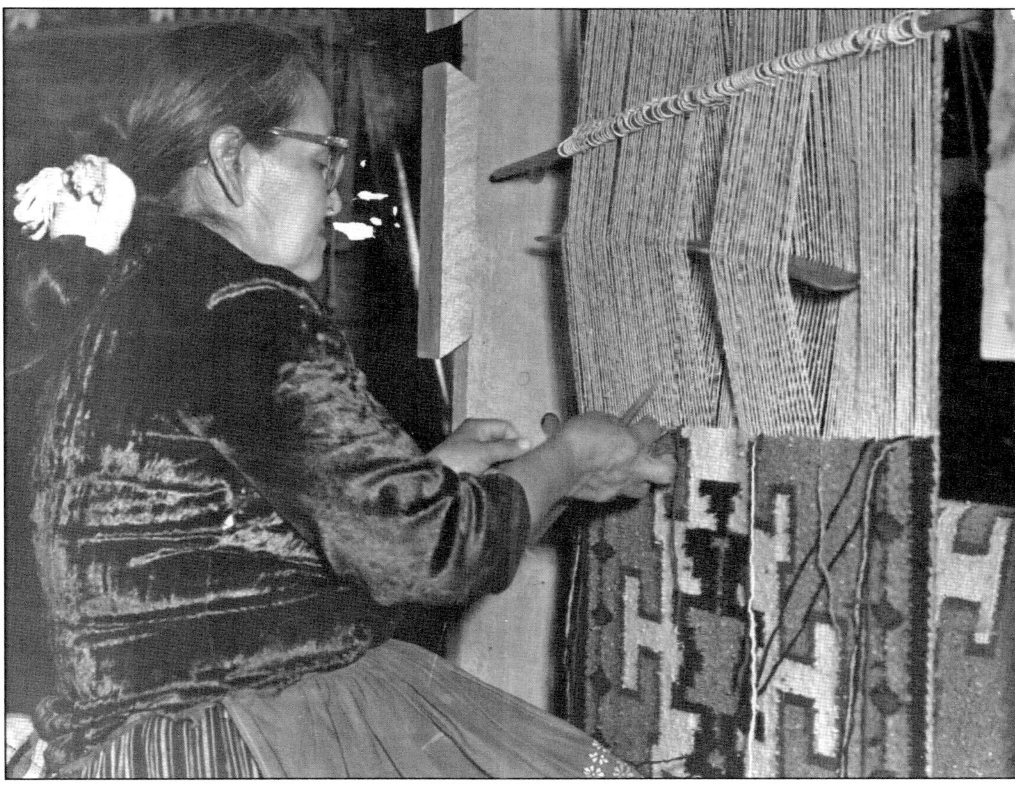

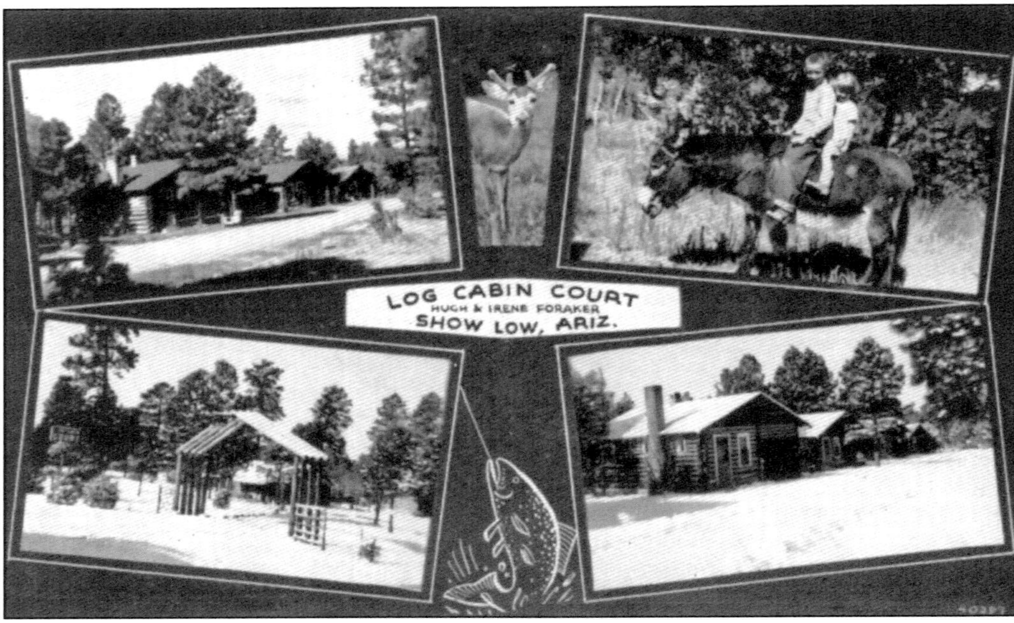

Hugh and Irene Foraker came to Show Low in the 1940s from South Bend, Indiana. They bought and operated the Log Cabin Court, a group of rustic log cabins across from the Paint Pony Lodge. Their children, Hugh Jr. and Diane, are pictured in the upper right. The Forakers also owned Show Low Drug, where Hugh was the pharmacist. (Ellis collection.)

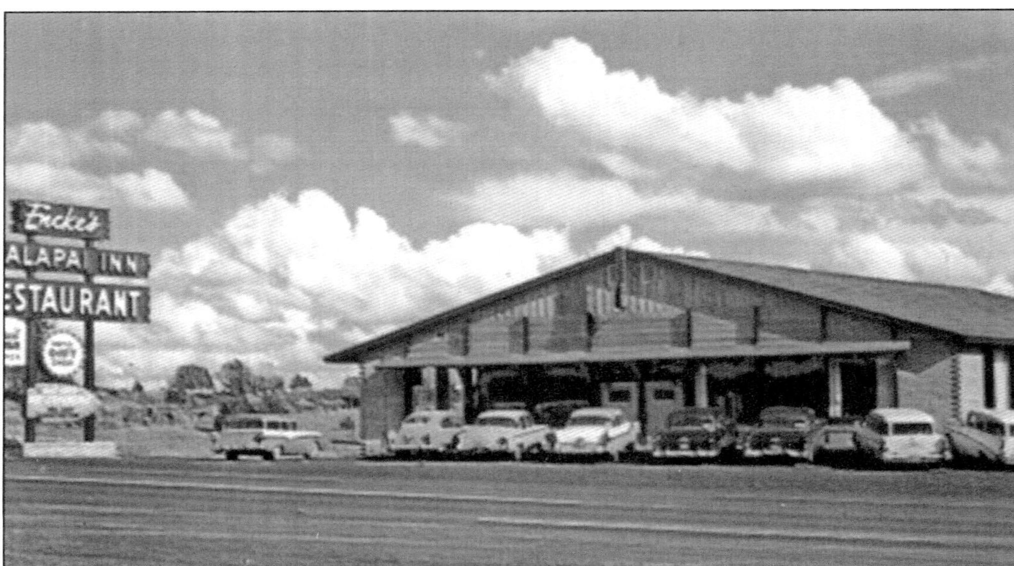

The Malapai Inn was constructed in 1957 by C. I. Robson of Mesa, who built it for Ann Encke. She operated it as a steak house and bar. If someone could eat a 52-ounce steak and all the trimmings, it was free. About one out of six who tried could do so; one man actually returned twice. Encke also taught several Show Low teens the culinary arts. (Huso collection.)

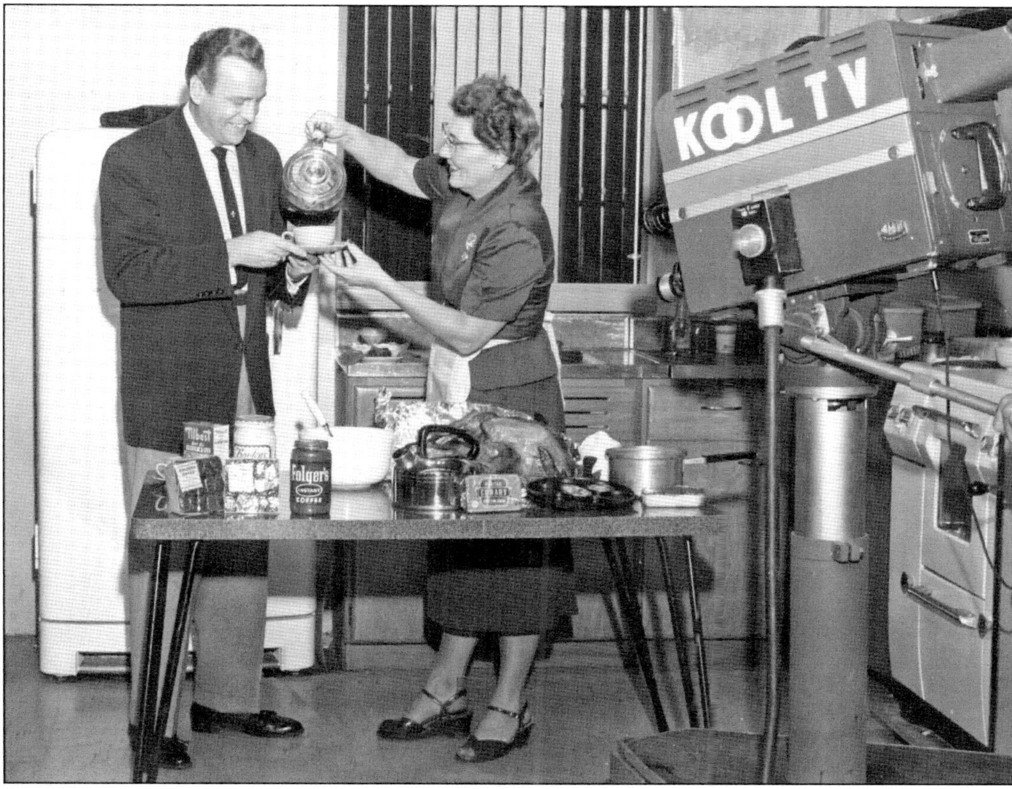

In the early days of television, Ann Encke (above with Wally Imes) was the hostess of Recipe Roundup on KOOL-TV in Phoenix. She was codeveloper of Rosarita Mexican Food Company and owned two restaurants in Mesa. In Show Low, she was a community activist and, in 1960, drove to Barry Goldwater's cabin in the White Mountain Country Club to ask for a donation for the hospital under construction, strongly hinting that it was yet to be named. In 1963 (below), she was named Show Low's Woman of the Year for her hospital fund-raising efforts. Mel Holladay (right) was Show Low mayor and named Man of the Year. Also shown here is L. C. "Jerry" Hall, Show Low realtor and president of the chamber of commerce. (Both, Steven Petrie.)

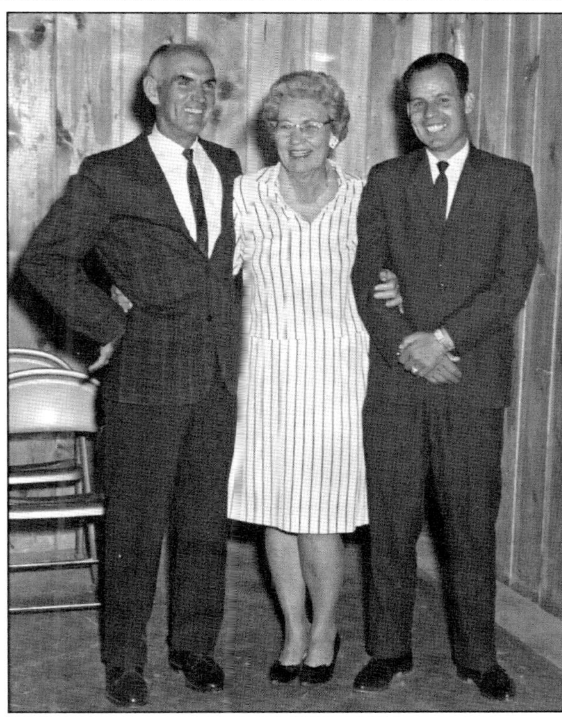

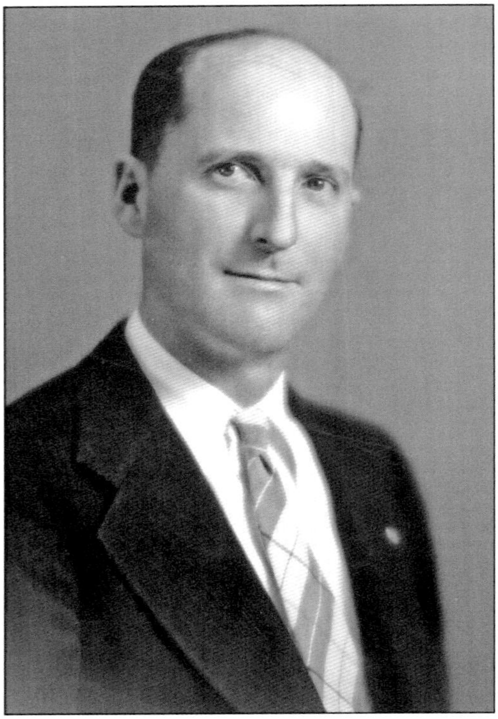

William R. Bourdon was born in Minnesota in 1894 and was awarded the Distinguished Service Cross during World War I. In 1927, he purchased 137,000 acres in Navajo County. At the time of this photograph, he served as state legislator. He was also a delegate to the Republican National Convention, and he ran for governor in 1948. During World War II, he first served on the draft board and then rejoined the army. The *Holbrook Tribune-News* reported, "A sissy is a guy who will resign from a draft board to join the Commandos." (Arizona State Archives 01-8042.)

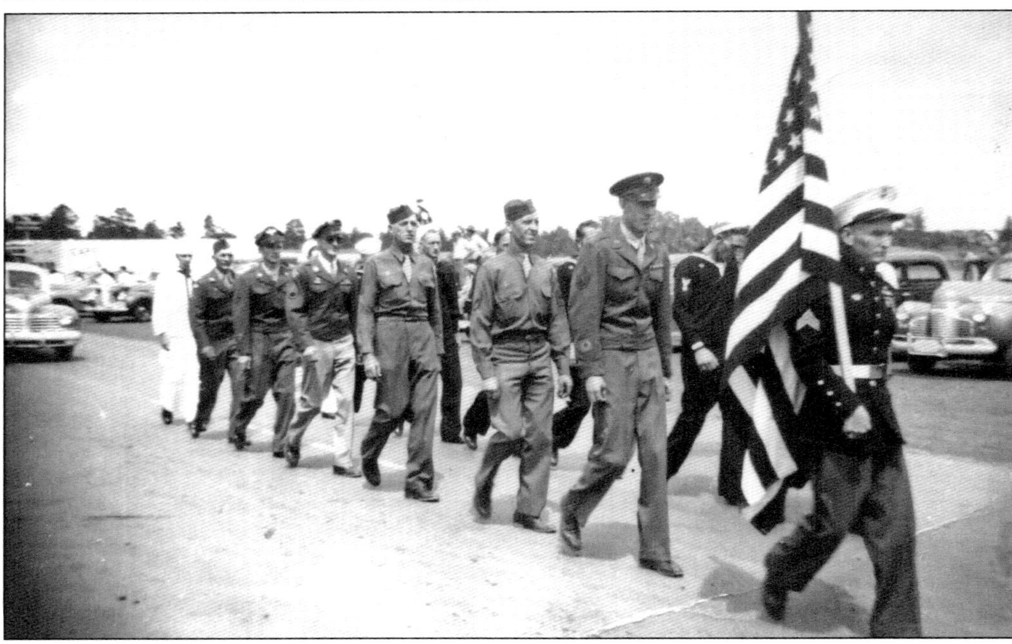

Almost all young men in Show Low served in the military during World War II. Marching in the Show Low parade in 1950 are World War II veterans, with the army vets in the first row. From left to right, the army vets are three unidentified, Otto Mills, unidentified, Clyde Rothlisberger, and Leland Nikolaus, lead by marine Hal Butler. The navy vets were in the second row. They are all unidentified except Lynn Kartchner, who is next to the flag. (Otto Mills.)

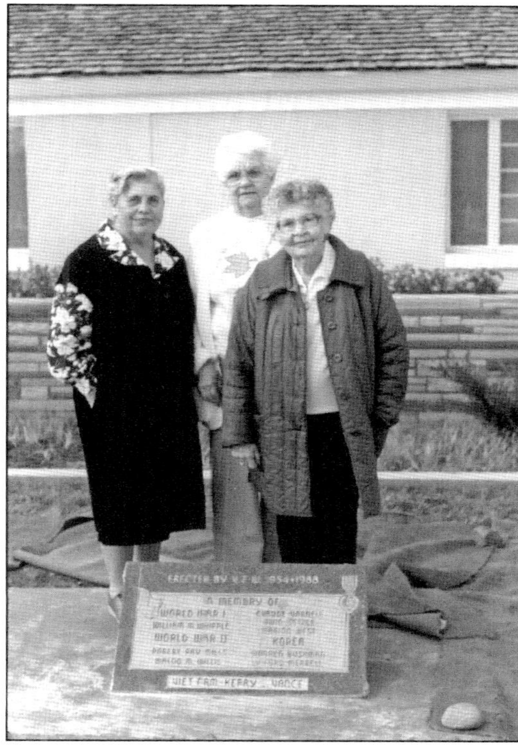

In 1954, the VFW erected this memorial to Show Low soldiers who died in the military: William M. Whipple in World War I; Robert Ray Mills, Waldo M. Willis, Claude Varnell, Owin Setzer, and Marion West in World War II; and Warren Bushman and Linford Merrell in Korea. In 1988, Kerry L. Vance's name was added for Vietnam. Pictured at right remembering Marion West are his sister Hazel; wife, Myrtle; and sister Marzelle. Below is Marion West, who died in France on December 26, 1944. (Both, Ray West.)

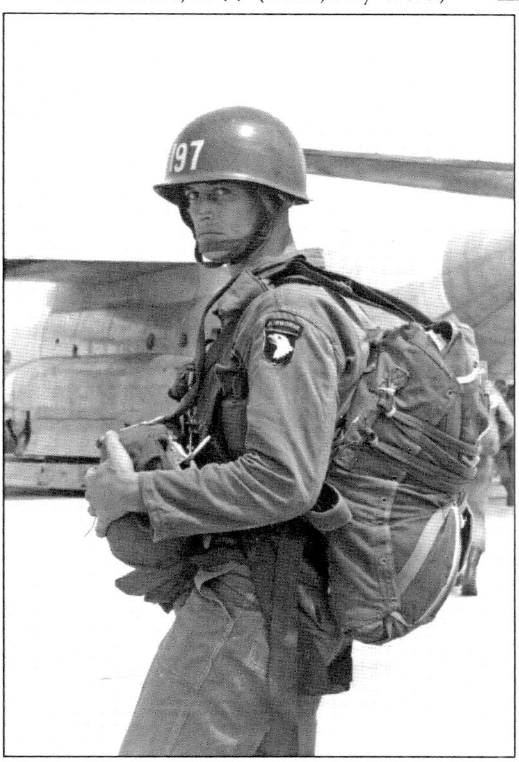

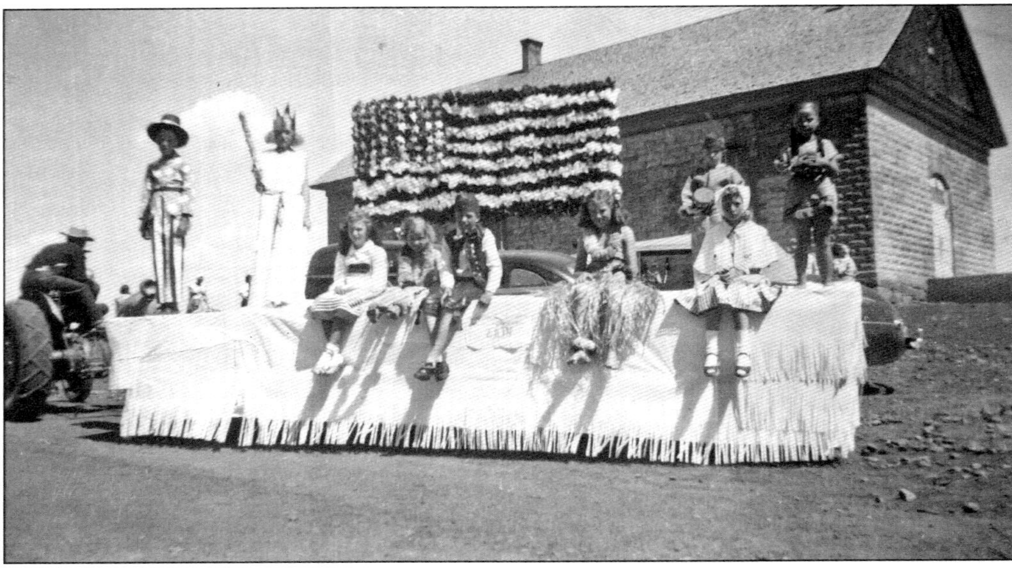

These two photographs show the original LDS church in the late 1940s. Above is a group of Primary children representing various ethnic groups for the Fourth of July parade, probably in 1947. Below, Bill Huso photographed the Shell bulk plant and old church after a 1946 snowfall. In 1935, church leaders began making plans for a larger building. Some money was raised, but construction was delayed with World War II. In 1945, the members started sponsoring the rodeo to raise funds. The old Relief Society building and church, on the north and south ends of "church house hill," were torn down, and meetings were held in the school gymnasium during construction. (Above, Elizabeth Nikolaus collection; below, Huso collection.)

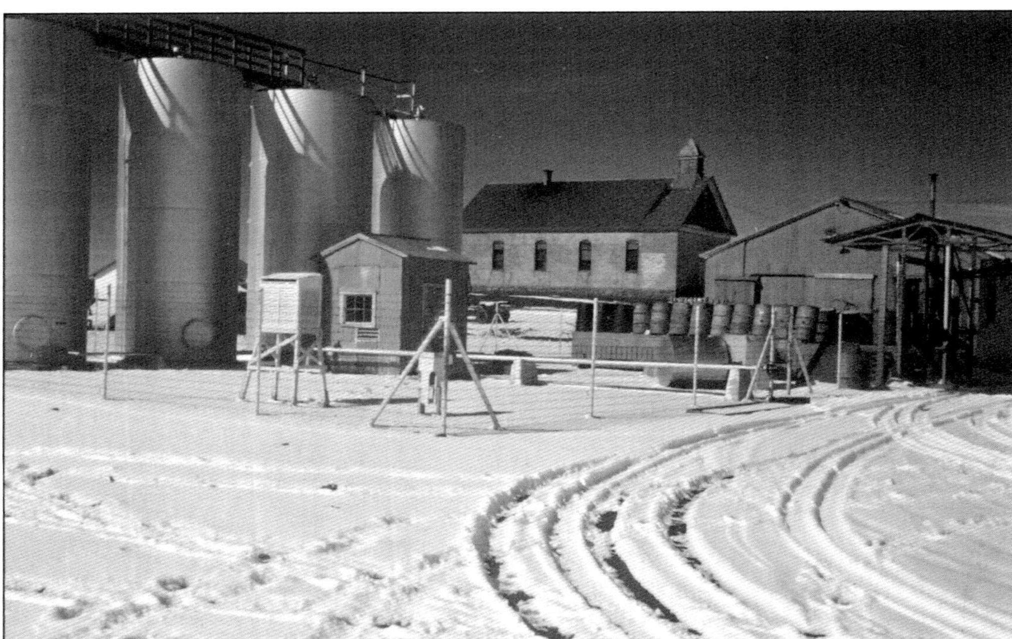

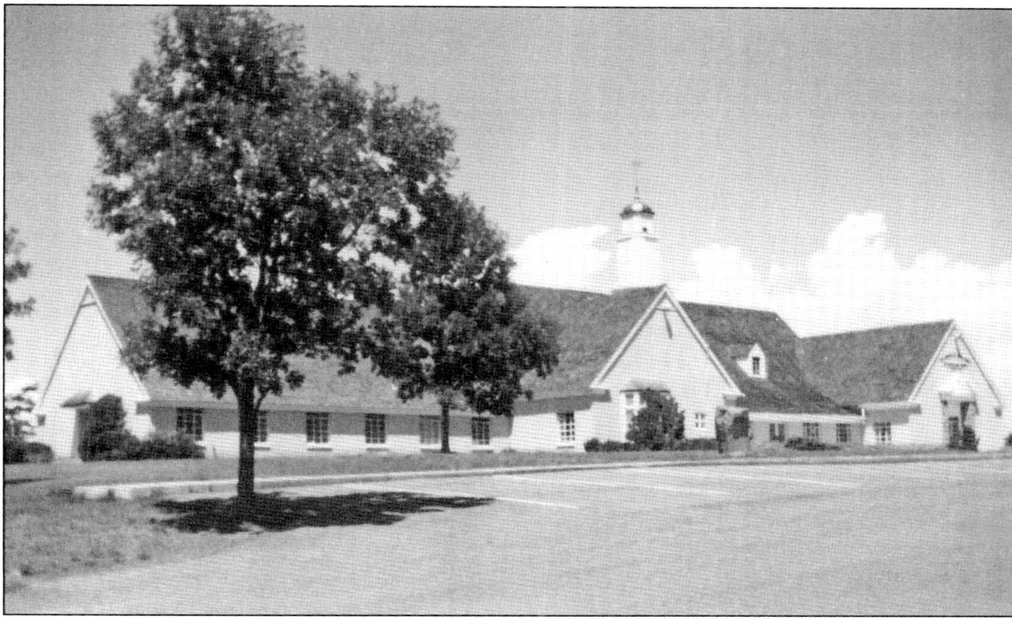

After several years of labor and fund-raising, the new church (above) was completed and dedicated in 1953. The cultural hall included a beautiful flagstone fireplace on the west side. Below is a Gleaner class (girls age 16-18) about 1952, standing in front of the fireplace. From left to right are Shirley Petersen, unidentified, Jean Zellner, Lucille Jaeger, Venla Whipple, Anita Joy Reidhead, Teddie Val Stock, Glenda Willis, and LaDawn Ellsworth. Elizabeth Nikolaus was their teacher. (Above, photograph by Dixie Stock Gillespie; below, Elizabeth Nikolaus collection.)

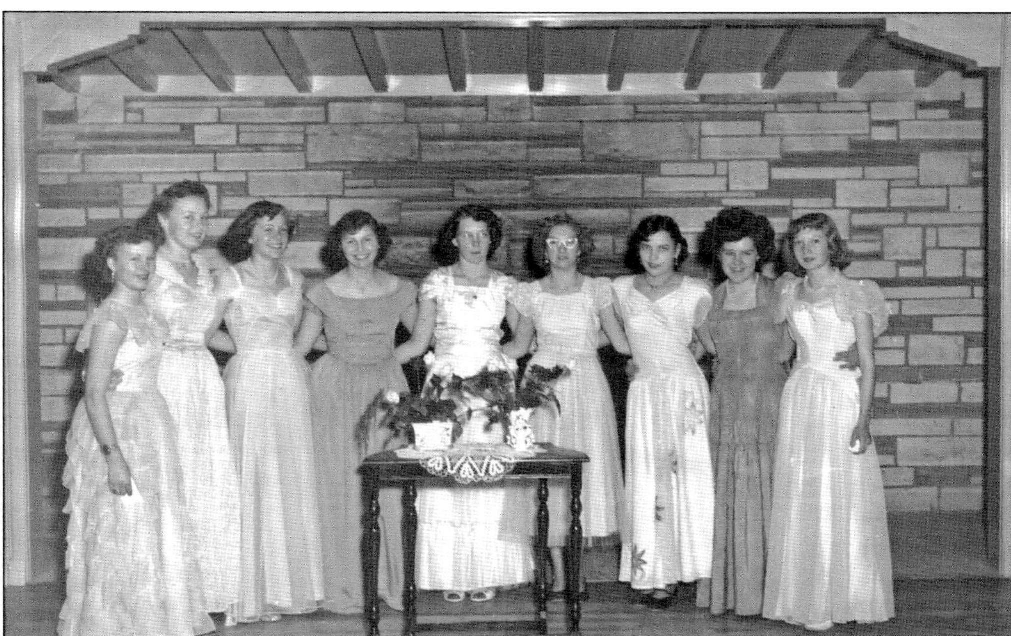

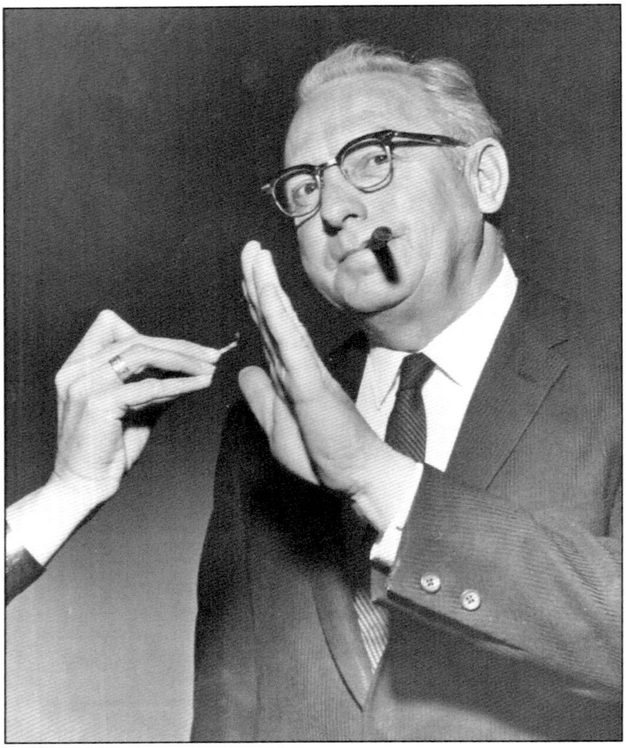

Bill Huso (at left) was born in Joice, Iowa, in 1909 and came to Holbrook in 1935 as a cashier/bookkeeper/credit manager for A&B Schusters. He met Irene Frost and married her New Year's Eve 1937. During World War II, Huso worked at the Gila River Japanese-American Relocation Center. In 1945, he made one last move, to Show Low, to operate the Shell gas station for John Scott, who was later a highway commissioner. Huso and Scott became partners, added onto the building, and sold everything for a one-stop family store. As Huso's son, Mike, wrote, "People came to buy gas, shoes, nails and visit. Dad became known as respected for his good advice [and] listening ear." Huso was active in civic affairs, becoming state senator. At Huso's Shoes (below), Bill and grandson Colt visit with Santa in 1969. (Both, Huso collection.)

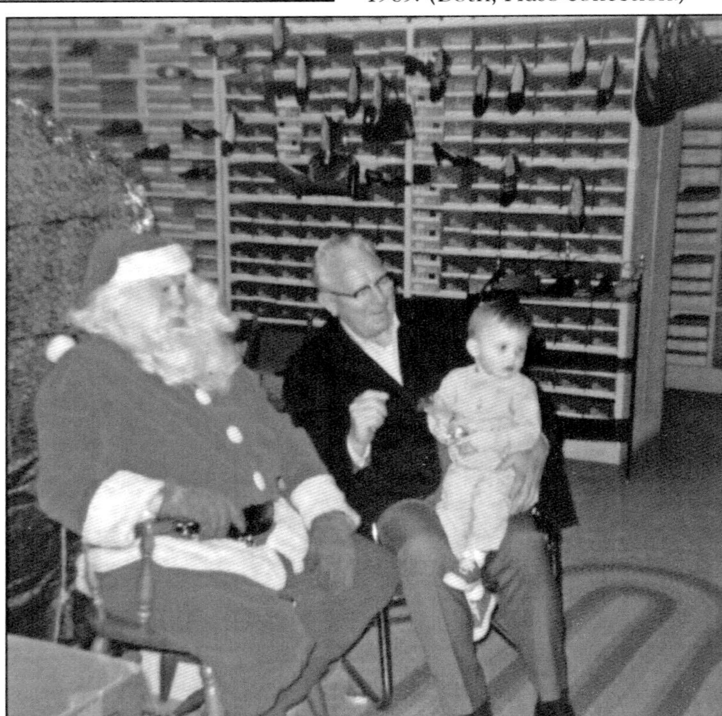

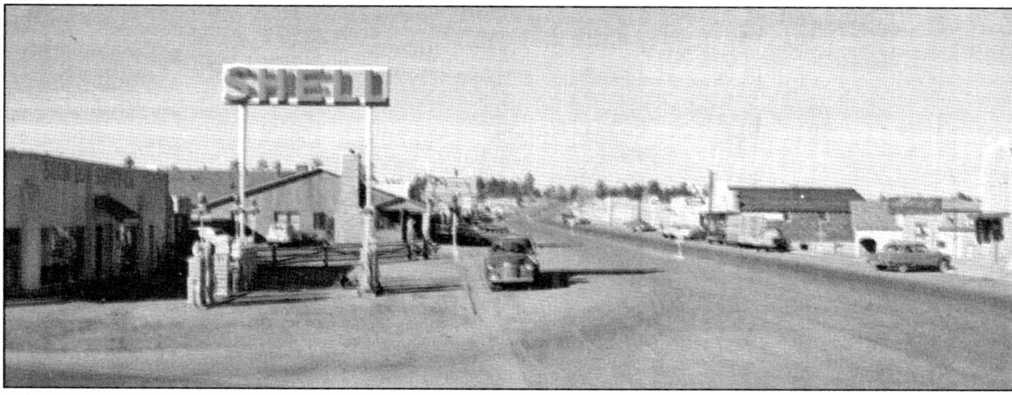

July 7, 1952, was a scary day in Show Low. The Shell tanker was dumping fuel into underground tanks at the Show Low Supply Company when a local lad, with firecrackers left over from the Fourth of July, lit one and threw it down near the tanks. The driver, seeing the fire, jumped into the truck to move it from the area, but the hose was still spewing gasoline. Adjacent buildings were saved by Show Low's volunteer fire department, townspeople, and the McNary Fire Department, which could pump water out of Show Low Creek. Because the business catered to sportsmen, rounds of ammunition were firing, along with Fuller paint and oil cans exploding. A most fitting sight the next day was the Shell sign with a fallen "S" (below). Irene Huso is kicking through the rubble of their business. (Both, Huso collection.)

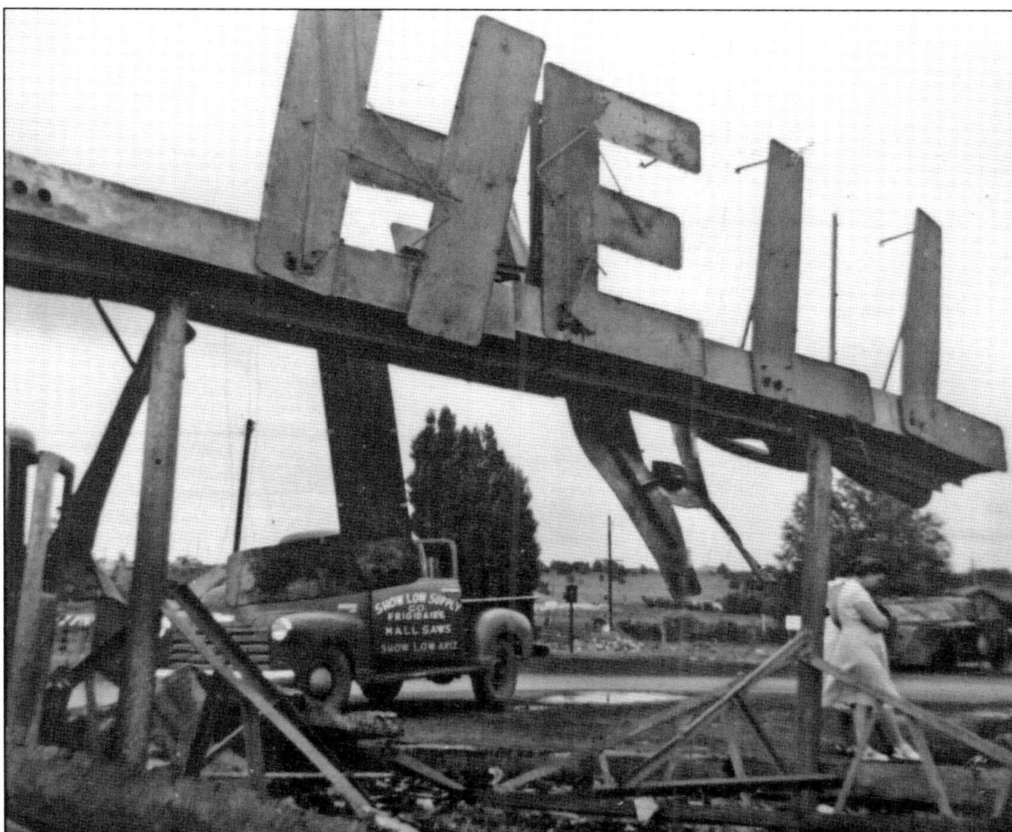

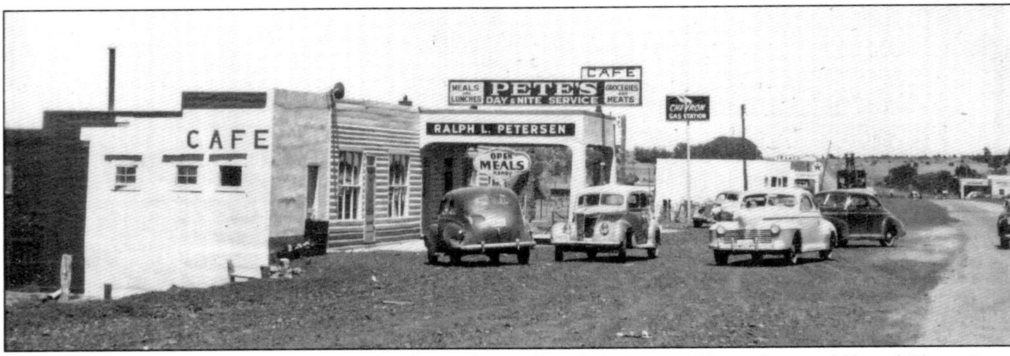

About 1940, K. B. and Irma West had a café south of Highway 60 in the middle of Show Low, which they moved across the street. In 1942, they sold it to Jim Stratton; his daughter, Shirley Jones, remembers the living quarters being converted into five motel rooms for construction workers. Later owners included Ralph and Ina Smithson Peterson and Arlee and Verdie Maxwell. The building was finally converted to Kings Market. (Deborah Austin.)

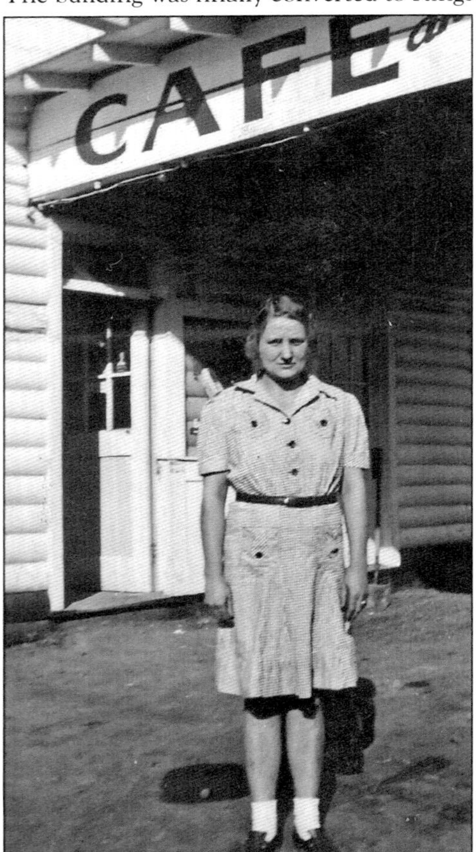

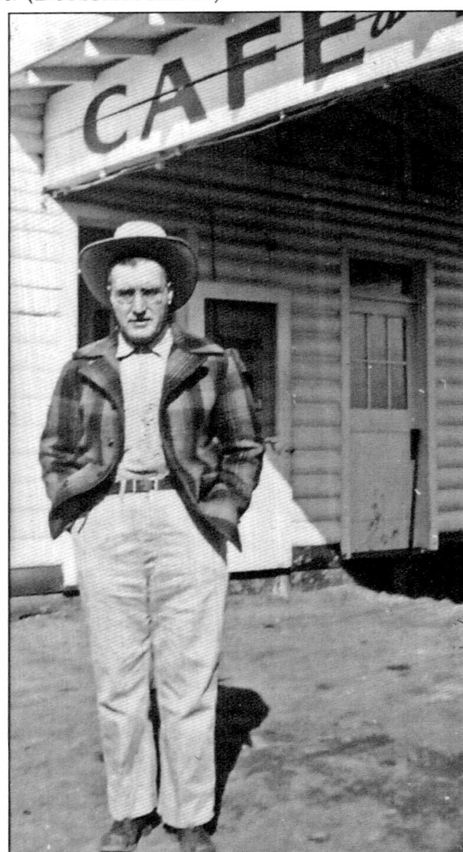

Wallace "Wal" and Alice Penrod (above) ran the night shift at K. B. West's café in the early 1940s. Seeing the need for another good eating place for construction workers, they opened the Wal and Alice Café in the Whiting Brothers building. They specialized in chicken-fried steaks, roast beef dinners, and Alice's melt-in-your-mouth cream pies. After operating cafés in Show Low and Lakeside, they retired in 1956. (Alberta Nikolaus.)

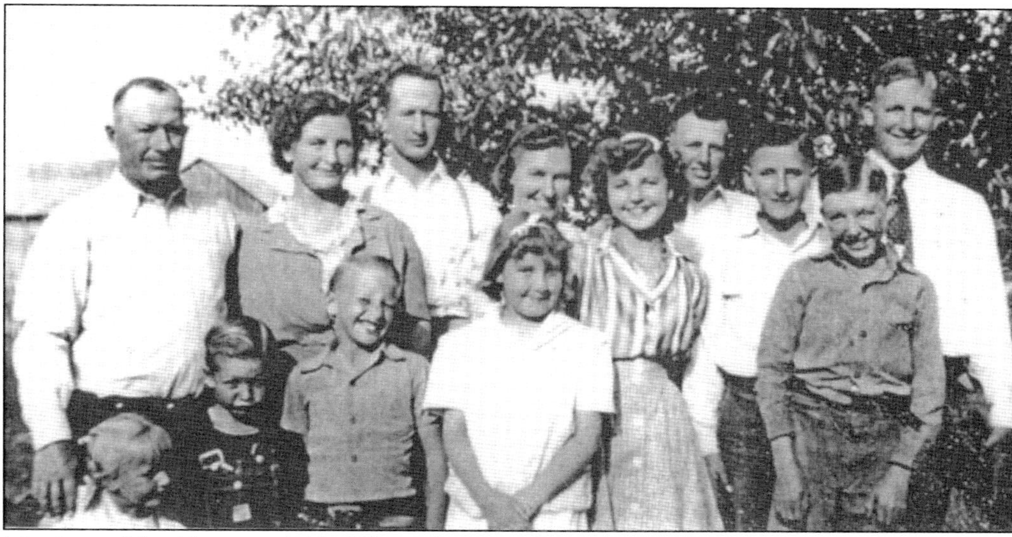

Members of the Almon and Alta Ellsworth Owens family have been involved in diverse vocations. Occupations of family members have included rancher, farmer, teacher, restaurant manager, and truck driver. Some worked at the paper mill, in the City of Show Low maintenance, and at the Shell distributorship; others owned a grocery store and trailer park. (Moylen and Joy Owens.)

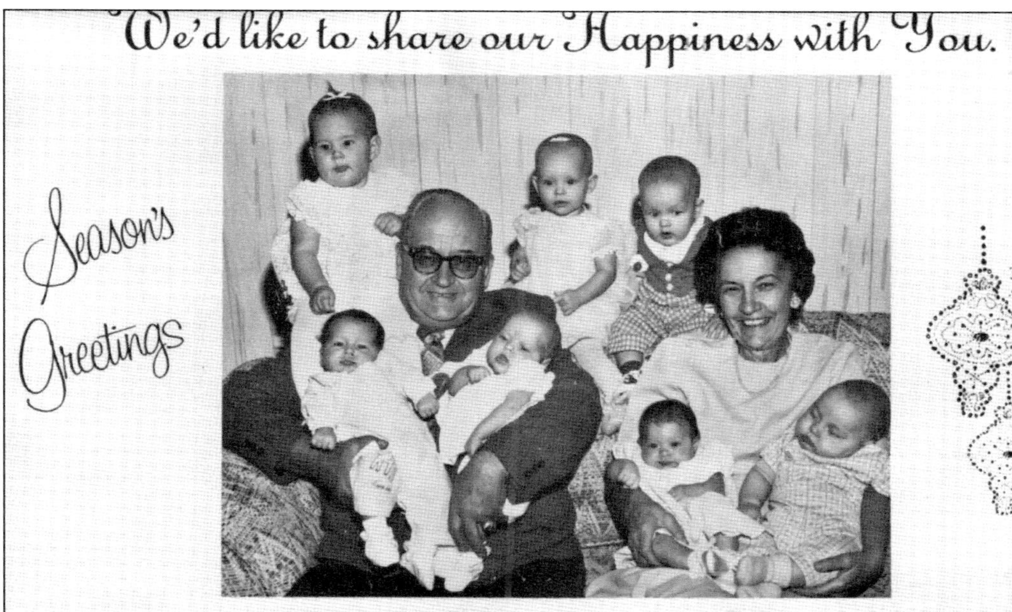

Orr and Roxie Owens celebrated 1977 with seven new grandchildren born. Roxie was a mainstay of Show Low music, directing and producing many operettas and road shows. In 2009, at 88 years of age, Roxie still teaches 35 piano and voice students. (Beatrice Jarvis.)

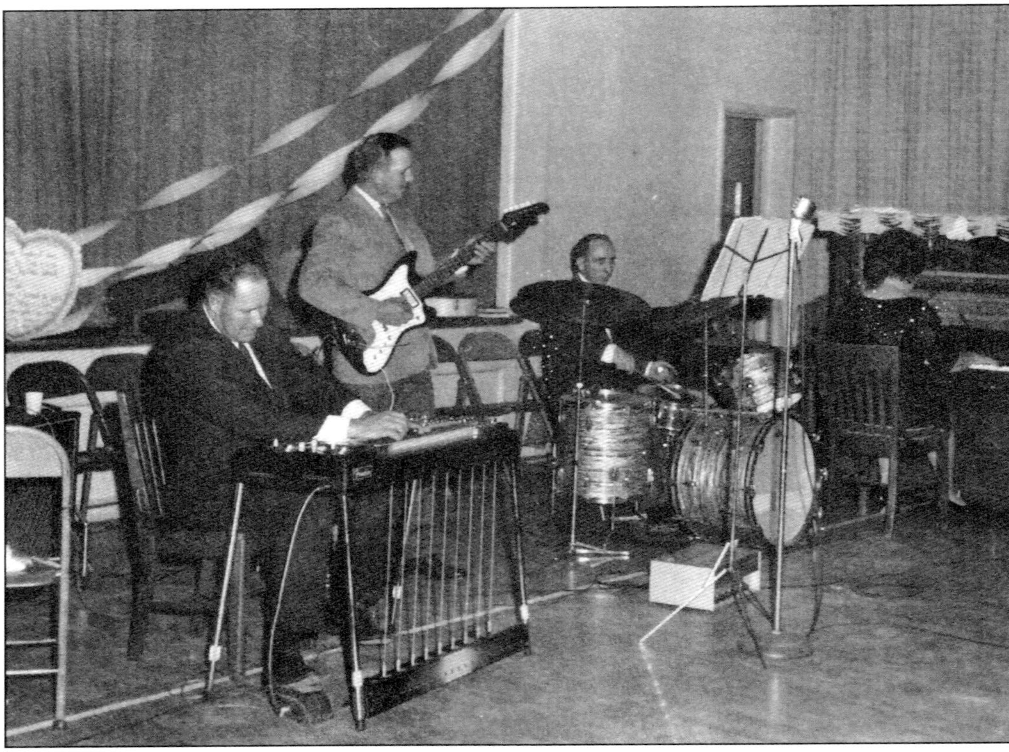

Garth Nikolaus and his Westernaires made music in the White Mountains for over 40 years. The photograph above includes, from left to right, Garth playing the steel guitar (although he usually played acoustic guitar when he sang), Milt Gillespie on lead guitar, Garth's brother-in-law Norman "Bud" Willis on drums, and Garth's sister Wanda Willis on piano. Ed Gillespie, Milt's brother, was the band's first lead guitarist. Nikolaus's wife, Alberta, said that Garth was "never so proud as when his son Brad played with him." (Alberta Nikolaus.)

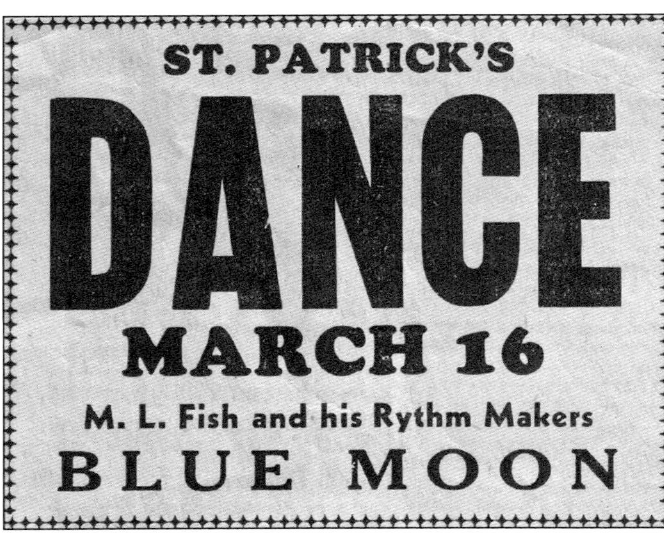

Dances were held every Saturday night at the Blue Moon, a unique hexagonal building west on Highway 60. Rupert Stock said, "I split wood for Joe West's pot-bellied stoves for dance tickets. All the teenagers in Show Low were pretty good dancers. Besides, we met lots of girls from the areas around Show Low there. This was the main menu for fun at the time." Mahonri Lazelle Fish and his wife, Minnie Adams, also played for many wedding dances (including their own). (Darla Baird.)

A patient horse and dog await their master at Bill's Bar (at right), the local watering hole for decades. Started by Bill Jennings, it was originally a café, bus stop, gas station, store, and bar. Later it evolved into a bar with a wood stove and wood chips on the floor (mostly to disguise the uneven floor). On the stage in the rear, local western bands crooned and played on Friday and Saturday nights. The dance hall was on stilts, and people standing outside during a popular western stomp questioned how it kept from collapsing. Below, Jennings (left) and an unidentified man prepare to install the beautiful parquet bar top. Many names and dates were carved into it; it served the same purpose as the old oak tree where lovers memorialize each other. (Right, photograph by Deborah Austin; below, Huso collection.)

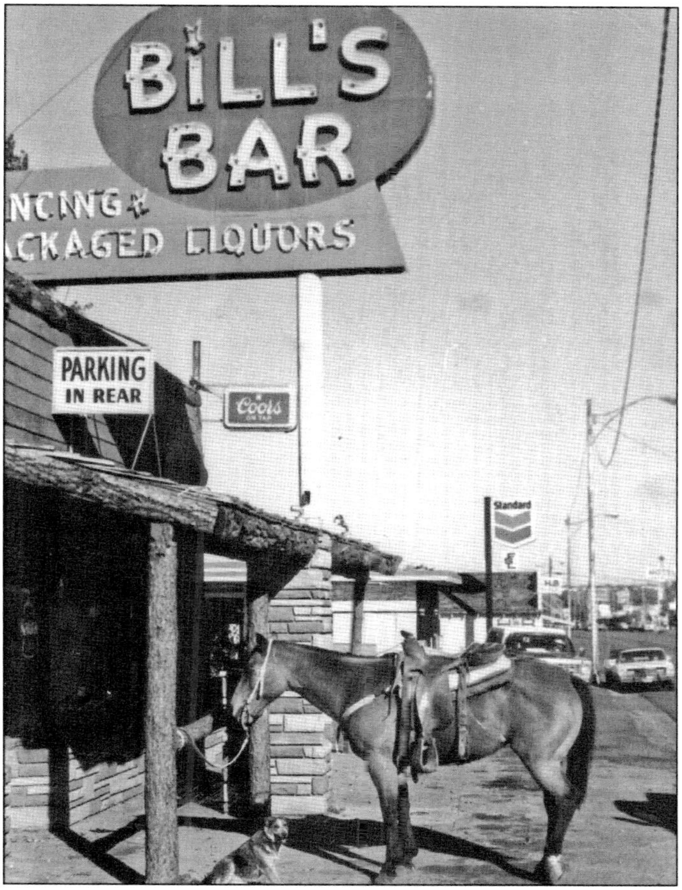

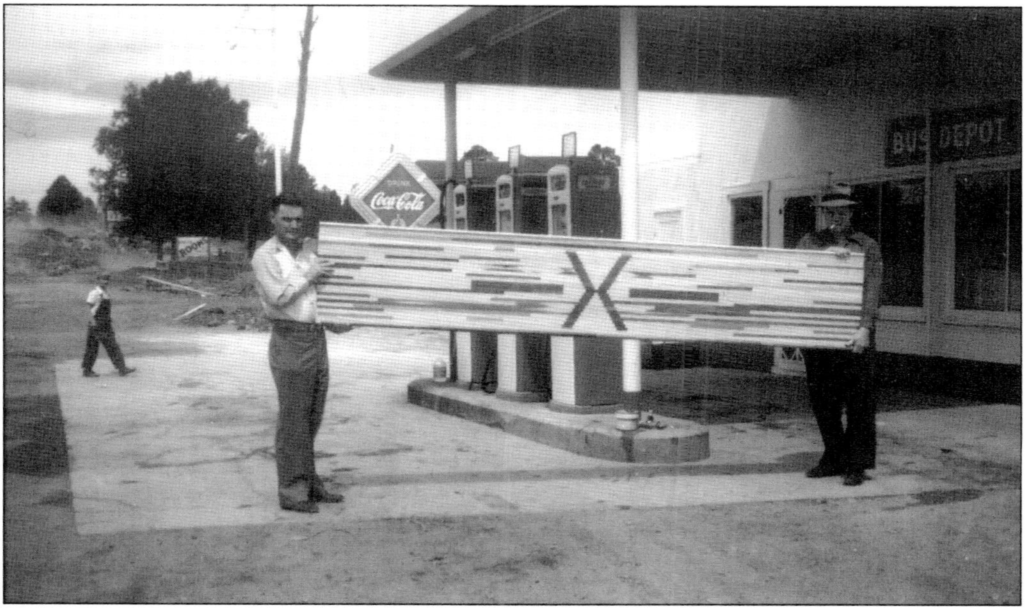

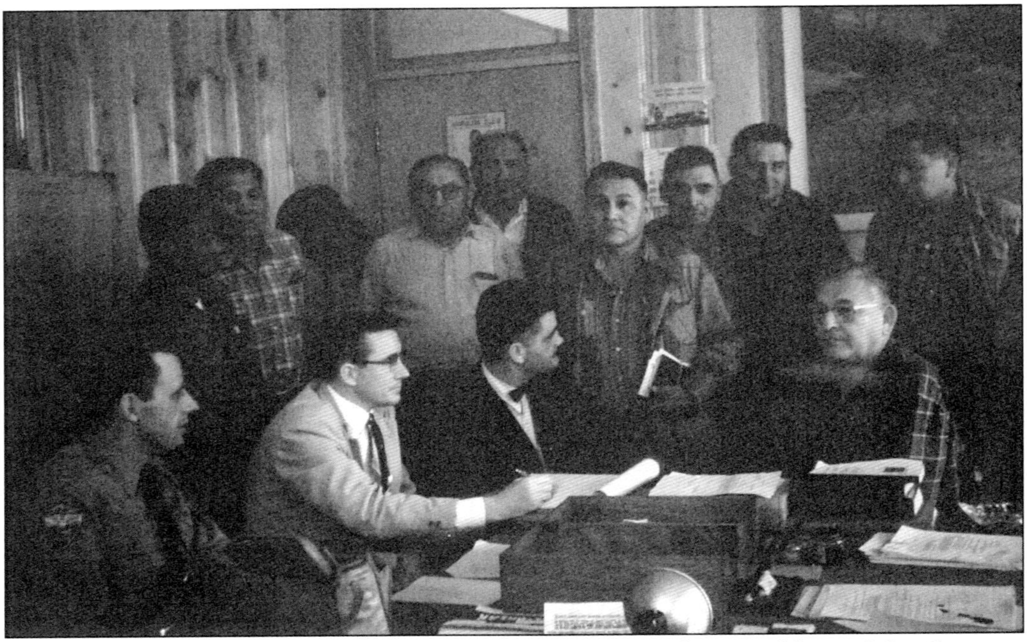

Winter sports enthusiasts, including Harold and Eleanor Vaughan, Paul Jones, John Consoni, and Jim McNeil, began in 1957 to work toward developing a ski run. The place they picked was just beyond the turnoff to Big Cienega on the Apache Reservation. They petitioned the Tribal Council to let them develop it. Pictured above are John Consoni (left) and Lamar Welker (second from left) with various tribal members at the signing of the contract. Below, Ed Vaughan (left) and Jim McNeil take advantage of a bonfire on a crisp day in January 1958 at Big Cienega Ski Run. (Both, Vaughan collection.)

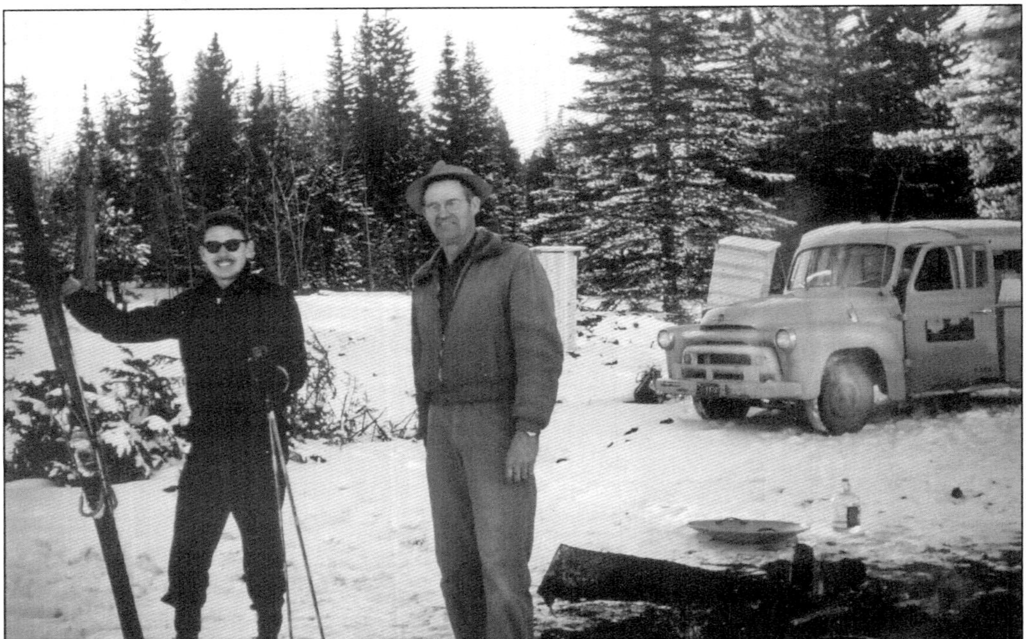

Pictured at right is Terry Doucet of Pinetop surveying the pristine winter landscape at Big Cienega in 1958. This photograph was reproduced in *Arizona Highways*. Lloyd Stock believes that the lift at Big Cienega was powered by Navajo County deputy Jim Stock's former patrol car, a 1939 Ford, because of a rectangular hole in the dash where the radio would have been and a round hole from the antenna. The lift was ingenious; the cable was wrapped around the rear rim, and the intact engine and transmission were used to advance and reverse the lift. Below, Jacque Vaughan (left) and Carrie Ellen Hughey have built a shelter from branches and logs in 1957 with hopes that no one uses it for a marshmallow roast when they take their next time on the ski hill. (Both, Vaughan collection.)

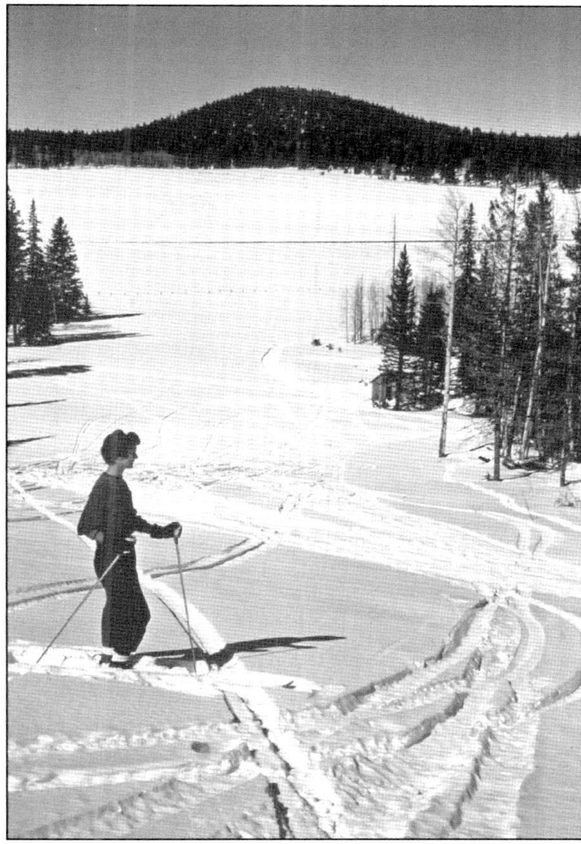

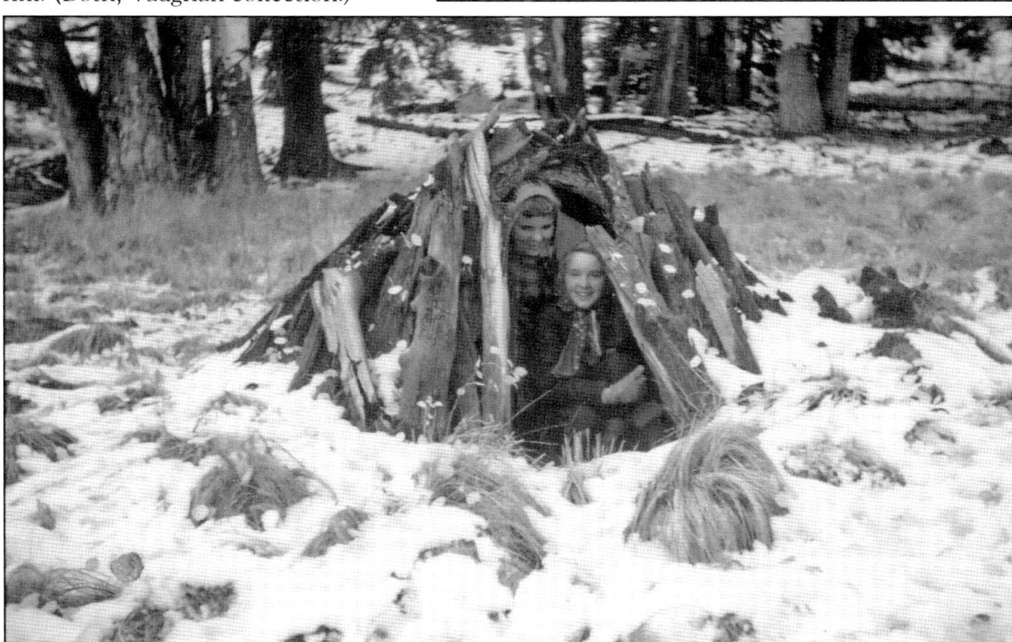

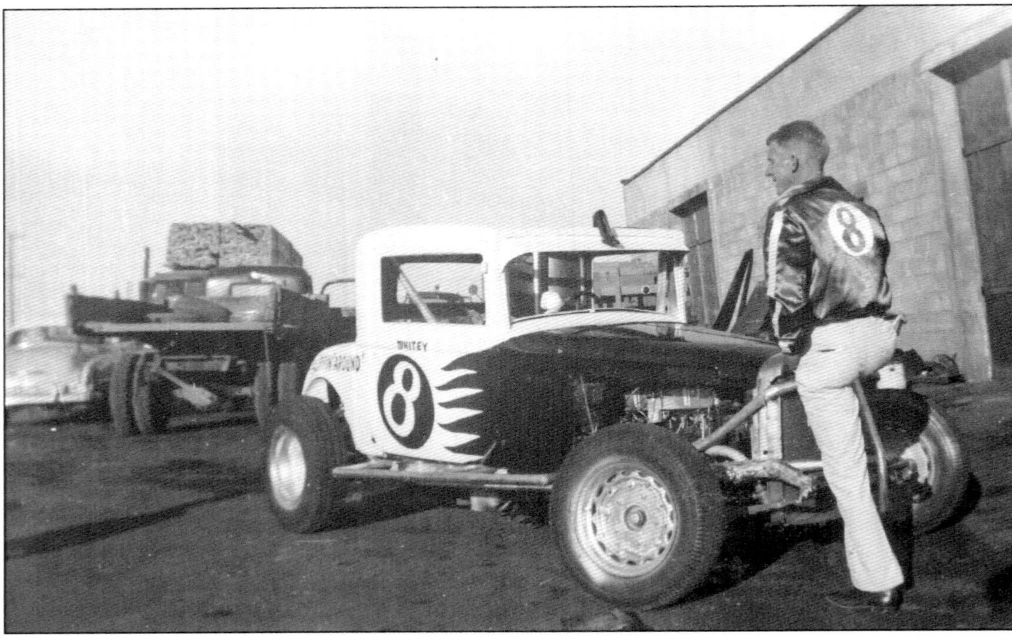

In the early 1950s, Arthur "Whitey" Adams (above), his brother Norman, and brother-in-law Lloyd Capps all had modified stock cars that they raced primarily in Holbrook. Whitey's "8-Ball" Ford (above) was well known for taking first place. Emma Adams wrote of the photograph below that Jim "H" Adams was inspecting to see that all was ready for the races because he well knew that as soon as the men had washed off the cement from a day's work at the ready-mix plant and had clean clothes on, they would be on their way, sandwiches vanishing as they traveled. Their first racecar was one found at the dump and transformed into the first No. 8. Betty Adams, married to Arthur's brother Gail, said she was amazed that Emma Hansen Adams, noted Show Low historian, had compiled so many photo albums of family cars and trucks. (Both, Lois Adams Lemons.)

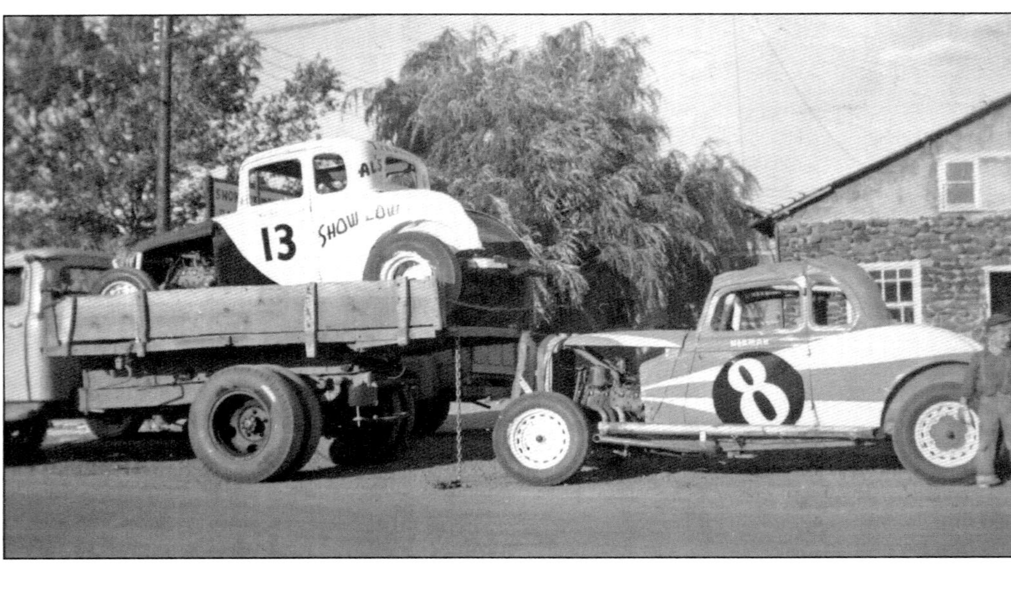

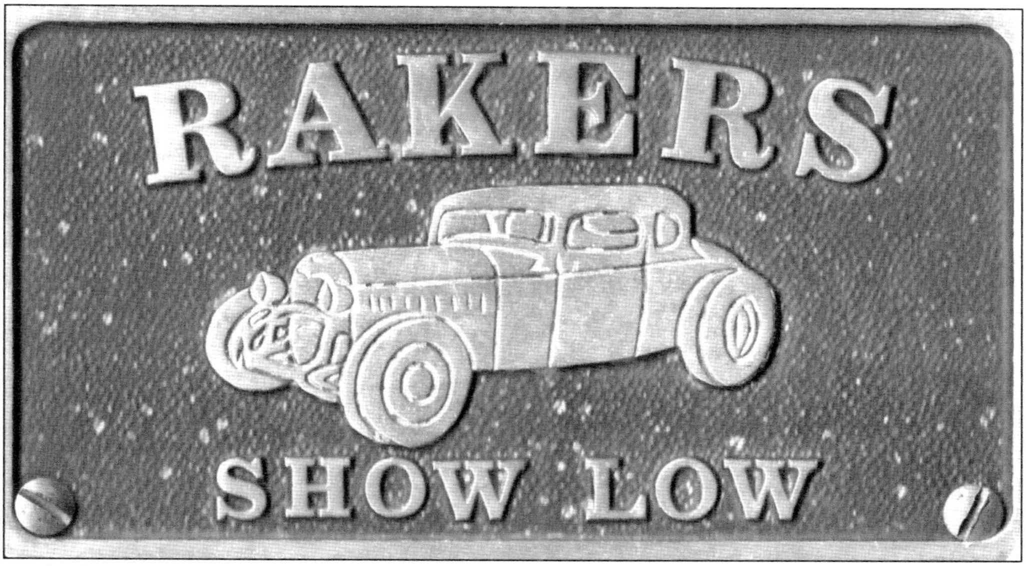

In the late 1950s, a spin-off of the Rakers Car Club of Mesa was formed in Show Low. The car enthusiasts talked street rods and drag races, taking their prized rides to drags in Winslow, Chandler, Deer Valley, Beeline, and other racetracks. Members included Howard Hansen, Mickey Pew, Don Roe Tanner, Larry Whipple, Doug Woolford, Mike Huso, Gail Adams, Arvel Adams, Lynn McNeil, Terry Holladay, Gary Nikolaus, Tony Jaeger, and John Stock. They gave out a card with this sentiment when helping motorists: "You have been assisted by a member of the 'Rakers of Show Low.' A car club organized by a group of safety-minded auto enthusiasts dedicated to the sport of safe hot rodding." Below, Huso's 1958 Chevrolet Apache carried club trophies on top of its tarp in a 1959 Fourth of July parade. Howard and Judy Hansen are driving the truck, complete with spinner hubcaps. (Both, Huso collection.)

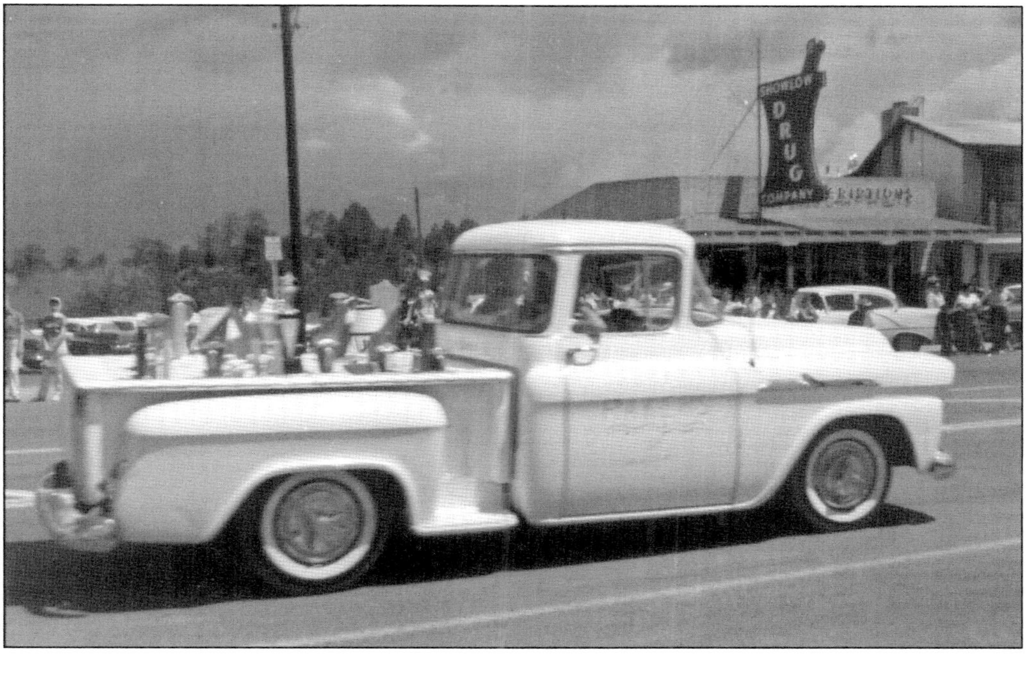

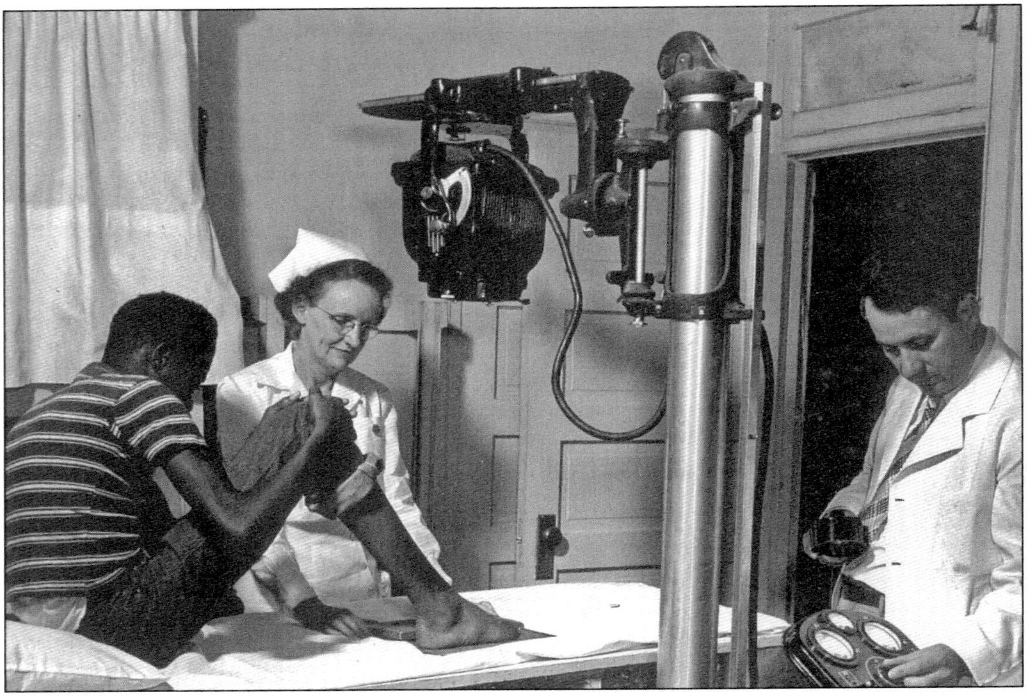

Arnold H. Dysterheft, M.D., and Zena Higgins, R.N., are x-raying a young patient in the old McNary Hospital in the late 1940s. Dysterheft, a Minnesota native, came to McNary in 1941 to provide medical care for Southwest Forest Industries employees. "Doctor D" was legendary on the mountain and was on call 24 hours a day for many years. His wife, Mildred, was a real estate broker in Pinetop. (SLHisSoc Museum.)

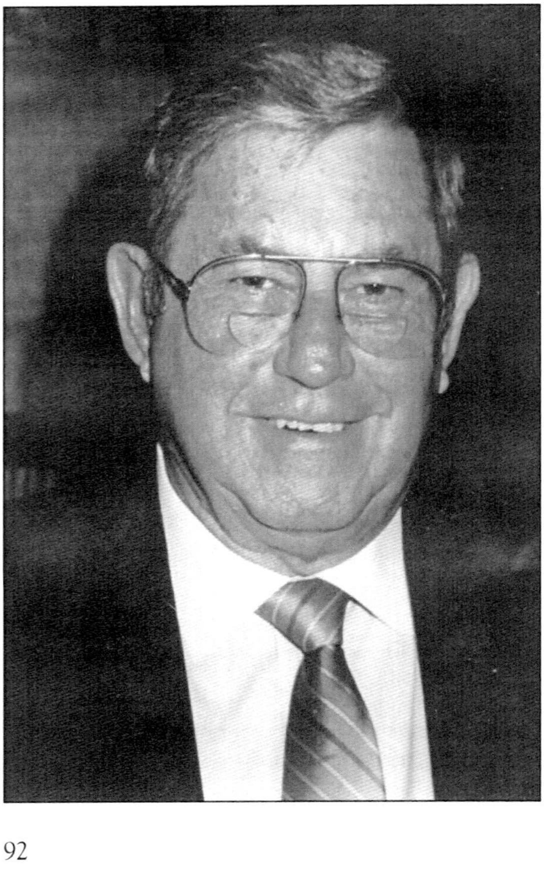

Al Armstrong, D.O., was from Joplin, Missouri, and came to Show Low and St. Johns in 1950. He used the St. Johns Hospital and Snowflake Maternity Hospital. He helped the community build the Josephine Goldwater Hospital but, in 1960, moved his practice to Mesa. Many loyal patients followed. After retirement, he returned to Show Low and was a founder of the Show Low Historical Society. (SLHisSoc Museum.)

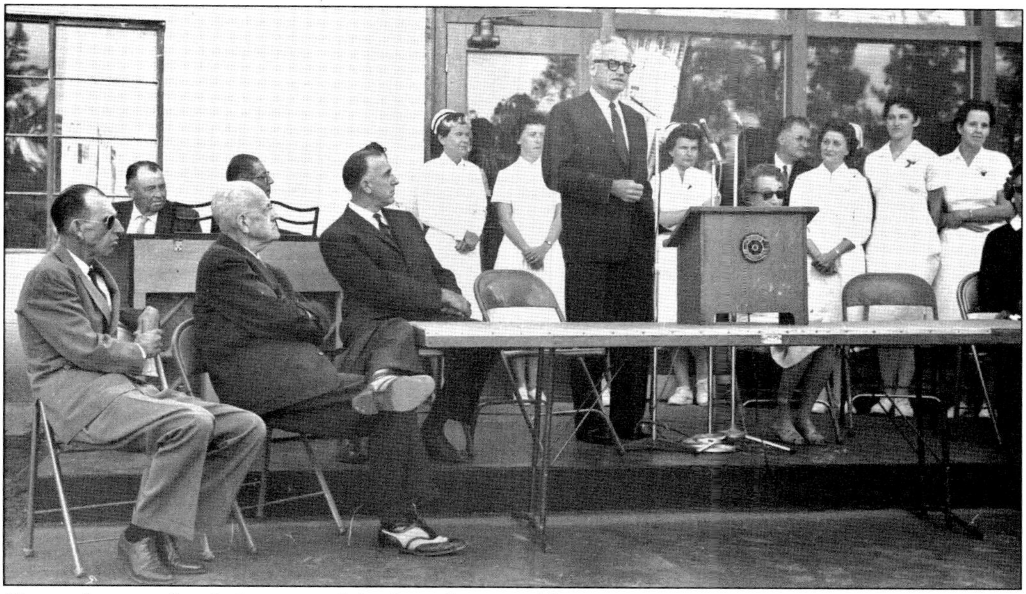

Shown here at the dedication of the Josephine Goldwater Hospital, April 22, 1961, are, from left to right, (first row) Mayor Bruce Reidhead, unidentified, Gov. Paul Fannin, Sen. Barry Goldwater, and Carolyn Goldwater Erskine (seated); (second row) Arlee Maxwell, Eric Marks, Eleanor Fossett, unidentified, Lillian Coon, Lloyd Rhoton, unidentified, possibly Joyce Reedy, and Leola Finney. Josephine Goldwater was a pioneer nurse in Arizona. (SLHisSoc Museum.)

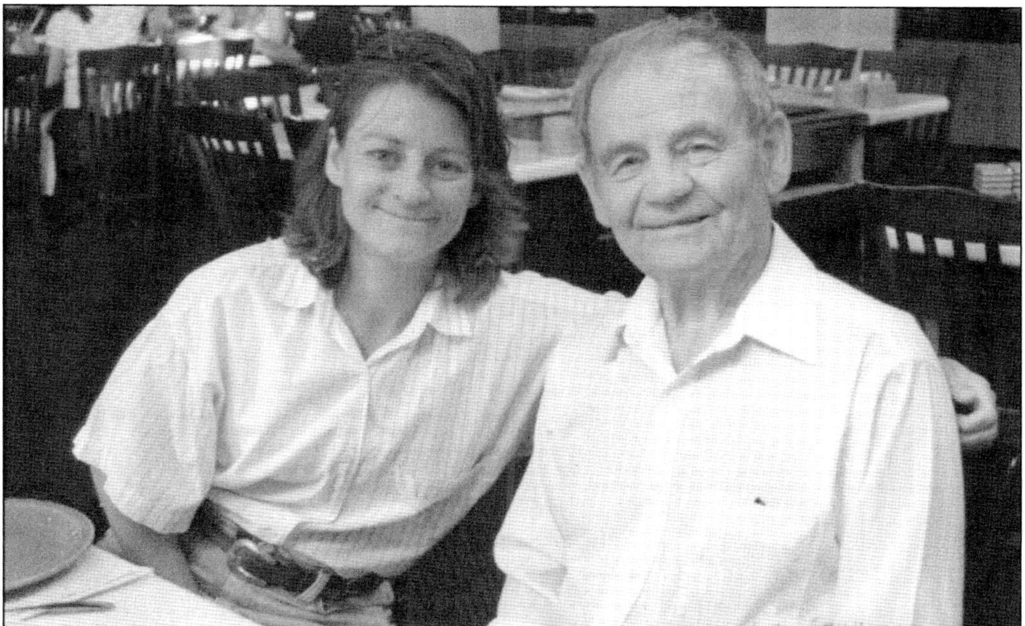

Paddy Ryan Garver, M.D., (here with daughter Toni) came to Show Low in 1966 at the urging of Hal Butler, who offered three months free rent if Garver would stay and practice medicine. Garver spent many long days and nights at the clinic and hospital, delivering babies and mending hearts and bones. He was an officer of the Network of Continuing Medical Education. (Gina Garver Crowe.)

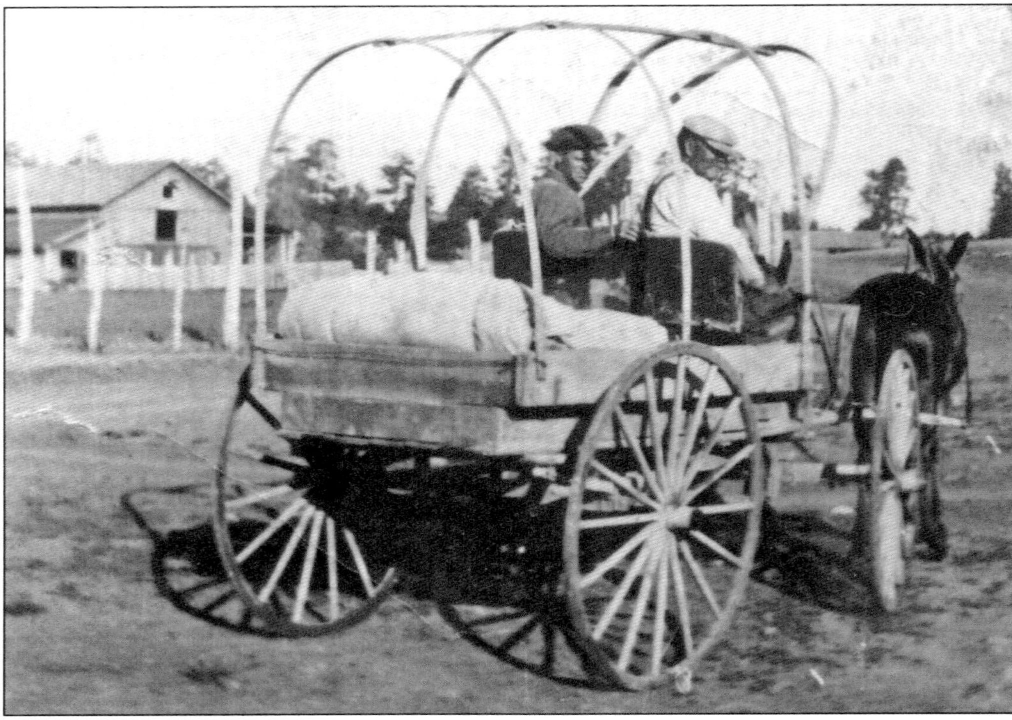

At first, mail came to Show Low from Fort Thomas; then, with the railroad, mail was delivered from Holbrook, and Dan Mills was hired. Here Joseph Brewer is delivering mail to Pinedale. Catching a ride with Brewer is William Henry Lewis (left). (Sheila McCleve Stewart.)

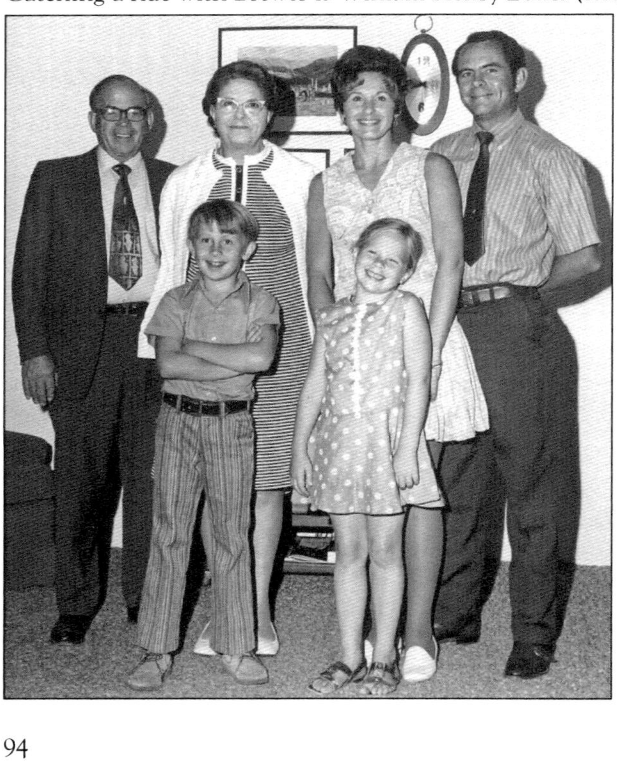

Originally the post office wanted one-word names for towns; today Show Low is spelled with two words. Don Carlos Tanner (above left) was appointed postmaster in 1931, and during his tenure, Show Low's post office changed from fourth class to second class and was the center of all mail delivered in southern Navajo and Apache Counties. Tanner is pictured here with his wife, Ecco, daughter-in-law Sandra, son Don Roe, and grandchildren Mike and Margo. (SLHisSoc Museum.)

Beatrice Jarvis is meticulously sorting mail at the Show Low Post Office about 1975. She is one of Show Low's consummate record-keepers. At 94 years, she is still photographing and cataloging Show Low history. Her albums include photographs of Fourth of July parades every year from their inception in the 1940s. She was born in Show Low and is one of only three Show Low natives older than 90. (Beatrice Jarvis.)

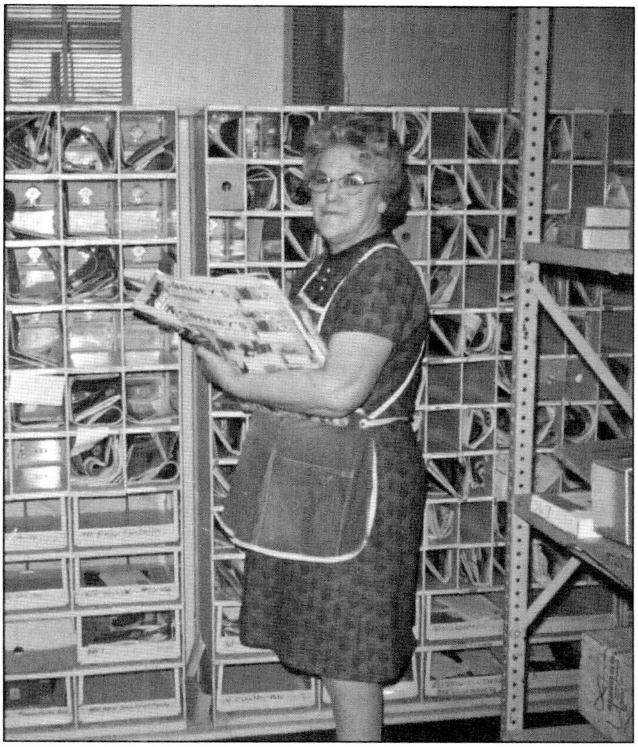

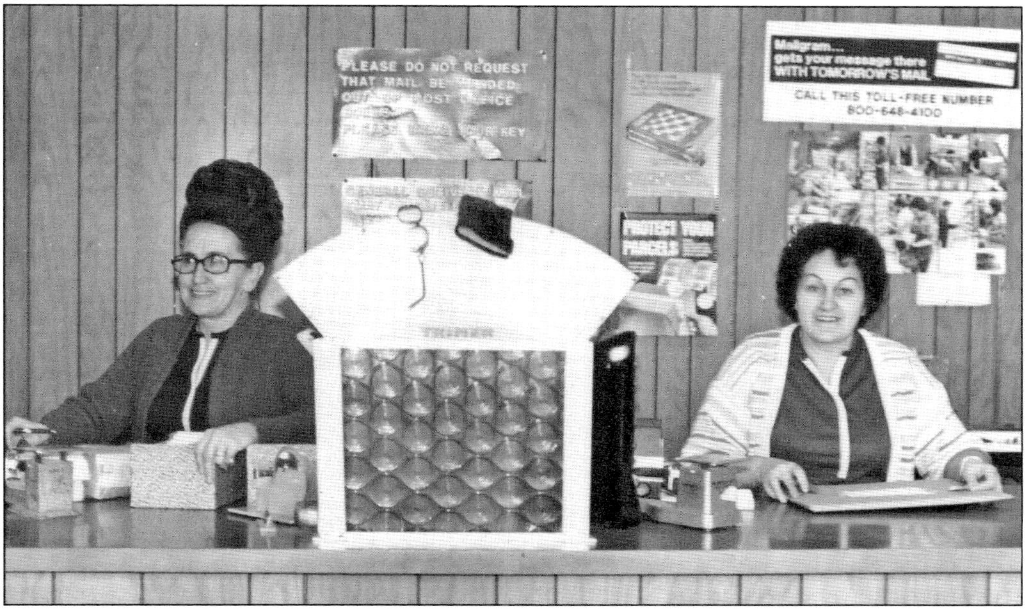

Betty Jo Ellsworth (left), Ione "Babe" Whipple (right), and Ruby Stock worked at the Show Low Post Office for many years. They made the post office a place to go if you needed to be cheered up or wanted to catch up on the latest news in town. Betty Jo moved to Show Low from Snowflake when she married Morley; their first home was a large tent on the Ellsworth Ranch. (Betty Jo Ellsworth.)

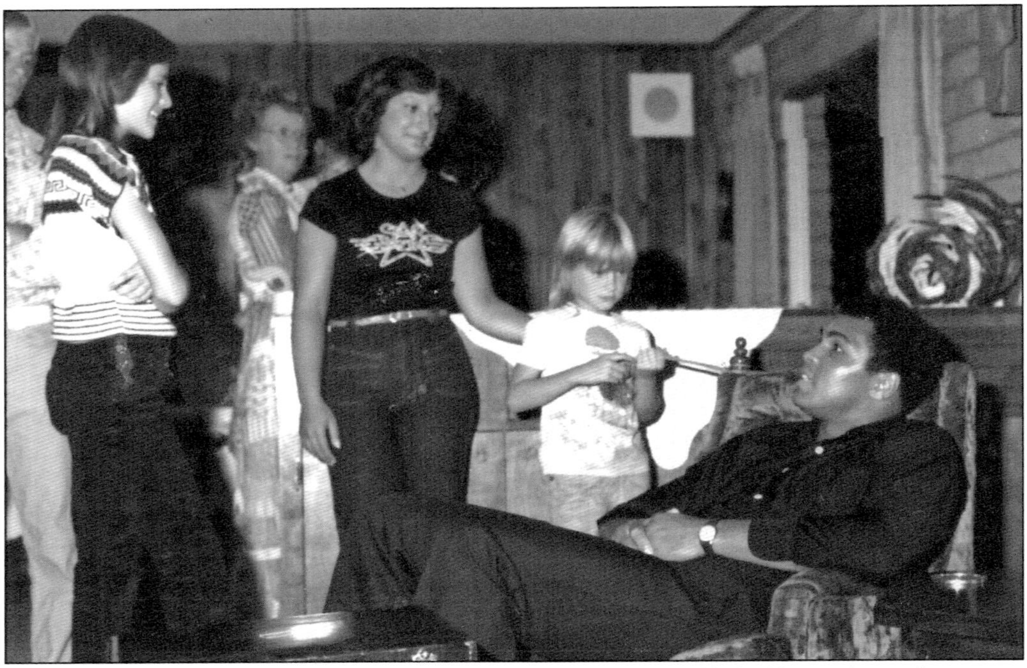

Before Dr. Paddy Garver and his wife, Marie, came to Show Low, Paddy had been a boxer, beginning at St. Anthony High School in Idaho and earning a boxing scholarship at Idaho State University. He then joined the navy and received a medical degree. Through his boxing connections, Garver knew Angelo Dundee, who in 1976 was training Mohammed Ali. Ali, 34, came to Show Low, training at the airport hangar for his upcoming $6-million fight with Kenny Norton. Above, Ali relaxes with, from left to right, Gina Garver, Barbara Jackson, Stella Ginoulis, and Greta Garver. When Ali was in Show Low, his entourage stayed at the Maxwell House. He became friends with Verdie (below left) and Arlee (right) Maxwell, including attending their 50th wedding anniversary party. (Above, Gina Garver Crowe; below, Arlee Tenney.)

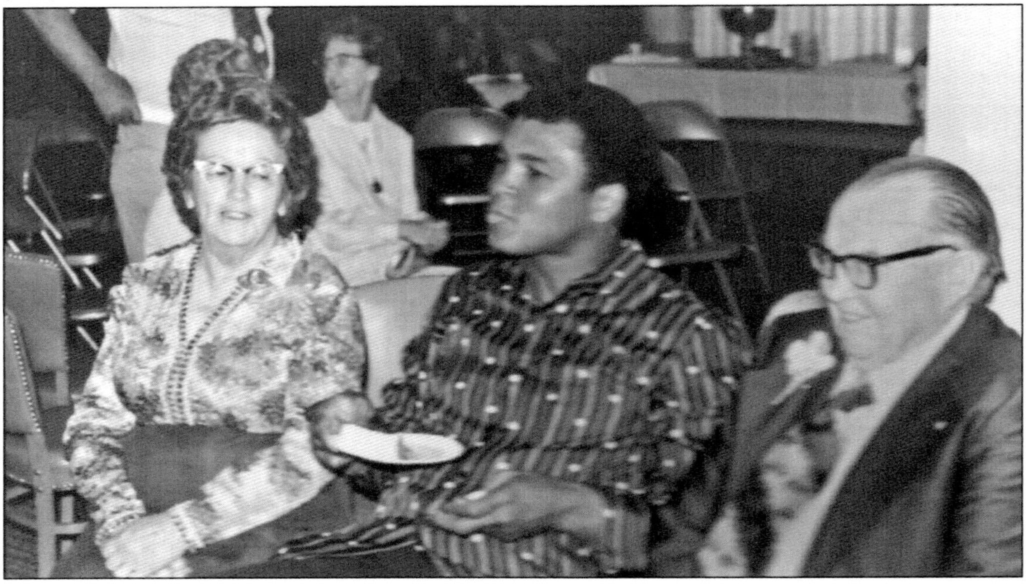

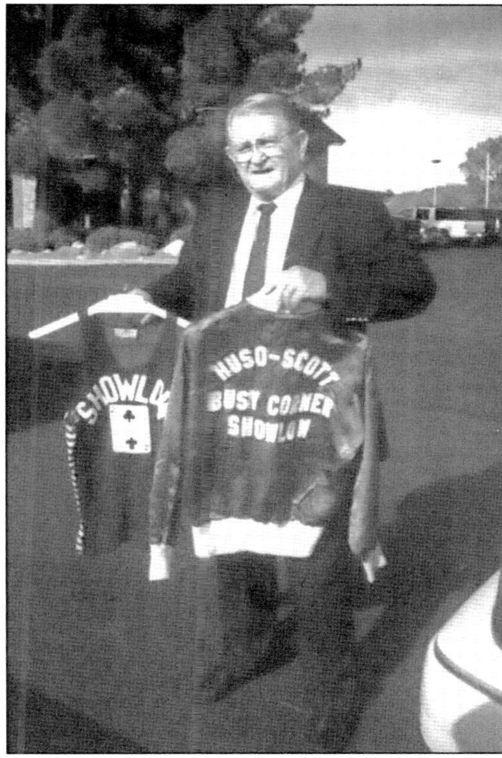

The "Deuce of Clubs" town basketball team was formed in the early 1950s. Purple and white satin jerseys and warm-ups were donated by Huso and Scott's Show Low Supply (at right with Ardell Ellsworth holding the jerseys). Another set was donated by the White and Jaeger Garage. Below are members of the team from left to right: (first row) Ronald Mills, Connie Graham, and Ronald Willis; (second row) Wade Butler, Ardell Ellsworth, Parley Stock, Morley "Pete" Ellsworth, Paul Willard, and Garth Nikolaus. Opposing teams were from neighboring towns. (Both, Ardell Ellsworth.)

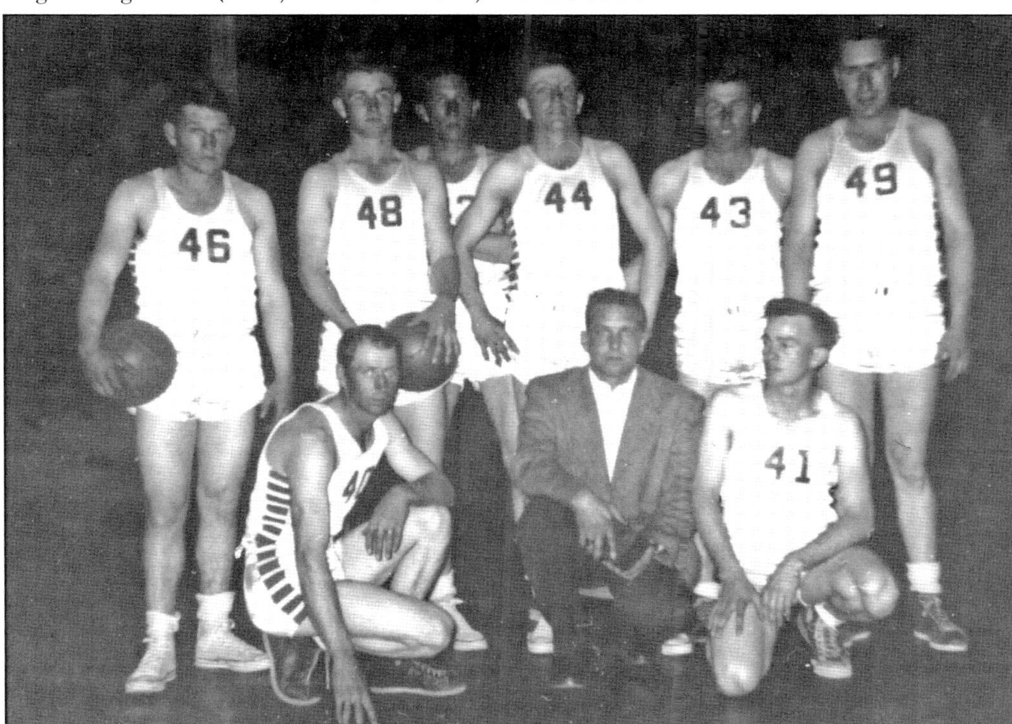

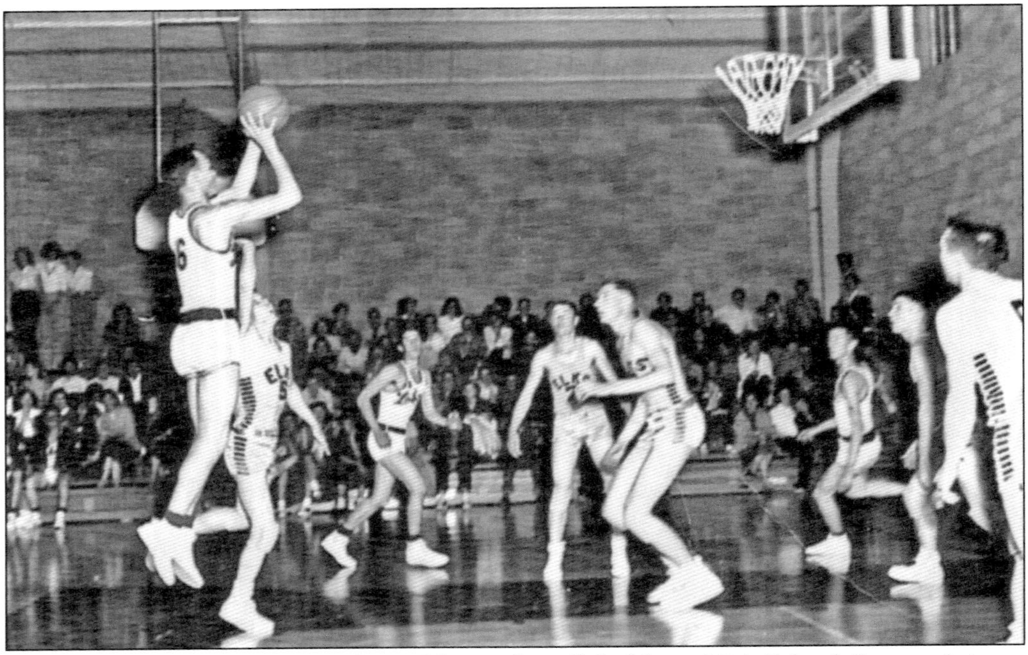

Dustan Everman was an outstanding athlete at Snowflake Union High School, Eastern Arizona Junior College, and Arizona State College (now Northern Arizona University) in Flagstaff. He was a basketball, track, and football star who was awarded All-State honors. Gerry, Gerald, and D. L. Nikolaus were also All-State athletes from Show Low. (Dustan Everman.)

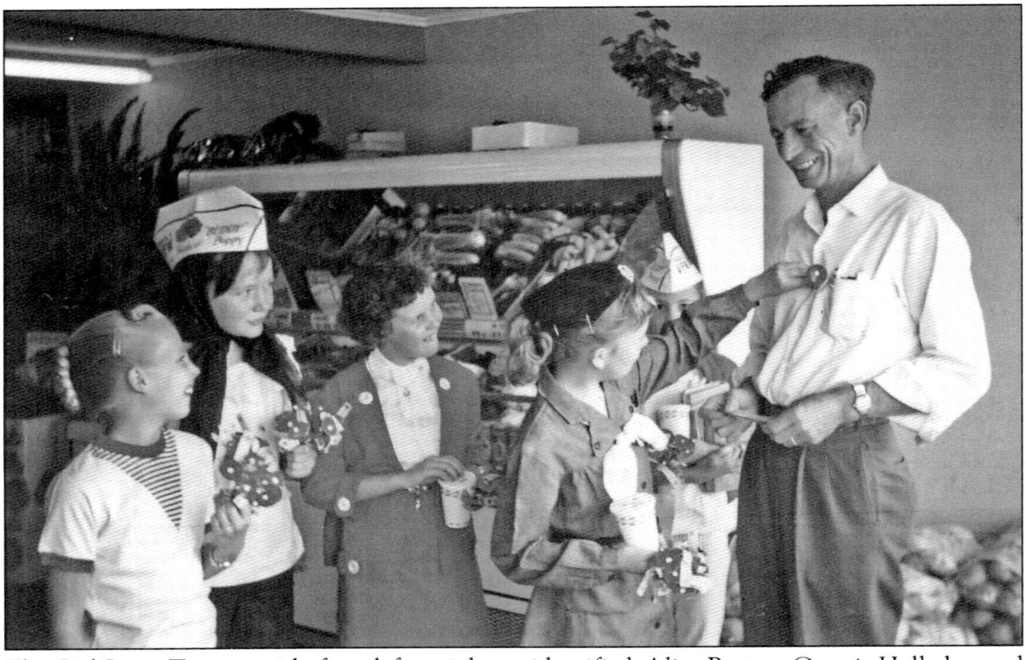

The Girl Scout Troop—with, from left to right, unidentified, Alice Barton, Connie Holladay, and unidentified—is selling Mayor Eugene King a Veteran's Day poppy in the late 1950s. The setting is the produce section of the mayor's store, King's Market. (Vaughan collection.)

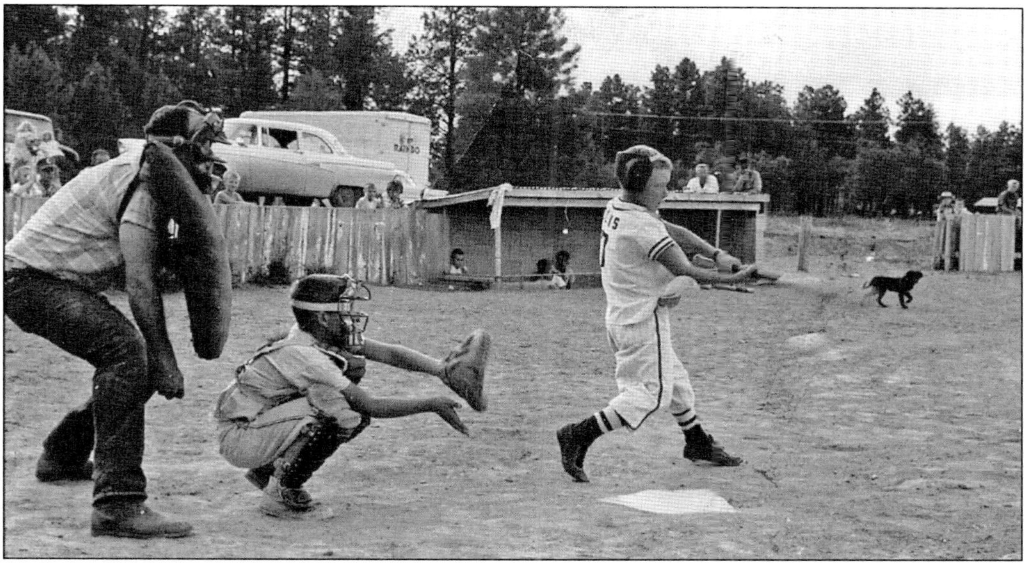

Walter Pew worked with his father, Clayton, and brother, Mickey, distributing restaurant supplies (note the Rainbo Bread van parked behind the fence), but here Pew is umpiring one of hundreds of Little League games. Eddie Hall is catching for his brother, George, who is pitching but not in this photograph. Arlee Tenney is at bat. Becky Hall (left) and Neta Savage are immediately left of the dugout, and Sandy Sweeter and Lloyd Capps (sponsors) are right. (Estelle Hall.)

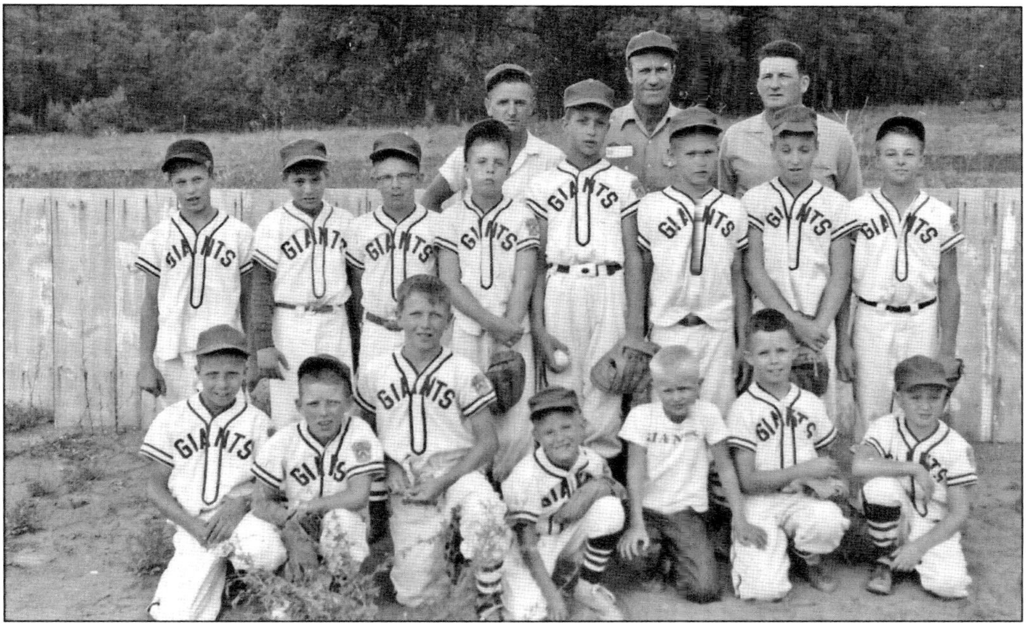

Gib Brewer was one of the founders of Show Low's Little League and was honored by having a monument erected at the park. The boys for this team in the early 1960s include, from left to right, (first row) Allen Stock, Gary Tenney, Karry Hansen, Art Savage, Eben Lewis, Mark Pew, and Charles Lewis; (second row) Danny Baldwin, Andy Coates, Deon Whipple, Lee Mathews, Leon Stock, Harold Maxwell, Tim Sturdivant, and Matt Abrams. Coaches were, from left to right, (third row) Ferrel Savage, Gib Brewer, and Clair Tenney. (Ardell Tenney.)

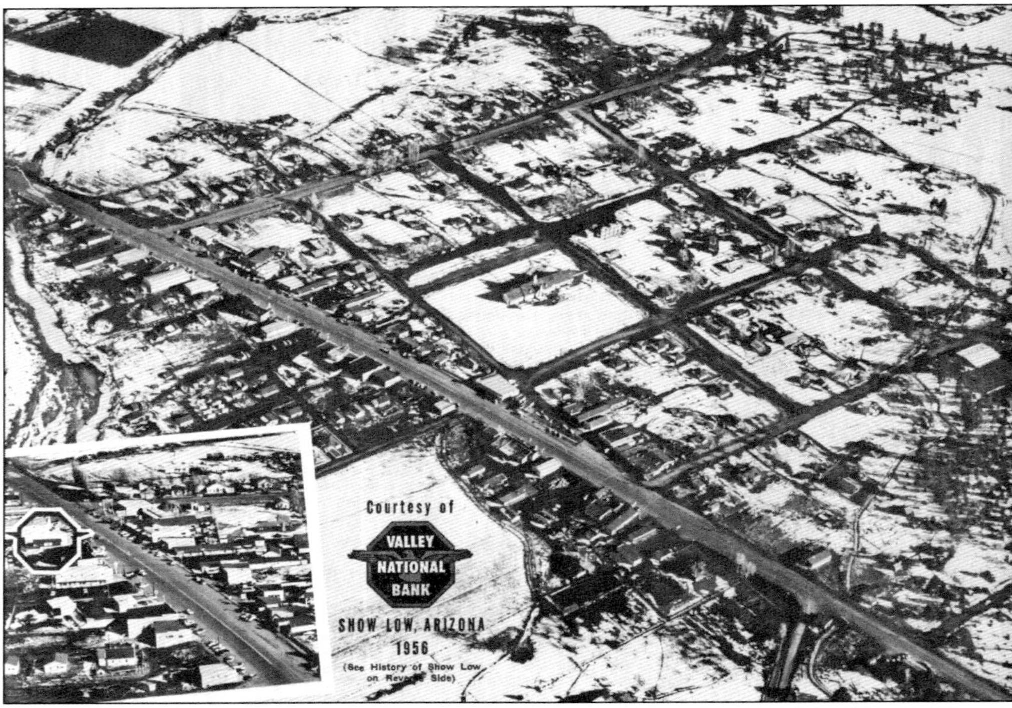

In 1956, Valley National Bank opened a branch in Show Low, just west of the Sho Lo Theater. The bank hired Bob Markow Photography from Phoenix to do an aerial view of the snow-covered town and turned the photograph into place mats to give away at the grand opening. Lamar Welker was the first bank manager. (Gail Adams.)

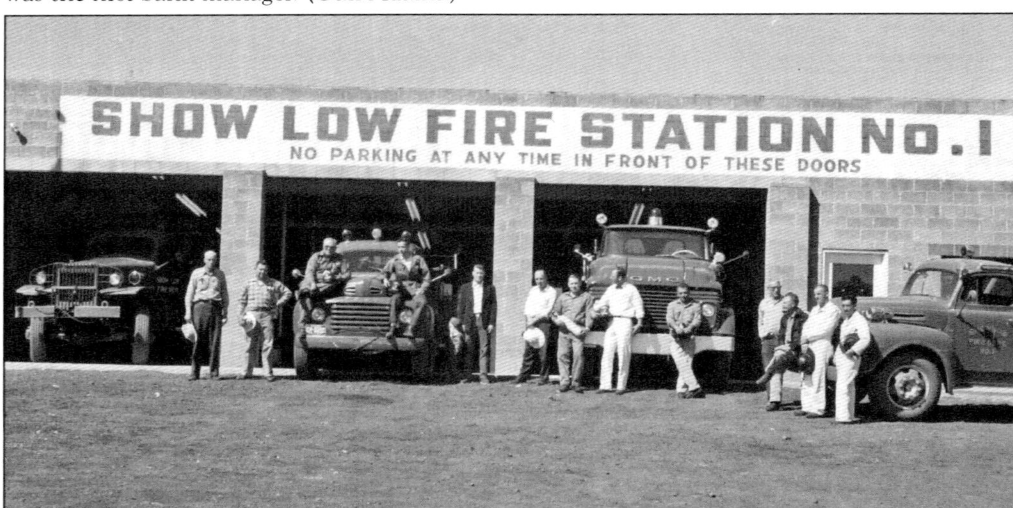

The Show Low Fire Department was chartered in 1949. Volunteer firemen in this early-1960s picture are, from left to right, Jim Stock (chief for 35 years), Larry Baldwin, Jim McMahon, John Stock, Don Umberger, Claude Butler, Wade Butler, Narvel Holladay, George Woolford, Aut Frost, Jerome Jaeger, Larry Frost, and Fred Baca. On snowy days when business was slow, many of the firemen gathered around the woodstove in the station to play cards. (Larry Frost.)

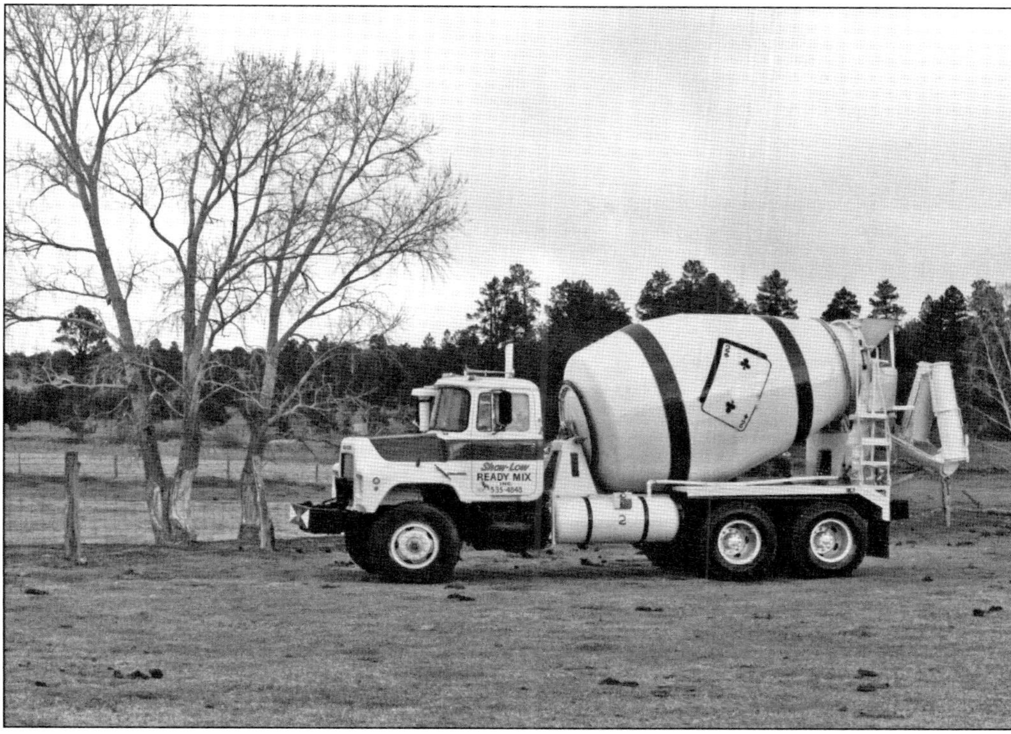

Show Low Ready Mix was owned by Fred Adams and his sons. When they moved to the Salt River Valley, Paul Seymore and Joy T. Pearce, both brothers-in-law of Arthur Adams, bought the business and expanded it. Note the Deuce of Clubs on the mixer and Show Low Creek in the background. (Dany Seymore.)

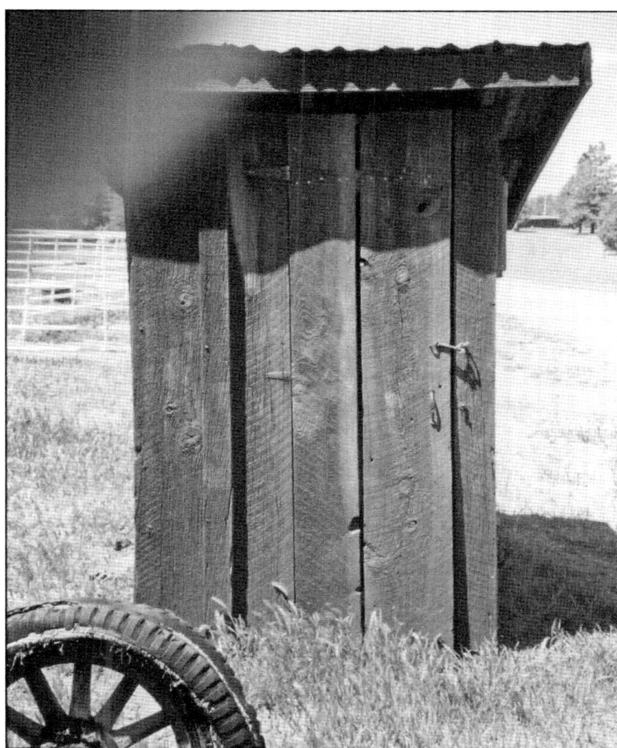

Although many young men in Show Low become Eagle Scouts, one unique project was the restoration of this outhouse by Paul G. Frost in 1992. He erected a plaque that read, "This outhouse was built in 1936 under the WPA by Arthur Burton. Mr. Burton also built a one-bedroom ranch house for Aut & Jayne Frost the same year." James Harrison Frost and Editha Smith homesteaded this ranch in 1910. (Jackie Frost Taylor.)

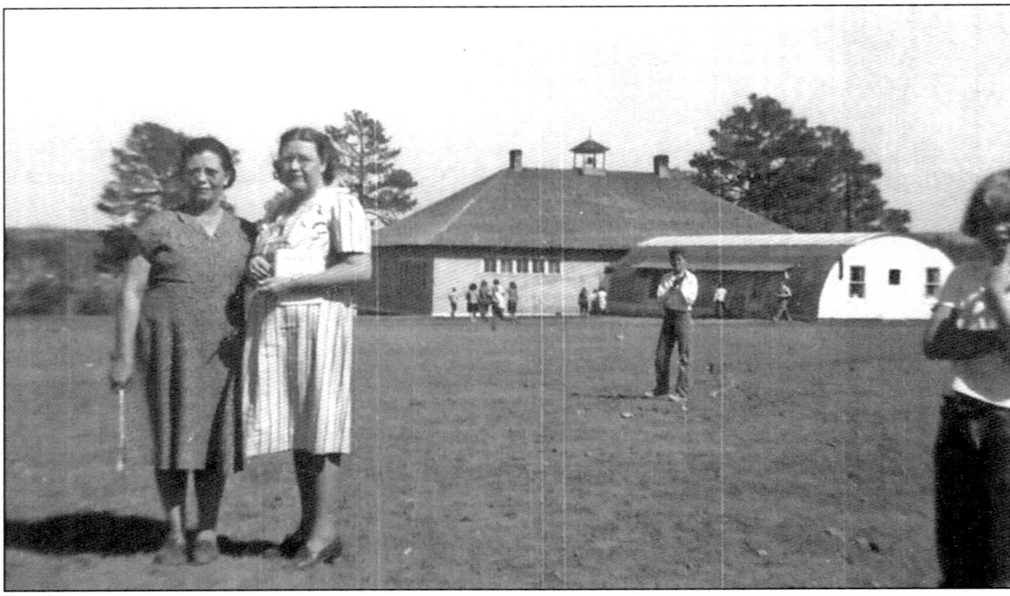

The photograph above seems to be the only one of the Quonset hut built on back of the old Show Low Elementary School. Teachers Jayne Frost (left) and Glenda Bushman here supervise recess; note the ruler or stick in Frost's hand, which will insure that Alan Peterson (center right) and Rita Kay Stock (right) do not misbehave. After retirement, Bushman traveled extensively, and Frost had Dutch oven cookouts for family, friends, high-ranking politicians, and businesspeople. Both ladies taught in Show Low for many years and were dearly loved. Below, Norlis McKay, principal, stands with a group of children in front of a later addition to Show Low school buildings. (Above, Lloyd Stock; below, SLHisSoc Museum.)

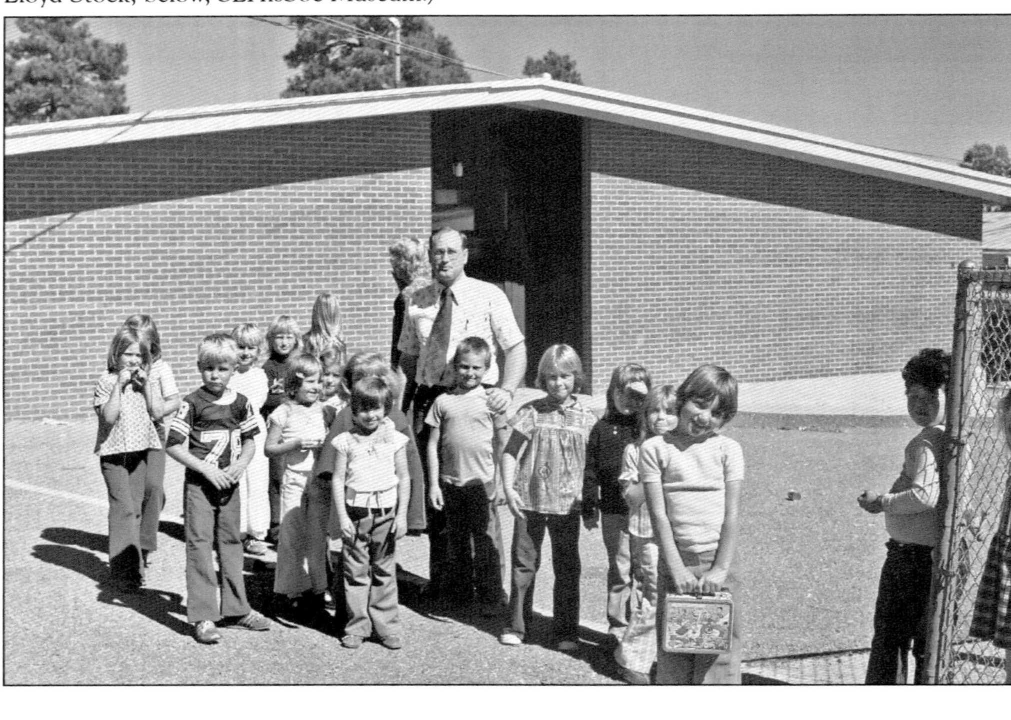

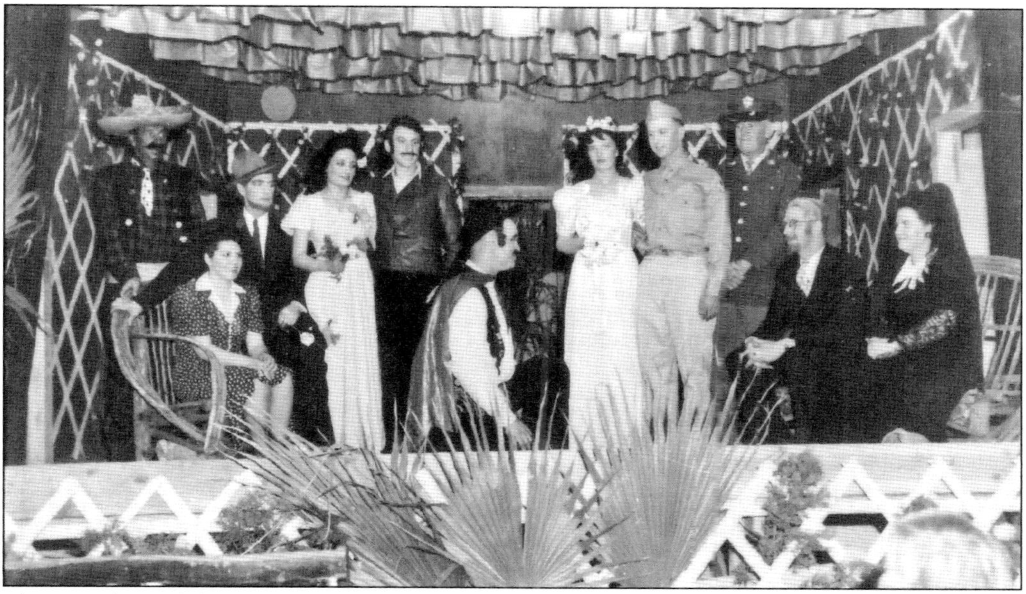

The story line of this 1940s operetta is forgotten, but Helen Adams Capps remembers they sang "de la vega" often. All participants colored their hair black with RIT dye, and some say that after the hall heated up, the dye started to run. Pictured here from left to right are Howard Whipple, Roxie Amos Ballard, Harvest Ellsworth, Dorma Penrod, Norman Adams, Mitchell Bushman, Maxine Ellsworth, Orr Owens, Bill Merrell, Charles Whipple, and Velora Ellsworth. (Helen Adams Capps.)

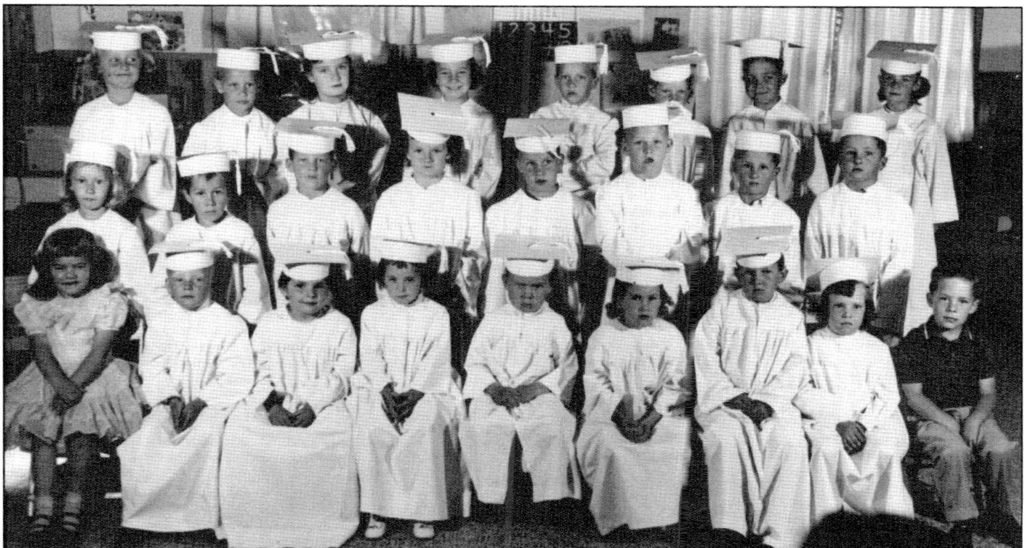

Lillian Coon, R.N., also held kindergarten in her home. This is the graduating class of 1959. Each child received a diploma and a kiss from Lil. Shown left to right are (first row) Laureen Palmer, Arlee Tenney, Lorraine Owens, three unidentified, Trent Adams, Heidi Huso, and Greg Cluff; (second row) Debbie Nikolaus, Harvey Wilson, four unidentified, Terry Whipple, and Gerry Whipple; (third row) Tricia Brewer, unidentified, Jolene Baird, Patty Stock, three unidentified, and Caroline Pew. (Caroline Pew Adams.)

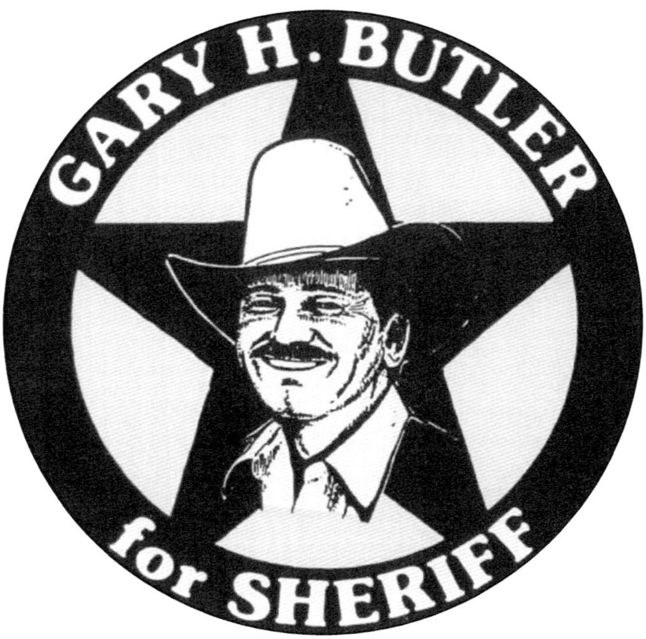

This logo for Gary Butler's Navajo County Sheriff campaign was designed by Steve Taylor of Show Low. Butler was born in Show Low, and after serving in the marines in Vietnam, he worked for the Scottsdale marshal's office. In 1971, he married Gail Nikolaus and began working for the Show Low Police Department (below). He was chief of police for 12 years and then took a six-year respite running the Timberline Ranch, a family venture. In 1988, he was encouraged to run for Navajo County Sheriff and won against incumbent Glen Flake. Twenty years later, he decided not to put his name on the primary ballot; he was the longest-serving sheriff of Navajo County. (Both, Gary and Gail Butler.)

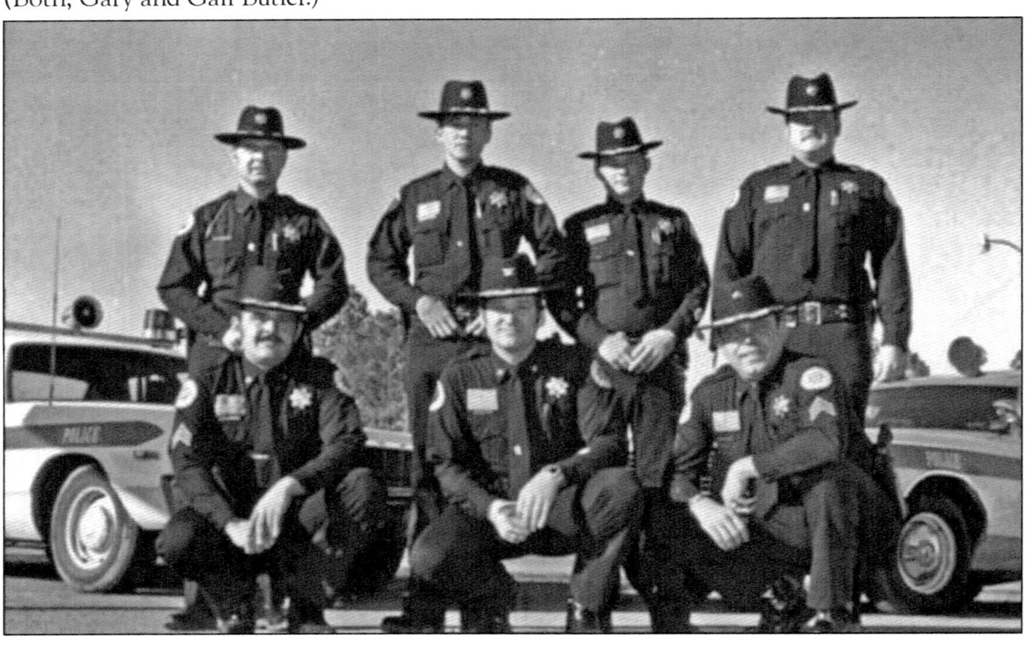

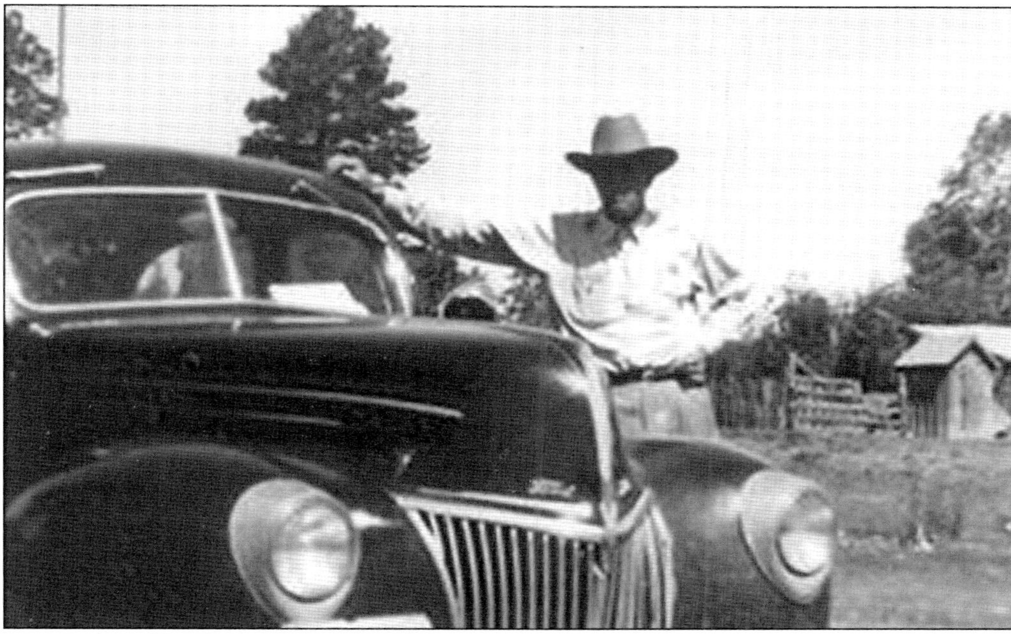

Jim Stock and his famous 1939 Ford patrol car provided law enforcement in Show Low for over 30 years. His mother, Jennie, ran the telephone switchboard from her home and put up with a lot of abuse from teenagers ringing her on crank calls asking if she had "been out feeding the chickens." Of course, she and her relief operators knew most of the "goings-on" in town. Jim and Thora Penrod Stock raised athletes: their sons, Jimmy, Johnny, Dallas, and Lloyd all excelled at boxing, and Dallas and Lloyd are competitive ropers. Lloyd has won a trophy saddle each of the last four years. Below, the Navajo County Sheriff's posse rides in the Fourth of July parade in the early 1950s. Note the Sho Lo Theater in the background, where Jerry and Gloria Rawlings lived upstairs with children Linda, Bill, and Lori. (Above, Lloyd Stock; below, Beatrice Jarvis.)

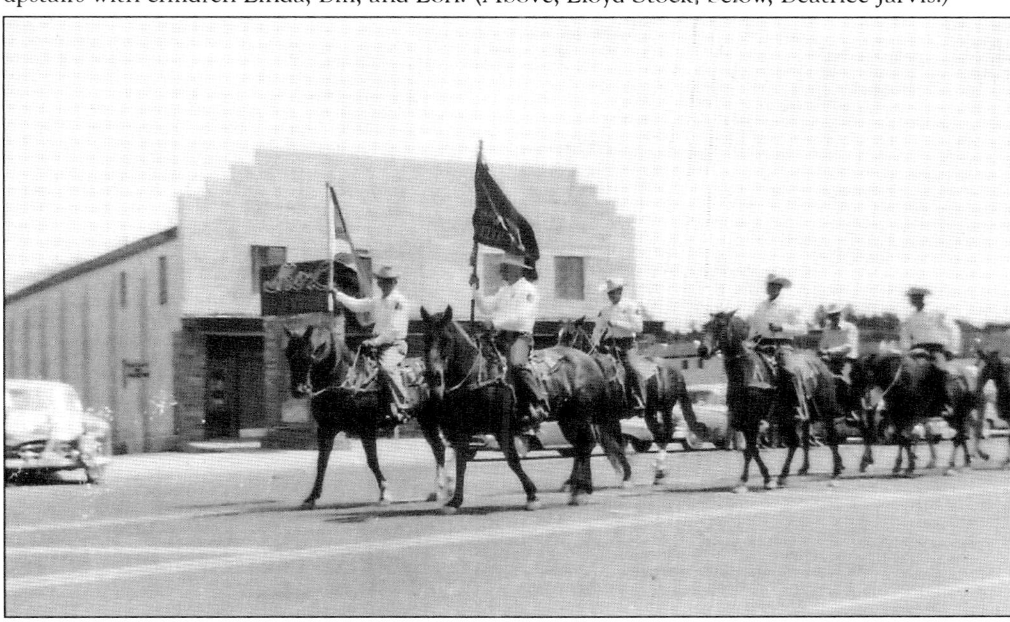

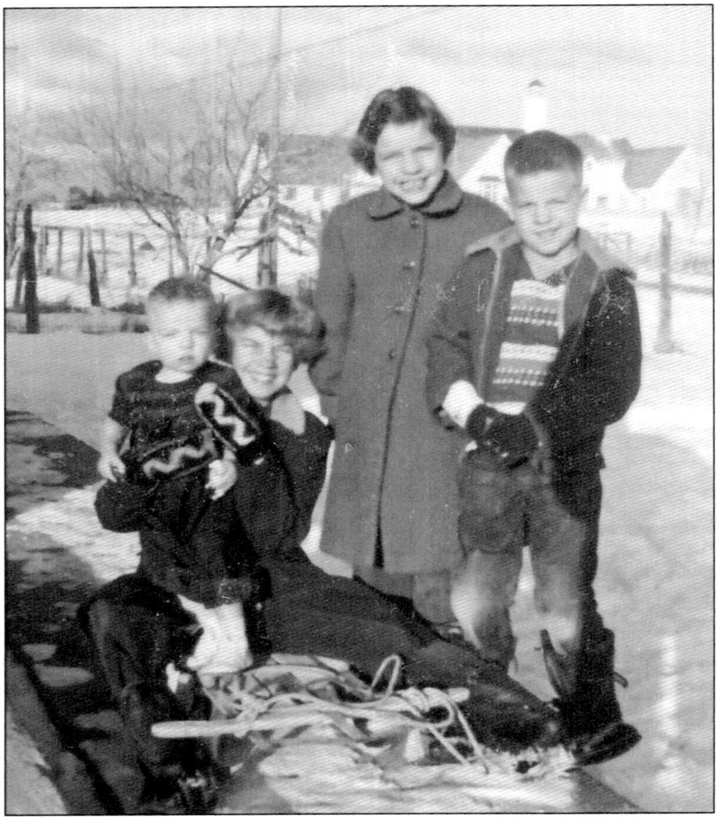

At left, a snowy day is welcomed by (from left to right) Kirk, Diana, Susie, and Eric Frost, children of Larry and Hilda Lewis Frost. They are in front of their home with the LDS downtown chapel in the background. Below, Lester and Ella McCleve's children are getting a little frisky on a swing set out by the barn. From left to right are Kathie with an unidentified boy she may have been babysitting, Sharon upside down, Connie in light dress, Marilyn as the Statue of Liberty on the top bar, Nancy Jane in the swing, and Nora on the end. (Left, Hilda Frost; below, photograph by Sheila McCleve Stewart.)

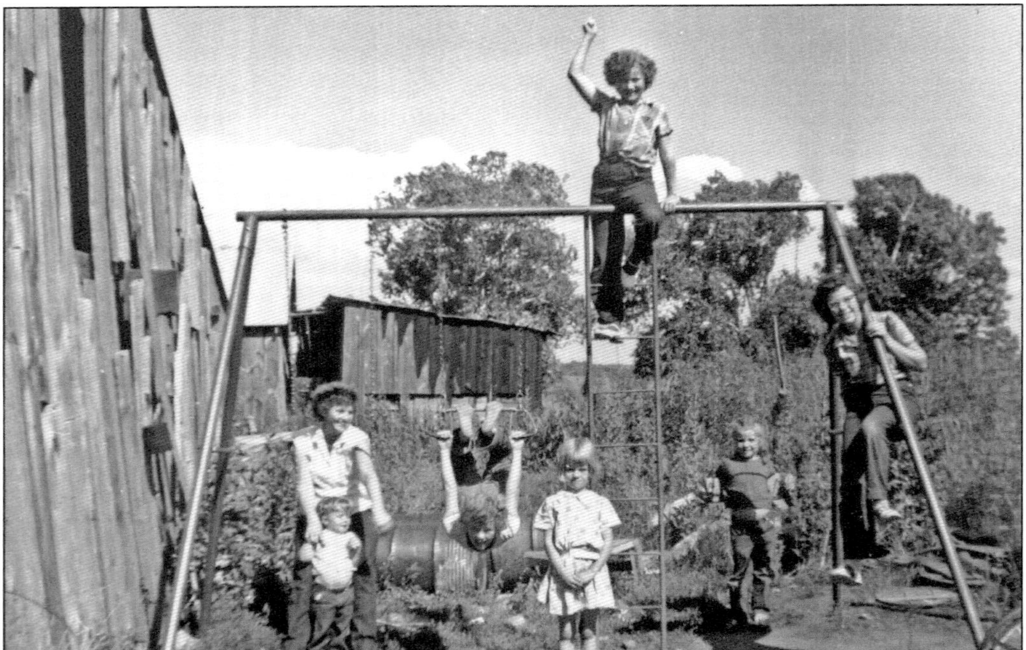

When Bill and Mary Sexton moved to Show Low in 1960, owning and operating the A&A Sporting Goods Store, the nearest Catholic church was St. Anthony's in McNary. So, in October 1961, their son Dan received first communion at McNary with Fred Baca as sponsor (right). In the 1950s, mass was sometimes said in Show Low at the Paint Pony Lodge. Then about 1963, St. Rita's Catholic Church was complete enough that services could be held in Show Low, although the congregants initially had to bring their own chairs. In 1968, Bill and Mary's son Jim (below) served as altar boy at St. Rita's. Today the White Mountains also host St. Mary of the Angels in Pinetop (which includes a Franciscan Sisters Convent). (Both, Mary Sexton.)

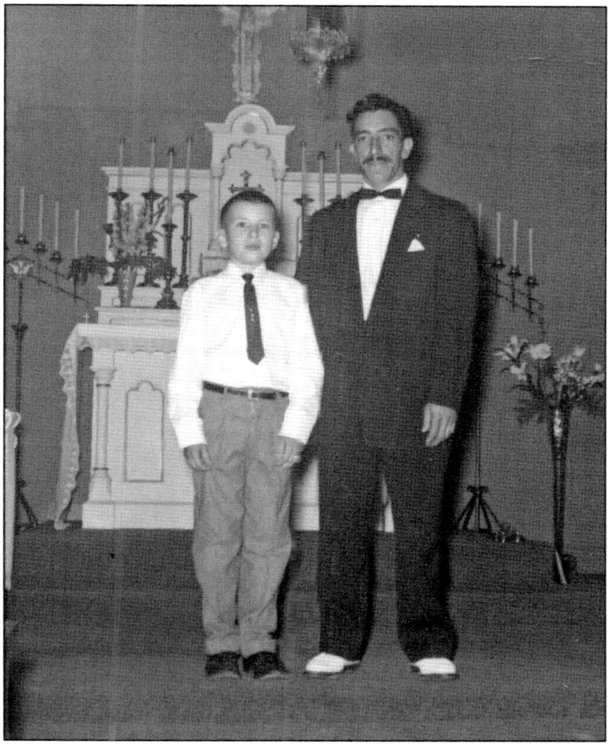

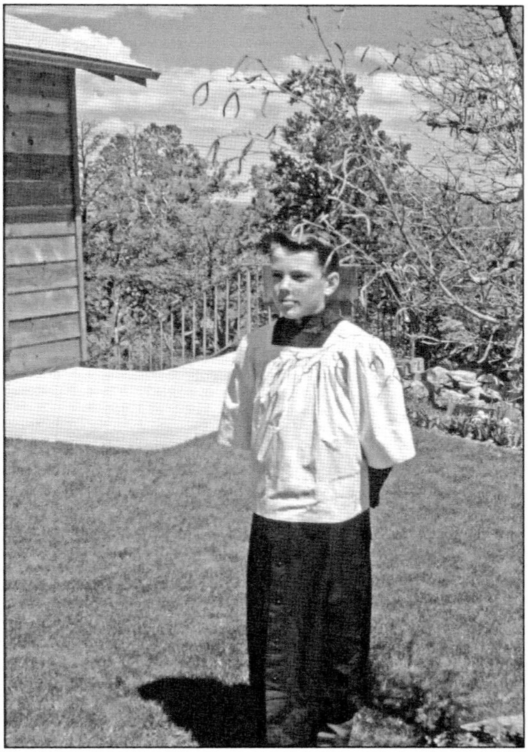

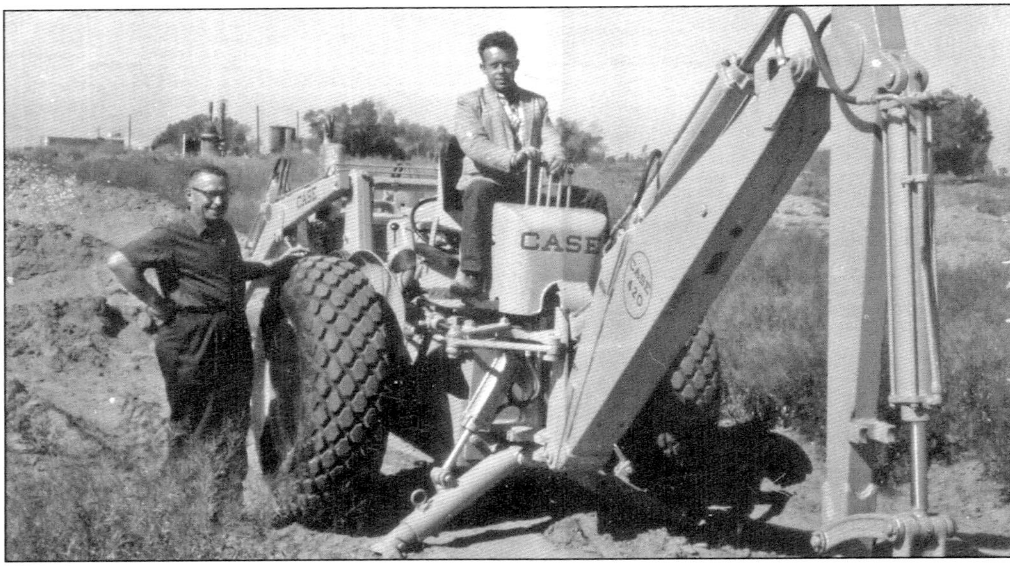

Jim McCarty first came to "the Mountain" to work on Show Low Lake dam in 1952. He married Doris Kay, and their three daughters are all named after queens of England—Elizabeth, Victoria, and Katherine. McCarty began the first solid waste business and a construction company that worked on the Pinetop Country Club, Pinetop Lakes, and Hawley Lake. He was a founder of Frontier State Bank and McCarty Realty. (McCarty collection.)

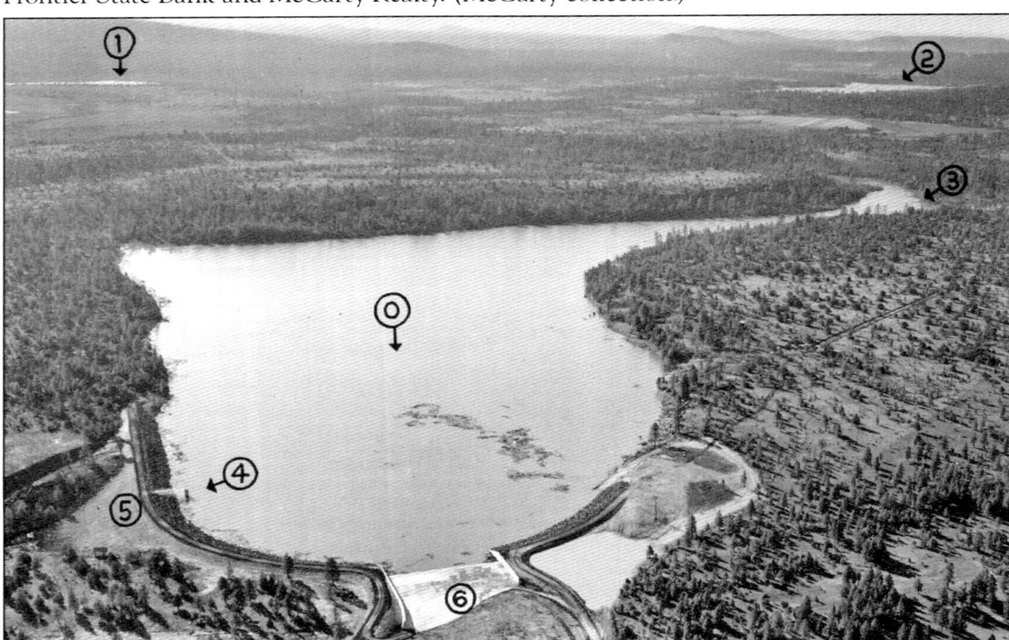

Phelps Dodge Corporation contracted with Isbell Construction of Phoenix to build Show Low Lake dam and spillway. This aerial view shows the following: (0) Show Low Lake; (1) Scott Lake; (2) Lakeside Lake; (3) diversion tower, control buildings, and pumps; (4 and 5) dam, control tower and outlet; and (6) spillway to Show Low Creek. Construction began in 1952 and was completed in 1954. (Used with permission of Freeport McMoRan Corporation.)

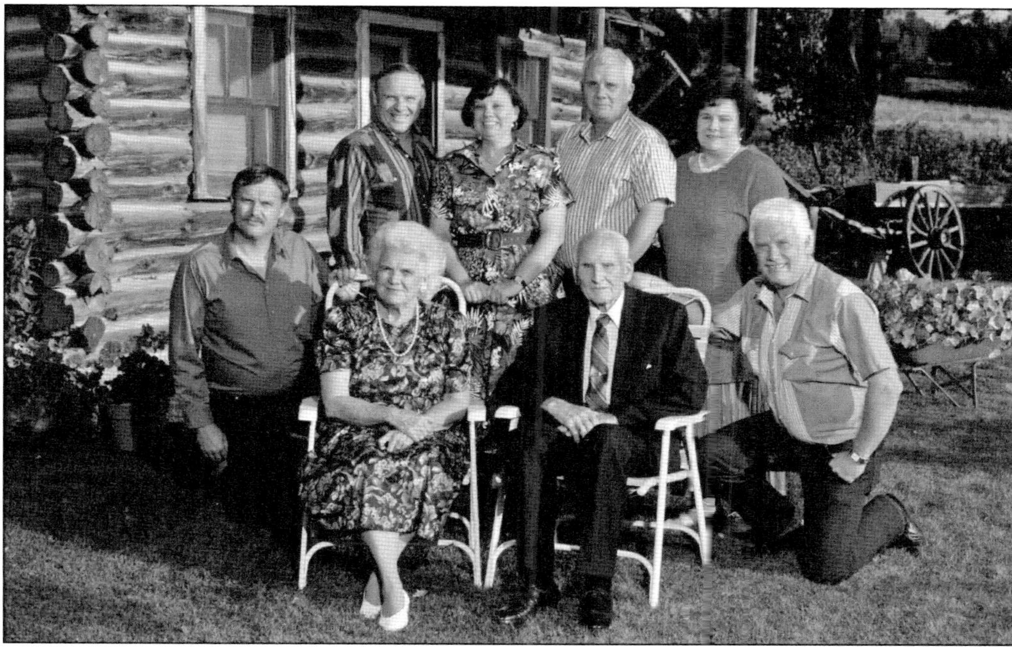

Ross and Georgia Reidhead Adams were both born in Show Low. When they got married in 1938, Ross drove a log truck in Vernon for Alfred Hansen, his brother-in-law. On Pearl Harbor Day, December 7, 1941, Ross began working for Smith Heywood Lines. Ross and Georgia bought a log cabin from Garnet and Gladys Adams Holladay and moved it to Show Low, just south of where they eventually built their larger home. After saving money for five years, Georgia took the advice of her mother, Lillie Reidhead, and bought land from Charley Woolford to build a restaurant. That began 33 years at Ross' Café. Below, this home belonged to George Mason Adams (who added the second story) and then John Oscar Reidhead. The land is still in the Reidhead family, although the home no longer exists. (Above, Georgia Adams; below, Darla Mills Baird.)

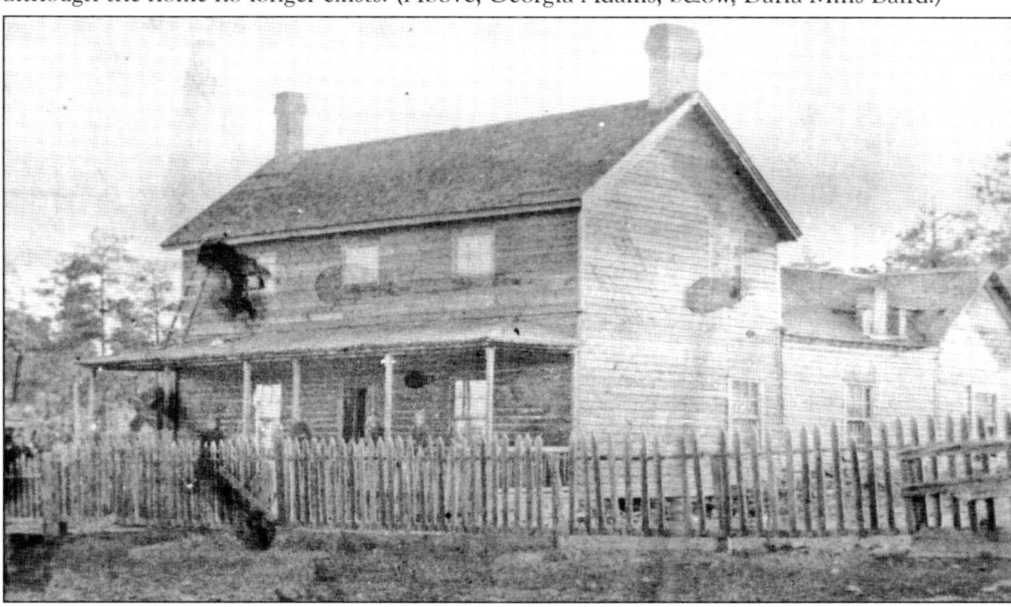

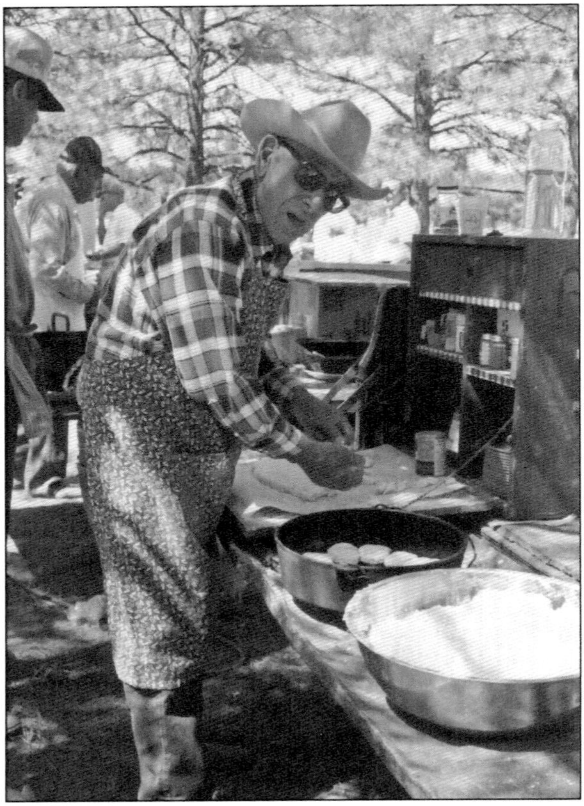

Austin "Aut" and Jayne Gibbons Frost entertained "under the pines" at the Frost Ranch. Aut (left) learned the art of Dutch oven cooking when he worked as a teenager with Spanish sheepherders. He made the biscuits, and Jayne fried the steaks. Jayne would say, "Grab a biscuit and don't mind the ashes—they season it." Frost worked in construction and served as a juvenile probation officer; Jayne taught school for 31 years in Navajo and Apache Counties. When she taught in Burton, a Baptist community, she had the children dance for a Christmas program. She said, "I didn't know Baptists didn't dance. We always danced." Below is the Frost family about 1960 from left to right: (first row) Aut and Jayne; (second row) Jeff, Smith Gibbons "Gib," Jerry, Jackie, and Nan. (Both, Jackie Frost Taylor.)

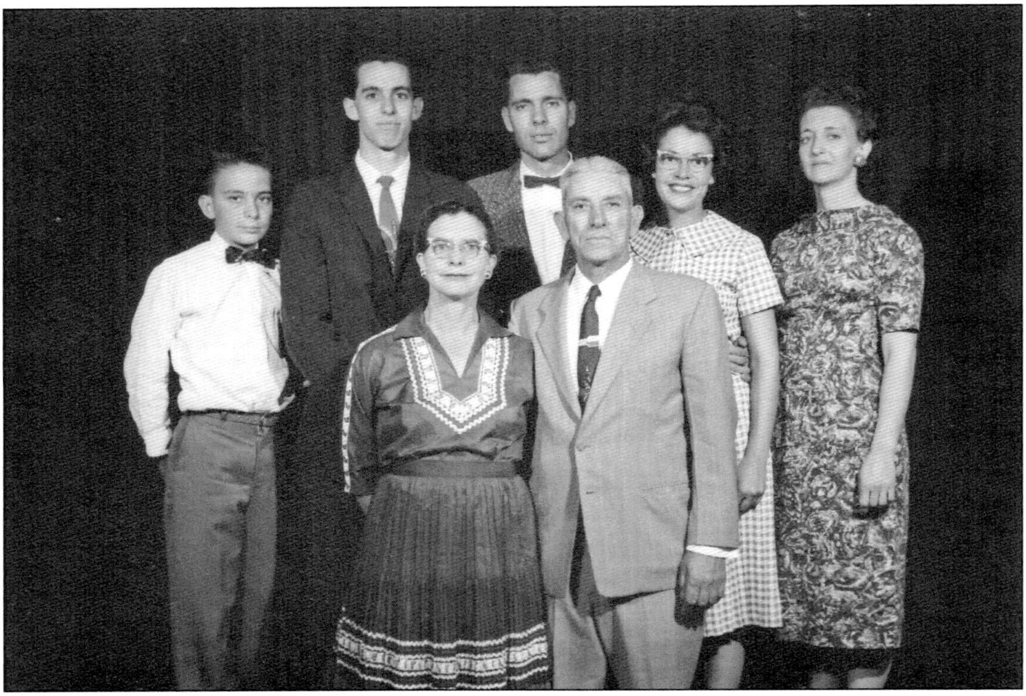

Five

Celebrating Show Low's Past

In Show Low, parades and rodeos have always been used to celebrate the past and show patriotic spirit. Each rodeo began with local ranchers, rodeo contestants and rodeo queens with their attendants posting the colors on horseback. Both the American and Arizona flags flew to the sound of scratchy music from a 45-rpm record broadcast over the loudspeaker from the announcer's stand. Sometimes the rough stock horses and bulls under the viewing stand would get rambunctious, and the needle on the phonograph would jump forward or repeat. Then the crowd would sing "The Star Spangled Banner." Women placed their hands over their hearts, and the men held their Bailey straw hats or felt Stetsons over theirs. Before any event started, a prayer was offered for the safety of all contestants.

In 1954, the Navajo County Board of Supervisors appointed the first Show Low City Council with Hal Butler as mayor; he was then reelected for two more years. From 1958 to 1968, Butler served on the Navajo County Board of Supervisors, representing Navajo, Coconino, and Apache Counties on the Arizona Department of Transportation Board for six years, and also served six years on the Arizona Oil, Water, and Gas Commission. Each of the subsequent mayors has supported Show Low, particularly with parades and rodeos.

But the spectacular ponderosa pine forest setting is what pulls everyone back to Show Low. In 1912, the *Arizona Good Roads Association Illustrated Road Maps and Tour Book* noted, "To the south [in Navajo County] you are attracted by the beautiful virgin pine forests . . . which will someday be the greatest pleasure and recreation spot in the western country, if not in the world. These forests are becoming noted for hunting and fishing. Bear, mountain lion, wolf, bobcats, coyotes, deer, and turkey abound throughout the forest, and the pure mountain streams are alive with mountain brook trout." The beautiful pine forests around Show Low continue to define the area.

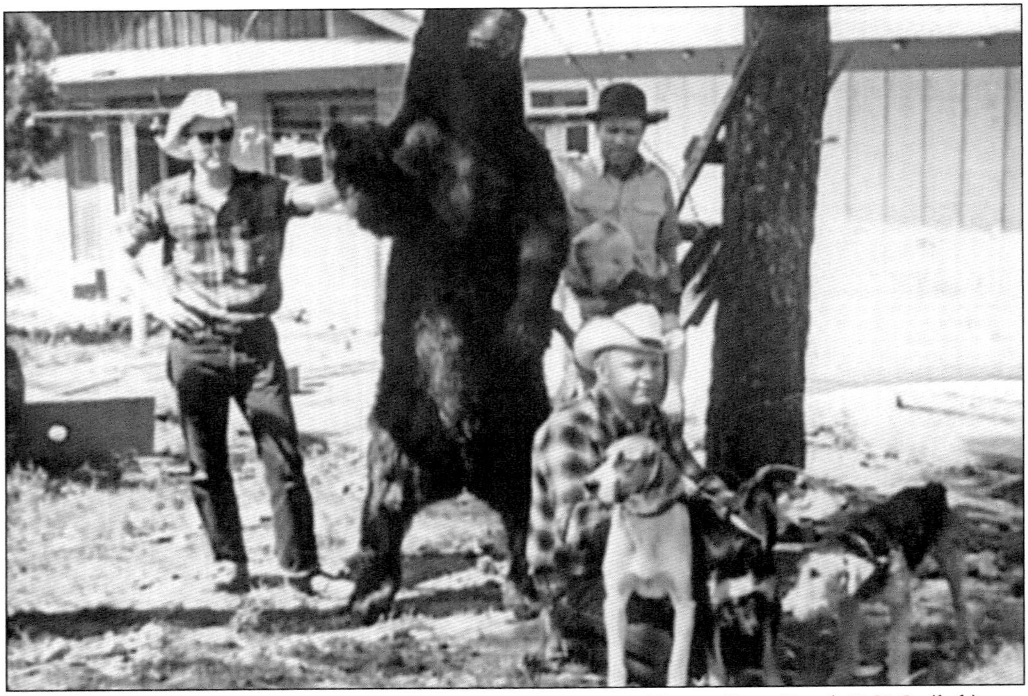

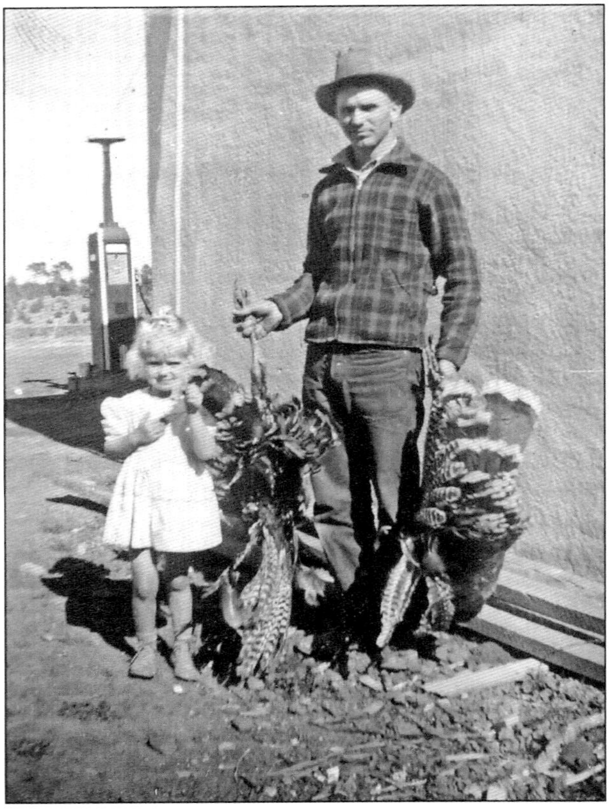

Above, Greg Boyd, D.D.S. (left), Gib Brewer (and his son Jeff, in front), and Pete Ellsworth (kneeling) show off the huge bear they killed at Hop Canyon on September 21, 1964. The skull measured 21 and 13/16 inches, which was a record for Arizona and only 2/16ths of an inch off the world record. Russell Colbreath, government trapper for the Fort Apache Indian Reservation, said that he had "been after the bear for three years because it had been killing calves in the spring." Boyd stated, "The bear weighed 464 pounds on the scales at the old Nick's Market and didn't have an ounce of fat on it." Below, Gib Mills and his daughter, Darla, show off the results of their turkey hunt in the early 1940s. They are standing next to the café that Mills and his wife, Neola, ran in the Jim Stock garage building. (Above, Greg Boyd; left, Darla Mills Baird.)

Lamell Ellsworth has been called "The Legend" for his hunting prowess. He bagged Arizona's "Big Nine" (mule deer, whitetail deer, elk, pronghorn, desert bighorn, javelina, black bear, mountain lion, and turkey) and actually had the "Big Ten" when it included buffalo. Commercial turkey calls are available, but Ellsworth preferred to suck air through the wing bone of a duck, an irresistible sound to a gobbler. In 1994 (right), Ellsworth killed a bull elk that scored 407 Boone and Crockett points. He used the "stalk and track" method for hunting and said he "would rather be lucky than good." Below, David Butler has snapped "the big one" at Show Low Lake. When the man-made lake was finished in the mid-1950s, the Arizona Game and Fish Department stocked it with larger-than-average fish. (Right, Pam Wood; below, Hal and Peggy Butler.)

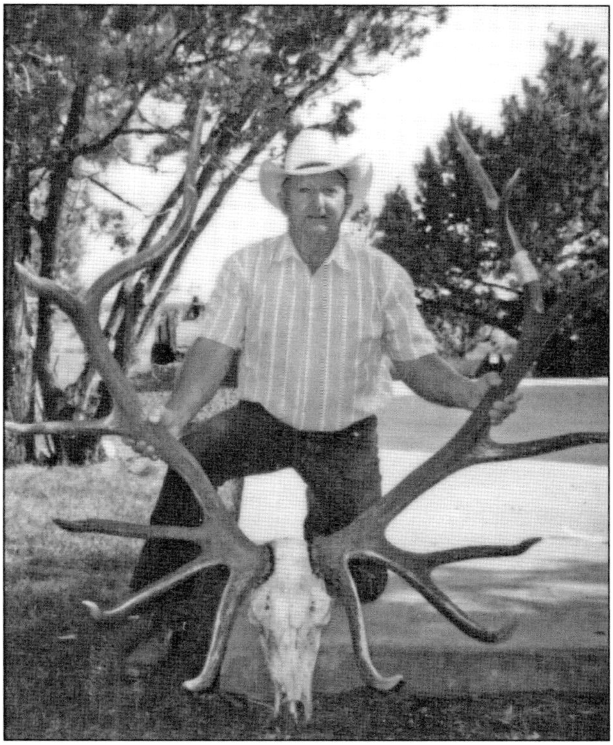

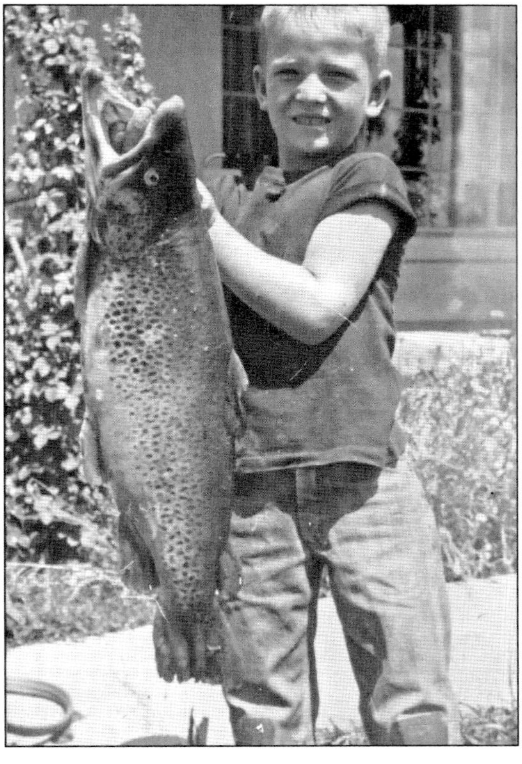

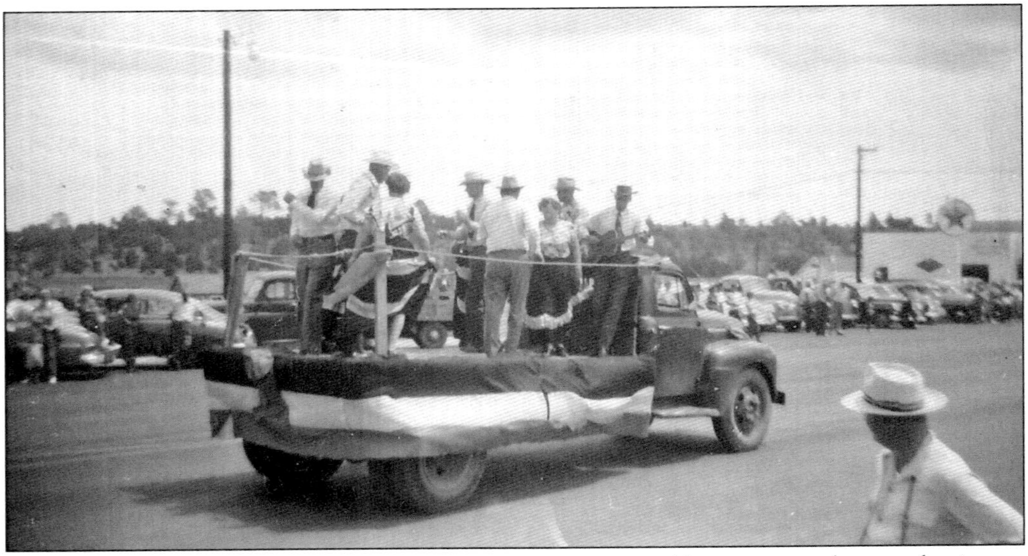

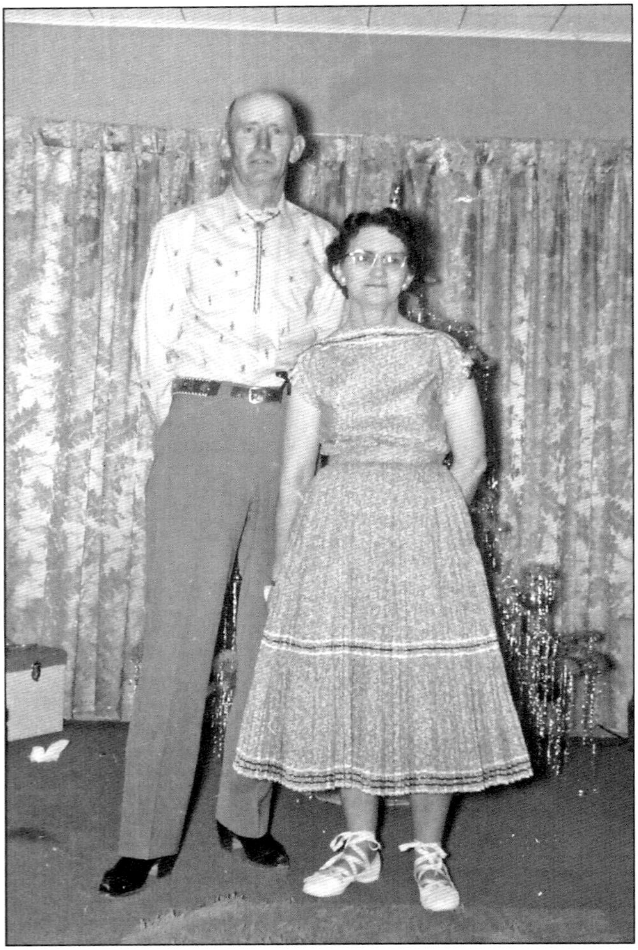

Above, square dancers do-si-do on a float in the 1948 parade (accompanied by Vigo McNeil, fiddle, and Warren McNeil, guitar). Arlee and Verdie Maxwell and Eph and Nell Mills began the Rainbo Square Dance Club in 1948, the White Mountains' first. They gave lessons and recruited 60 members. In 1952, all clubs in southern Navajo County were combined into the White Mountain Square Dance Club. Maxwell was the caller. Maxwell and Mills even taught a group of teenagers to square dance on horseback. (Kathy Mills Tippets.)

Eph and Nell Mills pose here in their "square dance togs." Eph was born in 1902 in Adair, an area now covered by Fool's Hollow Lake. At 15, he was driving a four-horse team and hauling freight. Eph farmed, ranched, and worked as a cowhand; ran cafés, gas stations, and stores; and built several homes with his sons. He was on the city council for eight years and on the school board for nine years. (Kathy Mills Tippets.)

Arlee and Verdie Maxwell moved to Show Low in 1945 from Lakeside. Their daughter, Imogene Brazieal, said, "The folks sold everything in Lakeside for $4000 and bought a café from Ralph and Ina Peterson." Eventually they bought the Show Low Café, upgraded it to the Maxwell House, and later purchased the Paint Pony. Arlee was inducted into the Democratic Hall of Fame, as was his daughter, Imogene. (Arlee Tenney.)

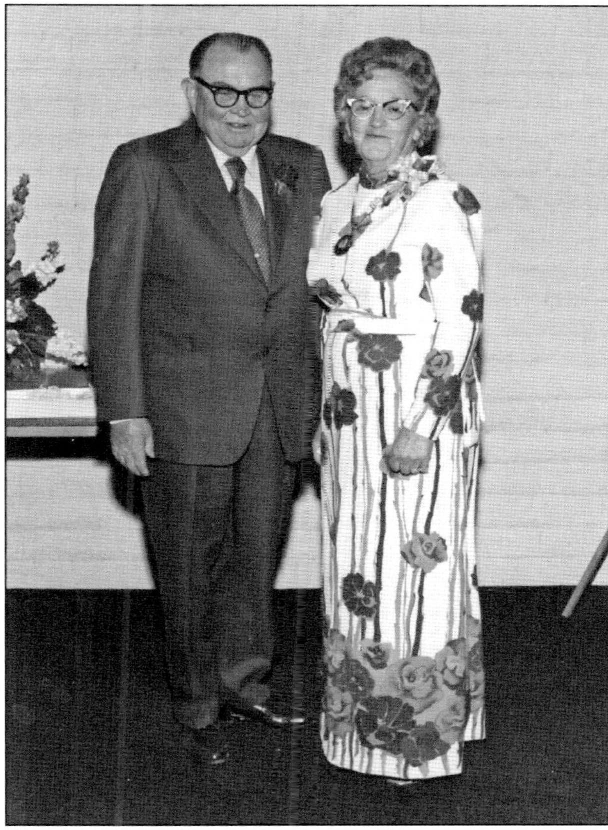

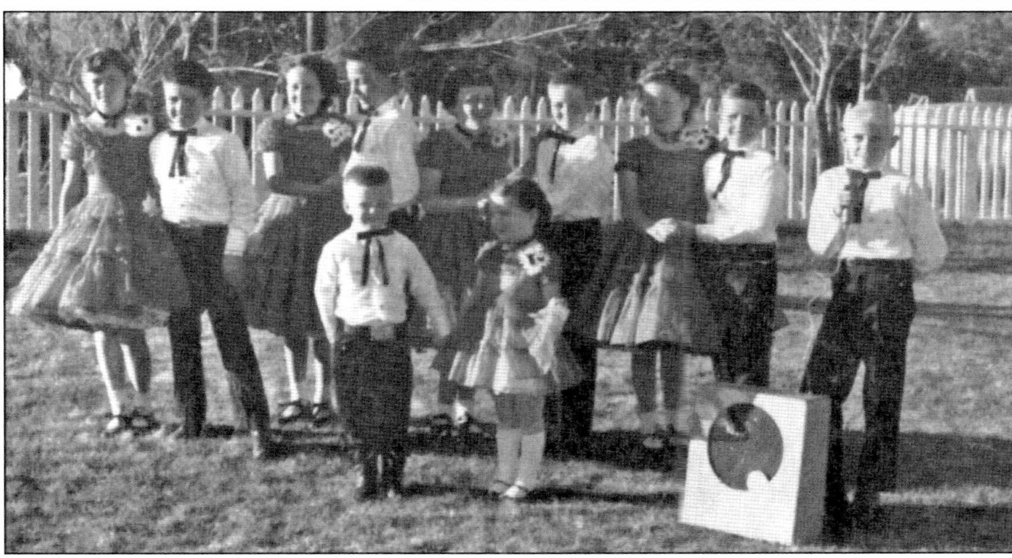

This group of young square dancers was trained by Arlee and Verdie Maxwell. From left to right are (first row) Arlee Tenney and Leta Smithson; (second row) Janice Nikolaus, Gary Smithson, Beverly Adams, Jeff Frost, Rita Tenney, Gene Coon, Loretta Smithson, John Payne, and caller Jimmy Welker. (Georgia Adams.)

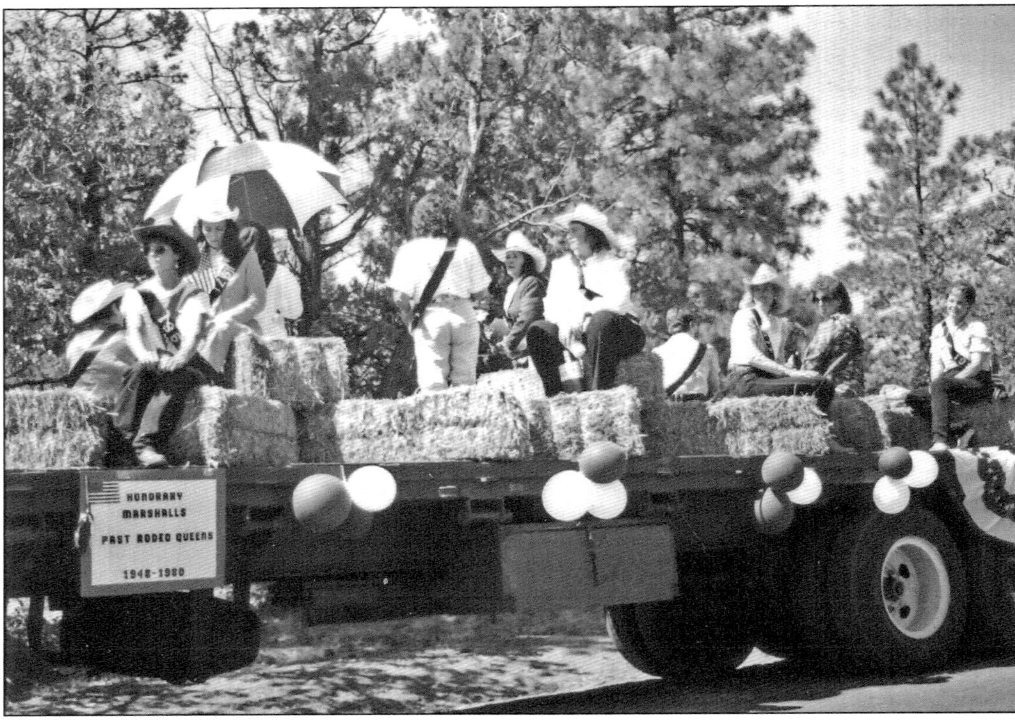

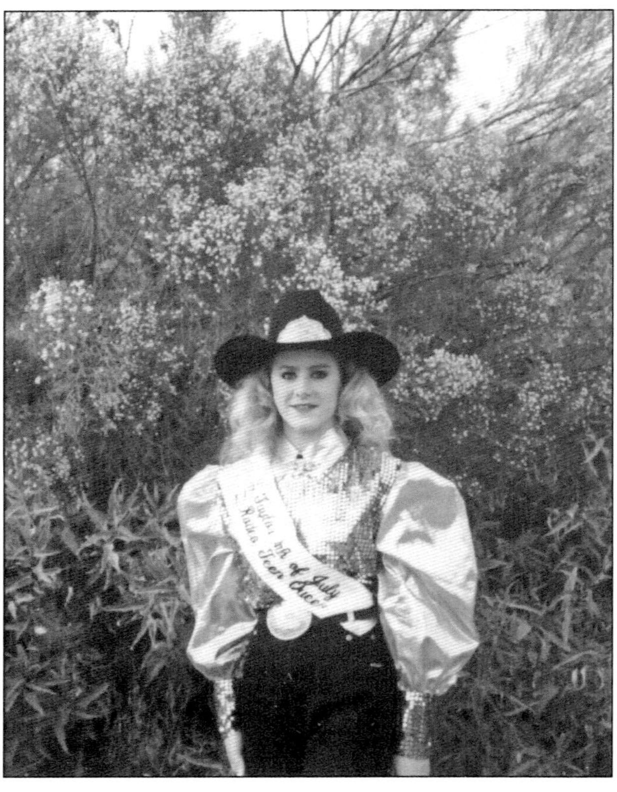

The method of electing rodeo queens used to be according to how much money each raised selling raffle tickets. In 1949, the bar crowd was determined to elect Dot McNeil, who owned the Navajo Inn. She was around 50 at the time and thoroughly enjoyed the honor. In 1989, all past rodeo queens were honored and rode in the parade as grand marshals (above). Meghan Baird (left) attended Show Low High School and was "Teen Rodeo Queen" for Taylor in 1994, but the rodeo was cancelled that year (a first) because cattle were being quarantined, so she called herself "Quarantine Queen." (Above, Beatrice Jarvis; left, Mary Sexton.)

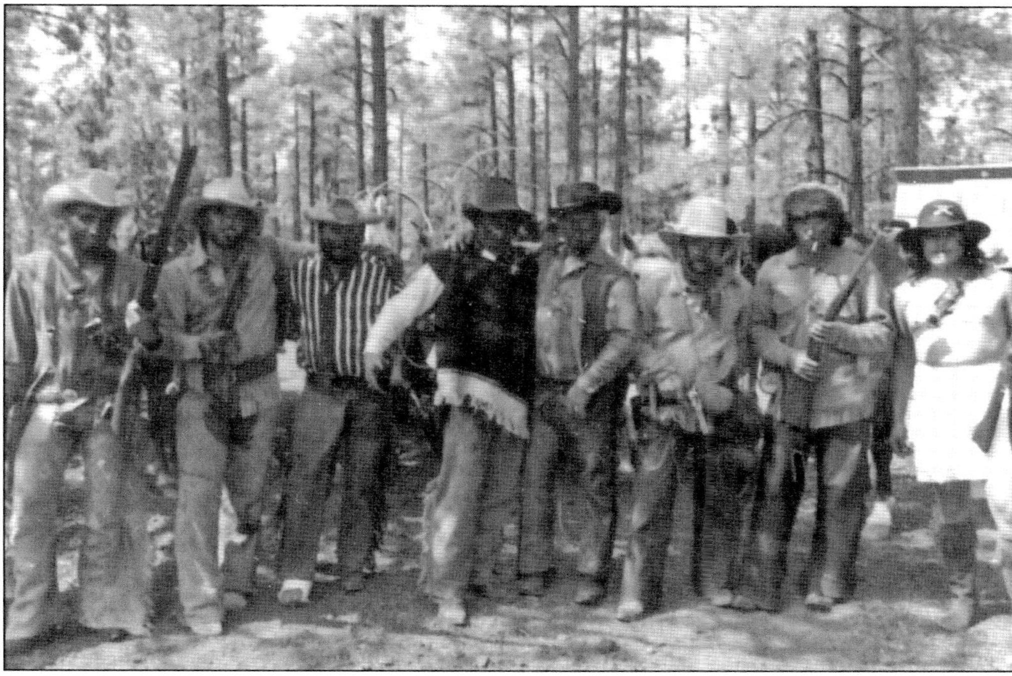

Gene Coon and his buddies, "The Wild Bunch," rode in the Fourth of July parade for 13 years. A much-loved entry, they made their way down Deuce of Clubs dressed in buckskins and serapes; their wagons had skins hanging and were trailed by hound dogs. They received a bit of a reprimand when one of them shot Woodsy the Owl with a black-powder blank and the fuzzy costume started to smolder. Members through the years have included Gene Coon, Bob Vollborn, Clifford Moya, Randy Brewer, Eddie "Cowboy" Brown, Victor Velasquez, Riney Maxwell, Bruce Rowell, and Bobby Barr. Unlike some other mountain men groups, this bunch did not just dress up and rough it one day a year. (Above, Clifford Moya; below, Huso collection.)

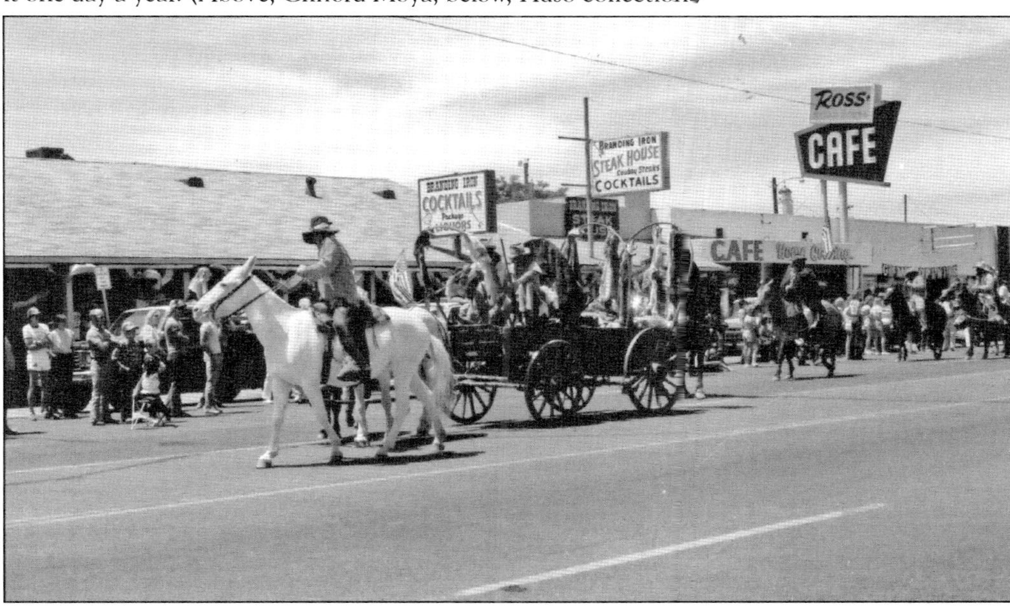

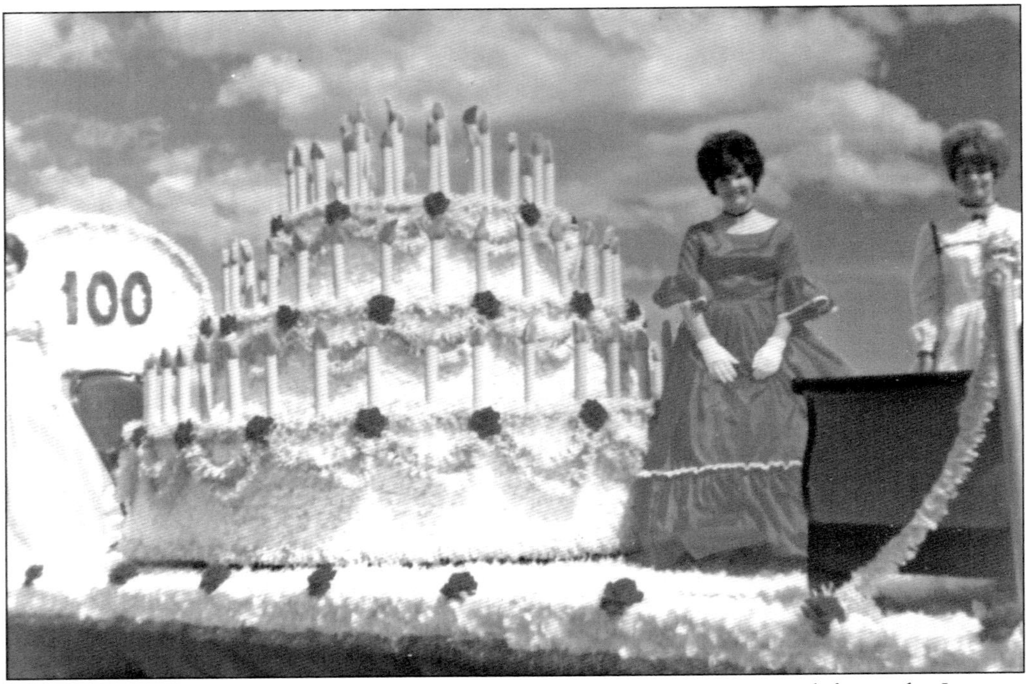

This was the Smithson Upholstery float for the centennial celebration. From left to right, Loretta, Leta, and Kathy Smithson were dressed in sherbet-colored gowns and rode next to the cake. If Eb Lewis got recognition for humor, the Smithson family deserved recognition for beauty and quality workmanship. When the children sent their parents to the Rose Bowl (for some tips), Velma was disappointed in the floats, saying, "They look much larger on television." (Huso collection.)

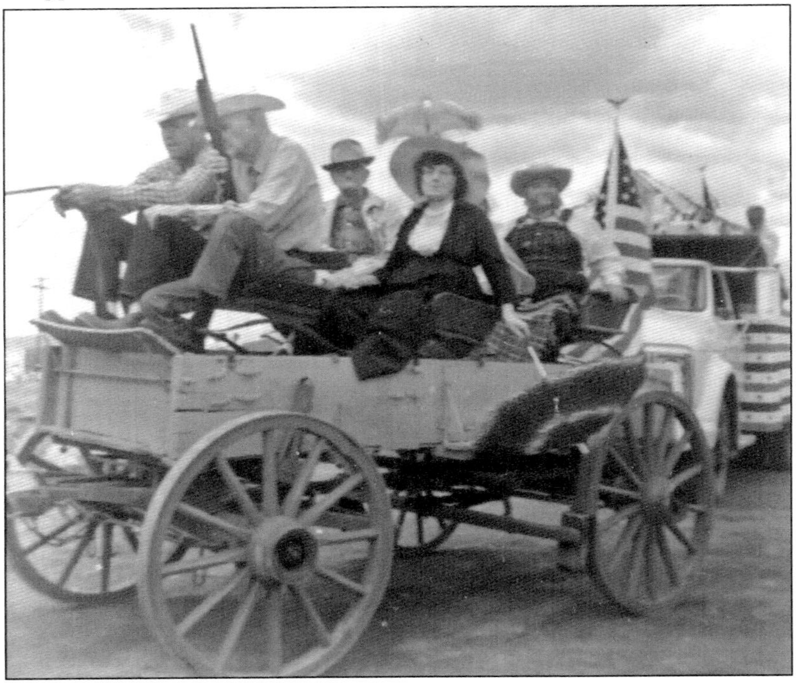

Jim Finney rides shotgun position in this wagon carrying pioneers for the Show Low Centennial Fourth of July parade. Sitting in the middle seat are Roy and Katy Adams Penrod; seated behind is Almon Owens. Vance Rogers may be the driver. There were over 125 entries in the parade in 1970; many were horse-drawn conveyances or beautiful floats. (Huso collection.)

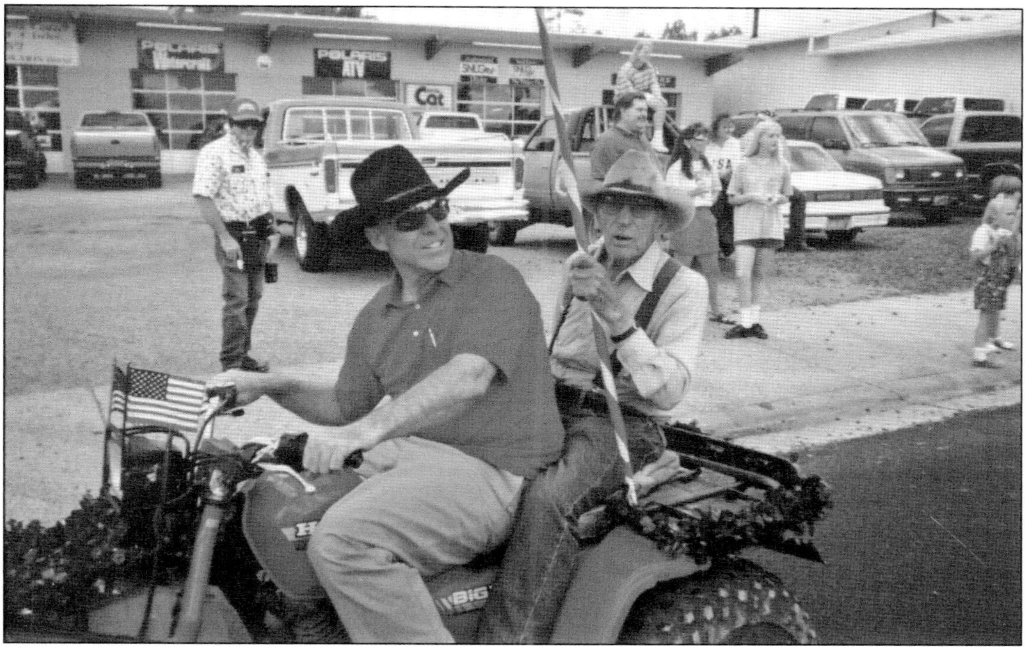

Here Gib Frost and his father, Aut, ride in the parade. One cold, rainy day in 1999, the 94-year-old Aut drove the three-wheeler, in third gear, for three wet hours to Christopher Creek, 60 miles away. Aut stopped at a real estate office, and the realtor called Aut's son, Jerry (and an ambulance). Aut said that he just "wanted to see how far he could get on a tank of gas." (Huso collection.)

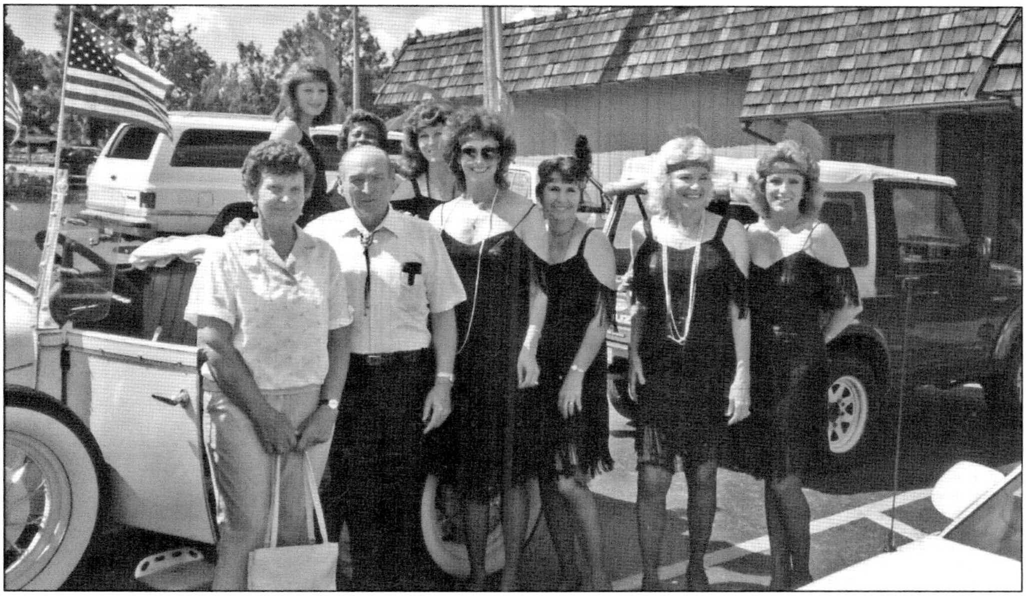

Peggy and Hal Butler pose here with members of the "Lucky Sevens," Show Low's ambassadors in the late 1970s and early 1980s. Next to Hal is Denise Butler, then Debbie Austin; other members of the "Sevens" were Almeda Fernau, CeCe Byington, Maxine Hudgens, Marcia Pagani, and Beverly Earven. The convertible belonged to Dan and Mary Ann Barton Simpkins. (Denise Harris Butler.)

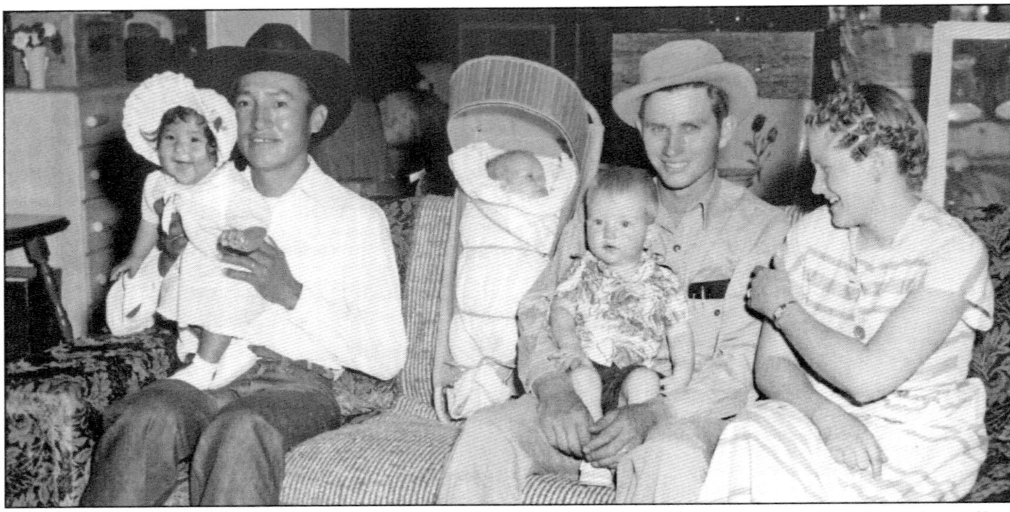

Elbert "Eb" Lewis's secondhand store was a potpourri of every imaginable item. Besides selling northern Arizona merchandise, Lewis would take a truck to the Midwest and purchase interesting antiques for resale. However, he is remembered for his sense of humor. About 1954, he was at Bert's Trading Post and thought of reversing the babies' "cultural dress." Above, from left to right, are unidentified, Howard Wahlin, Eben (in cradleboard), Charlie, Eb, and Geraldine Lewis. Below, Lewis is pictured on a unicycle at his store. (Both, SLHisSoc Museum.)

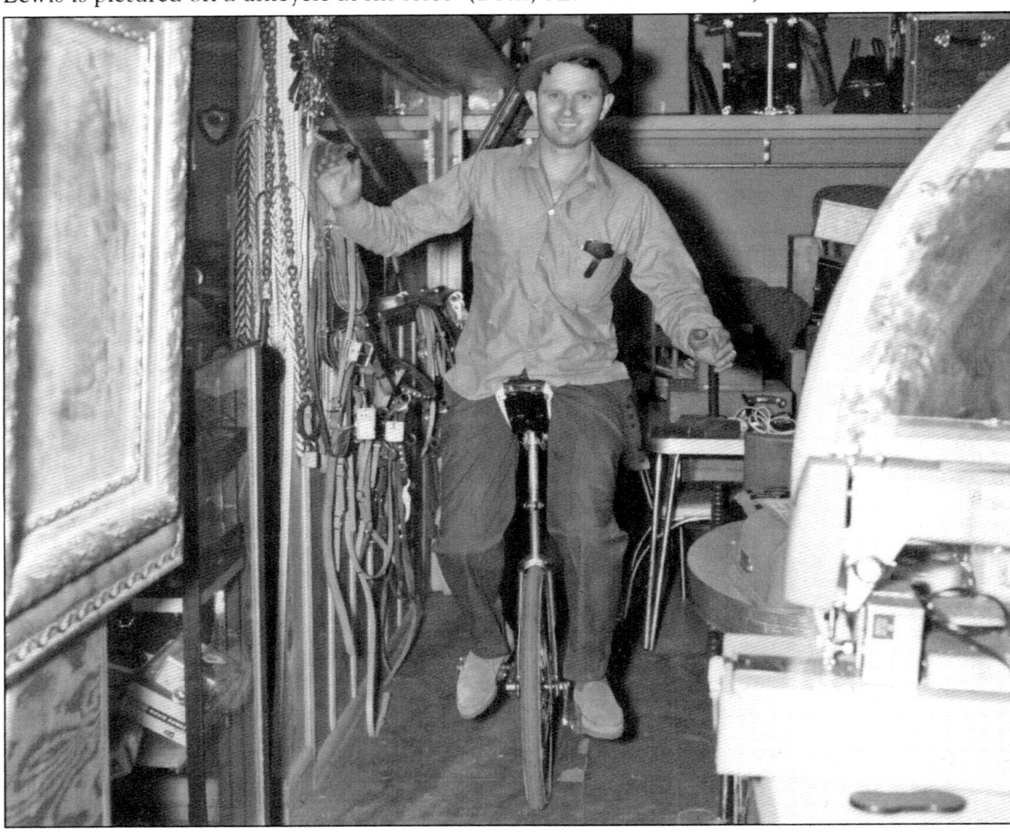

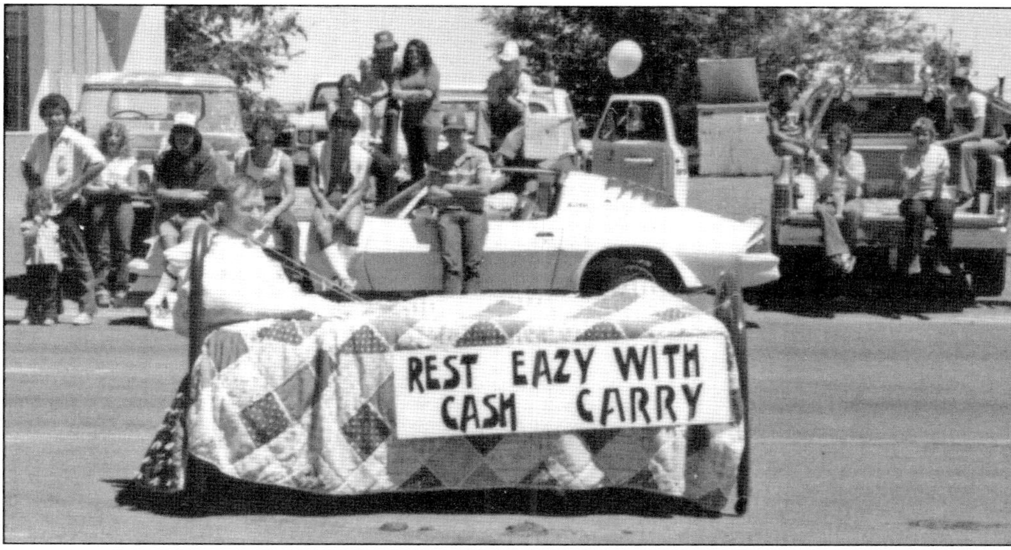

Lewis's entries in the Fourth of July parades often included store items put on wheels and independently propelled, including Lewis in a bed—"Rest Easy With Cash and Carry" (above). Other years included a live bear and wash tub—"No cash, no carry" (1963), walking carrying a live baby pig and bottle of milk (1978), Lewis on crutches—"I'll walk a mile for your business" (1979), Lewis playing a piano—"We play your tune at Cash and Carry" (1983), and a large trash can on wheels—"There's No Trash, Lewis Antiques" (1989). Below, Lewis (left) is dressed as an undertaker—"Old Man Gloom [Lewis] can be banished when Old Man Cheer [unidentified] takes the reins." The Vaughans purchased the Spudnut Shop from LeRoy Ellsworth about 1956, renamed it the "Spudnut Corral," and installed a neon sign with a cowboy lassoing a traveling spudnut. They also built a miniature golf course. (Above, SLHistSoc Museum; below, Vaughan collection.)

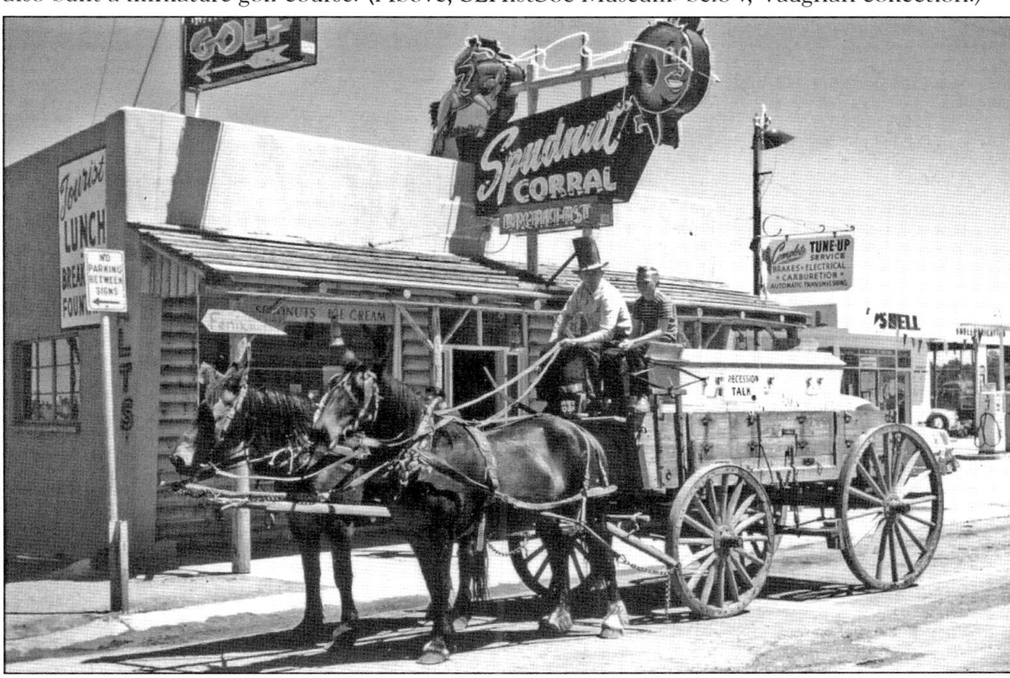

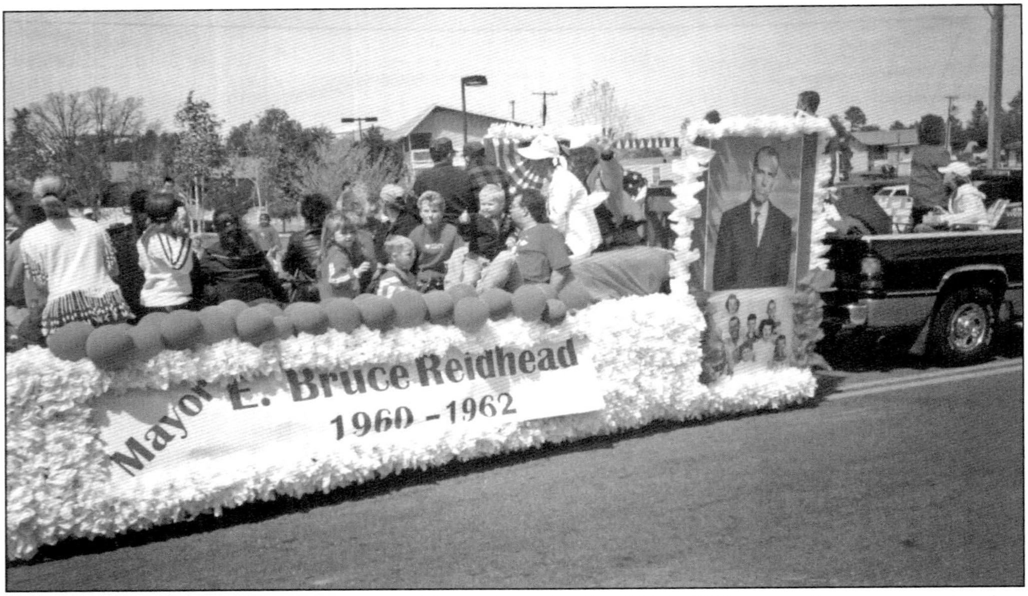

Bruce Reidhead was elected mayor of Show Low for the 1960–1962 term. Bruce was a lumber dealer who owned and operated the Reidhead and Chlarson Lumber Company and also owned the B&R Lumber Company. Bruce was also a member of the Elks Lodge and served for nine years on the Show Low School Board. (SLHisSoc Museum.)

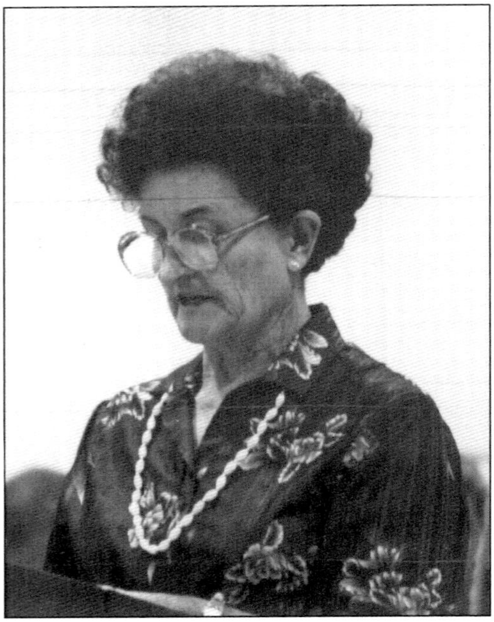

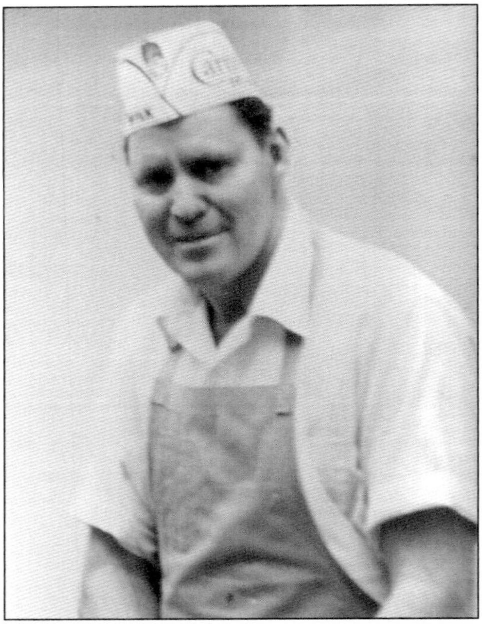

In September 1987, Show Low celebrated the constitution's bicentennial with a parade and civic program. A replica of the constitution was placed in the post office. Those who read it were then allowed to place their signature, along with the original signatures, at the bottom of the document. Elizabeth Nikolaus (left) participated as the entire constitution was read. Lamar Nikolaus (right), first mayor of Show Low, is in his butcher clothes. (Left, SLHisSoc Museum; right, Elizabeth Nikolaus collection.)

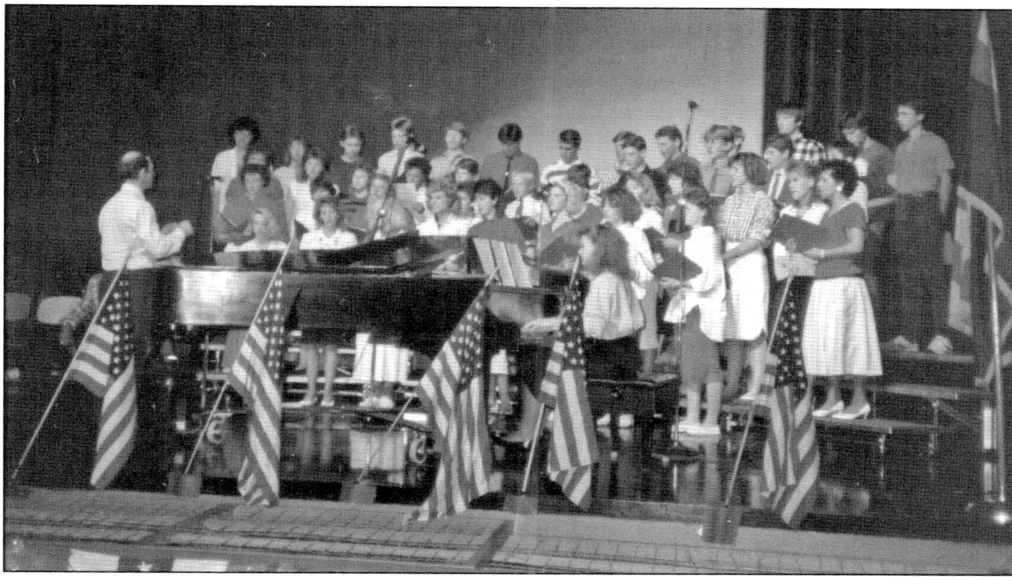

Scott Gentry, music teacher, led the high school chorus in "Shenandoah" and "The Battle Hymn of the Republic" (above). As part of the program, the Scouts of the White Mountain District recited the preamble to the constitution using sign language; the Cub Scouts can be seen below. On Saturday, a Bicentennial Grand Ball was held with the Garth Nikolaus Band providing the music. Those attending were encouraged to come in early American costume, and songs and dances from 200 years earlier were presented as a floor show. (Both, SLHisSoc Museum.)

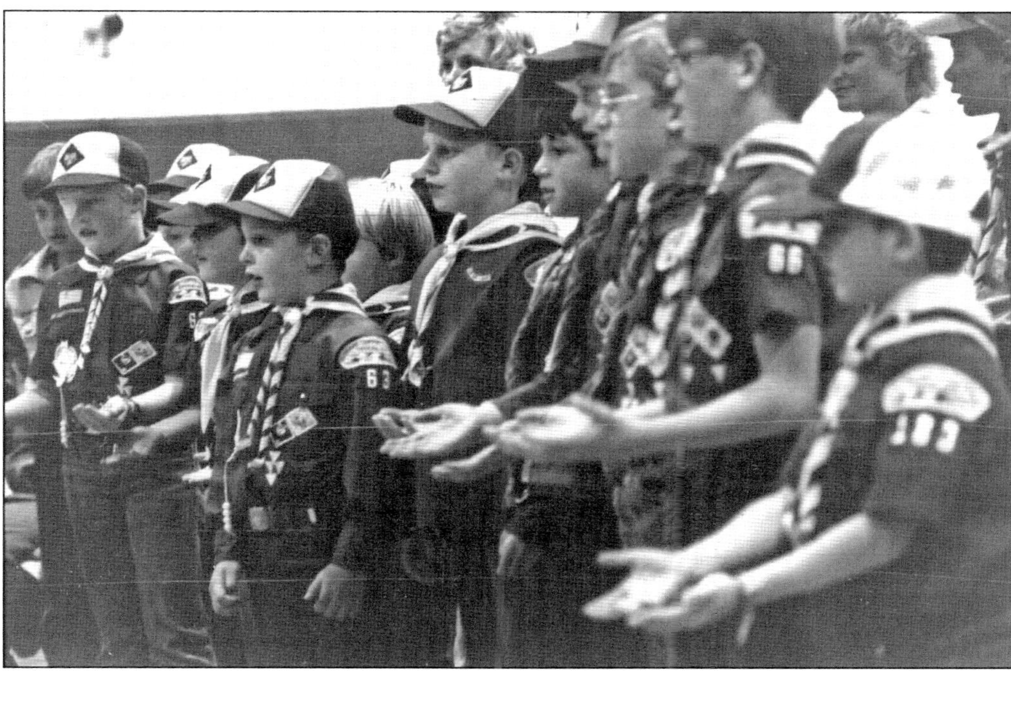

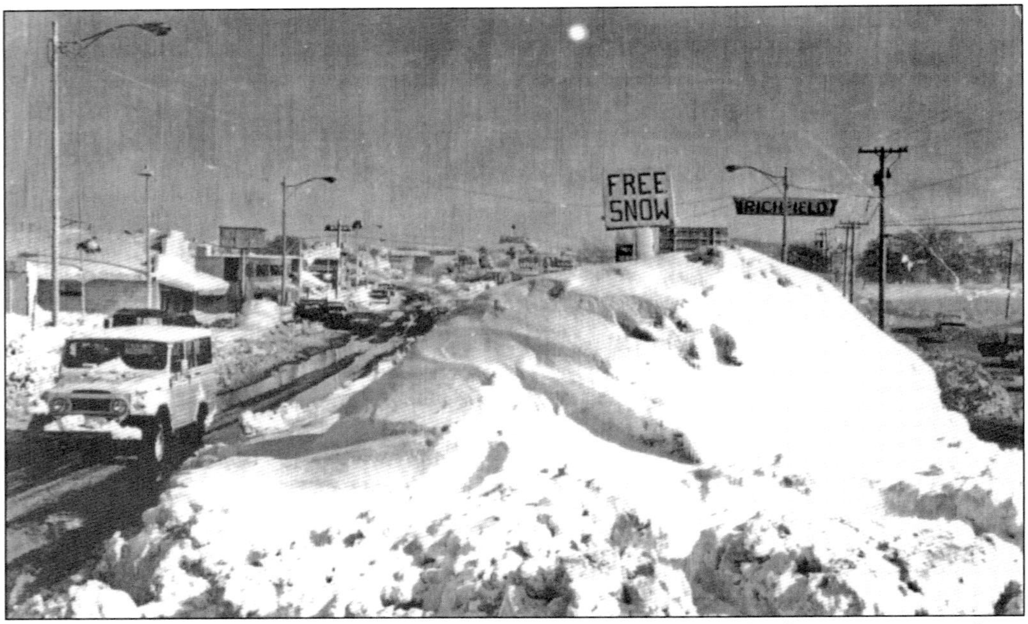

The winter of 1967 is remembered for snow falling for 13 days straight, leaving most residents home-bound, businesses and schools closed, and cars buried in drifts. Snow was deposited in the middle of the street, some places 10 feet high. Denny Thompson, Navajo County investigator, snapped a picture of the "Free Snow" sign near Louis Jones's Chevron station, showing someone had retained a sense of humor. (Howard and Judy Hansen.)

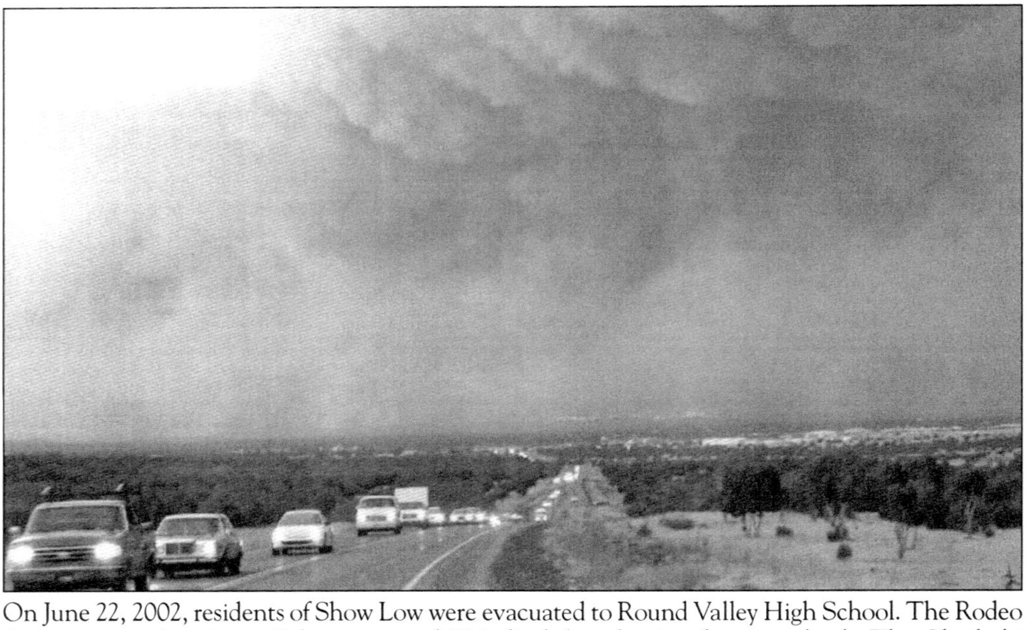

On June 22, 2002, residents of Show Low were evacuated to Round Valley High School. The Rodeo fire was started on June 18 by a seasonal BIA firefighter hoping for a paycheck. The Chedeski fire was built by a stranded motorist on June 20 trying to signal a helicopter. The fires merged and grew to 467,000 acres before the Rodeo-Chedeski fire was under control on July 7. (Navajo County Public Works Department.)

Clarence "Clad" Reidhead, the 11th child of John Oscar Reidhead, was born and died on the same property; he only left to serve in the army during World War II. Reidhead said, "I learnt to ride at the age of eight," and he was running the 80-acre farm at age 15 with the help of a sister and three horses. "These guys now think they need three tractors," Reidhead lamented. (Photograph by Deborah Austin.)

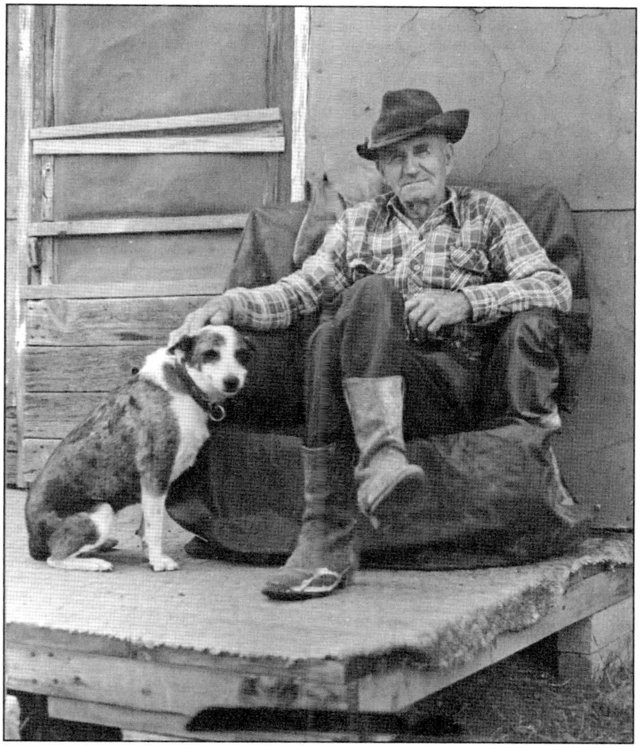

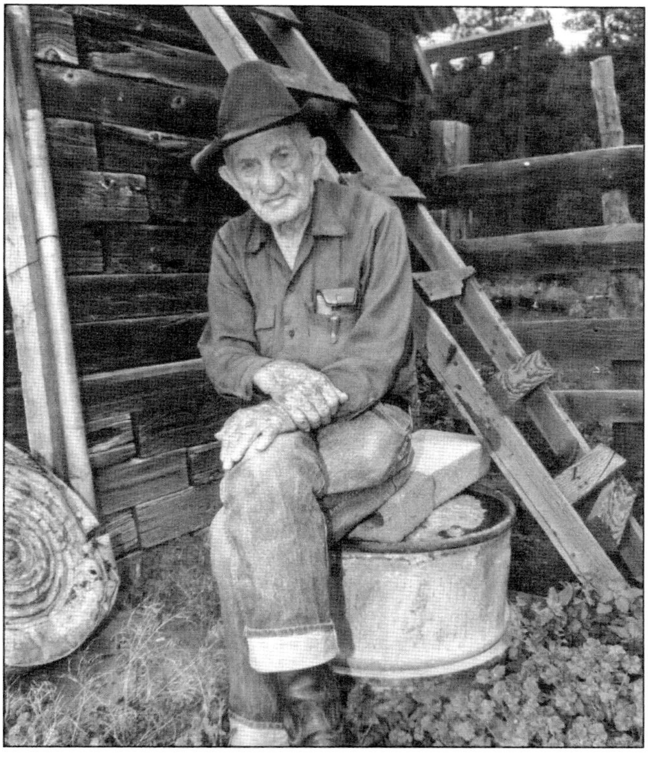

Lavern West was an old cowboy who lived in three centuries. Born in 1898, he died in 2000. His second wife was a White Mountain Apache woman named Clara. This Apache connection meant he could live at Forestdale and run his cattle on the reservation. (Photograph by Deborah Austin.)

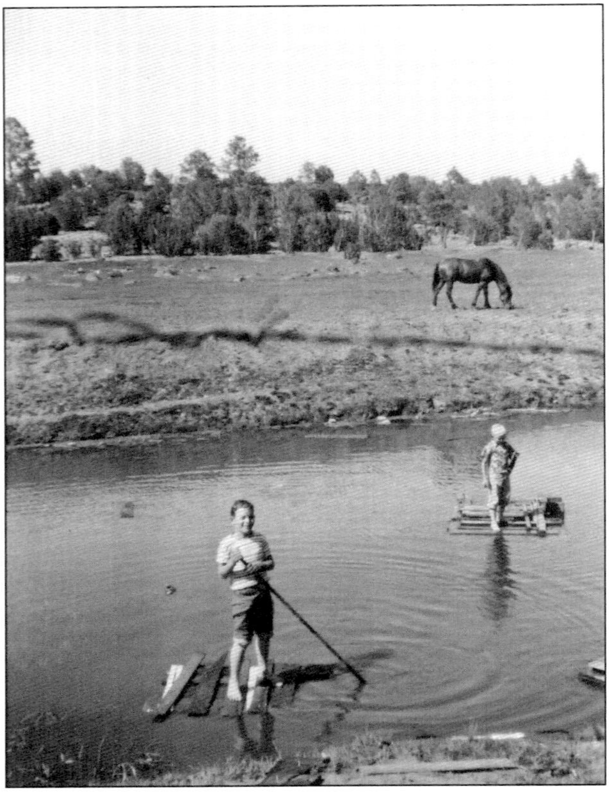

Show Low Creek has been a place to escape for generations of Show Low residents—a horseback ride, a swim, a leisurely walk, or a place to test rafts as Mike Huso (foreground) and Nolan Potts are doing in the late 1940s. The boys would go to the Reidhead Lumber mill and scavenge cutoffs long enough to make a raft. Then they would go to the Show Low Supply (belonging to Huso's father) to get enough rope to lash the boards together. The water was only about 5 feet deep when this picture was taken. Below is a serene view of Show Low Creek shot from Moylen and Joy Owenses' property north of Show Low. Although the mood of the creek is not always this peaceful, the creek defines Show Low today. (Left, Huso collection; below, photograph by Hilda Frost.)

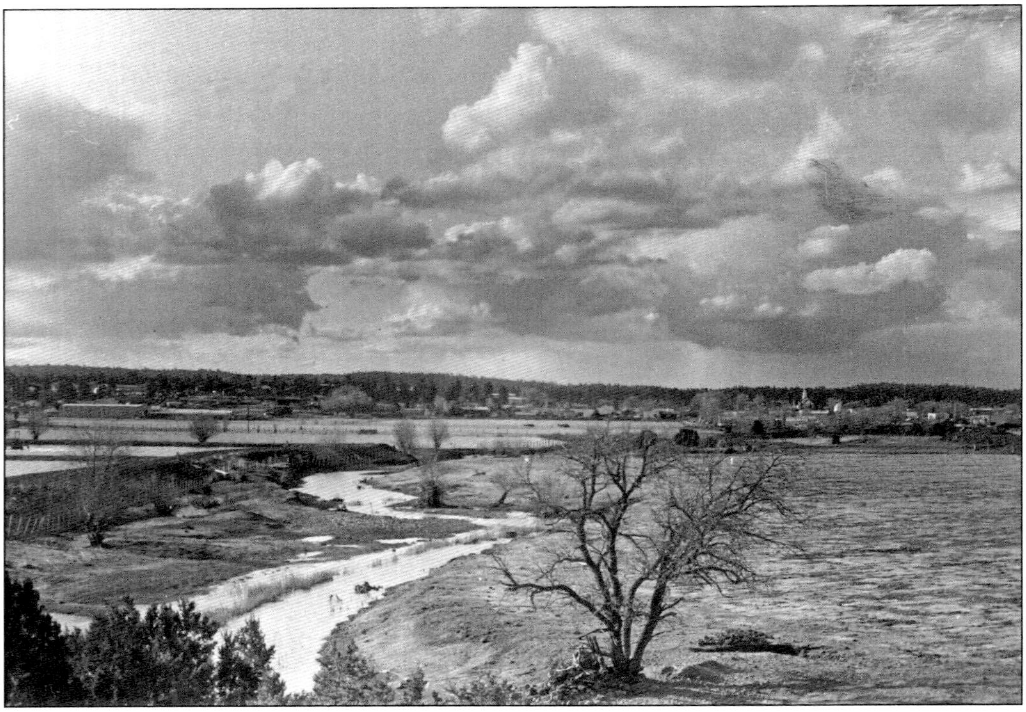

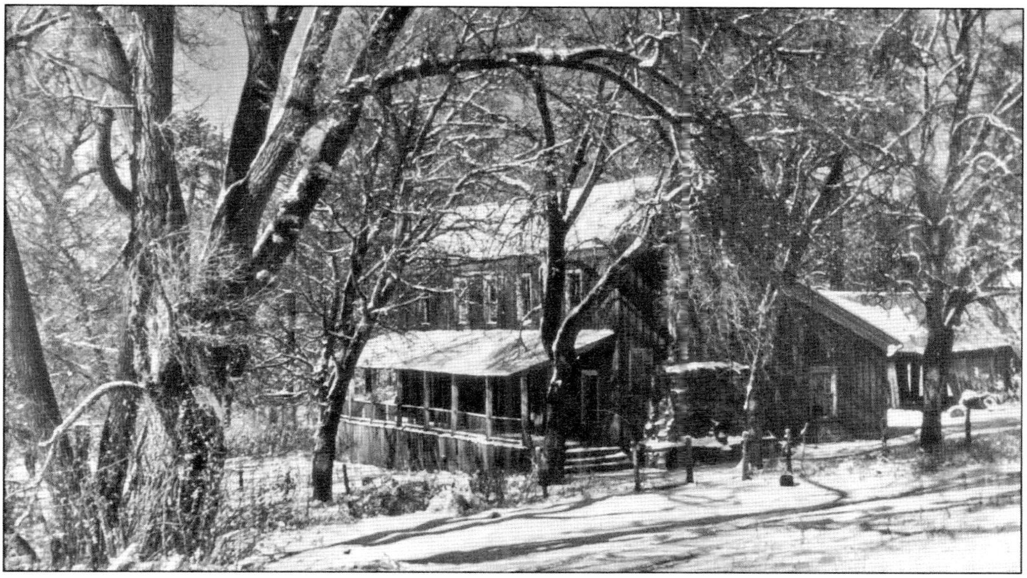

When Corydon Cooley left Show Low, he built a ranch-style home just south of Hon-dah. It was still intact in the 1960s, but not long afterward, it caught fire and was destroyed. This photograph was taken in 1956 after a snowfall. (Darla Mills Baird.)

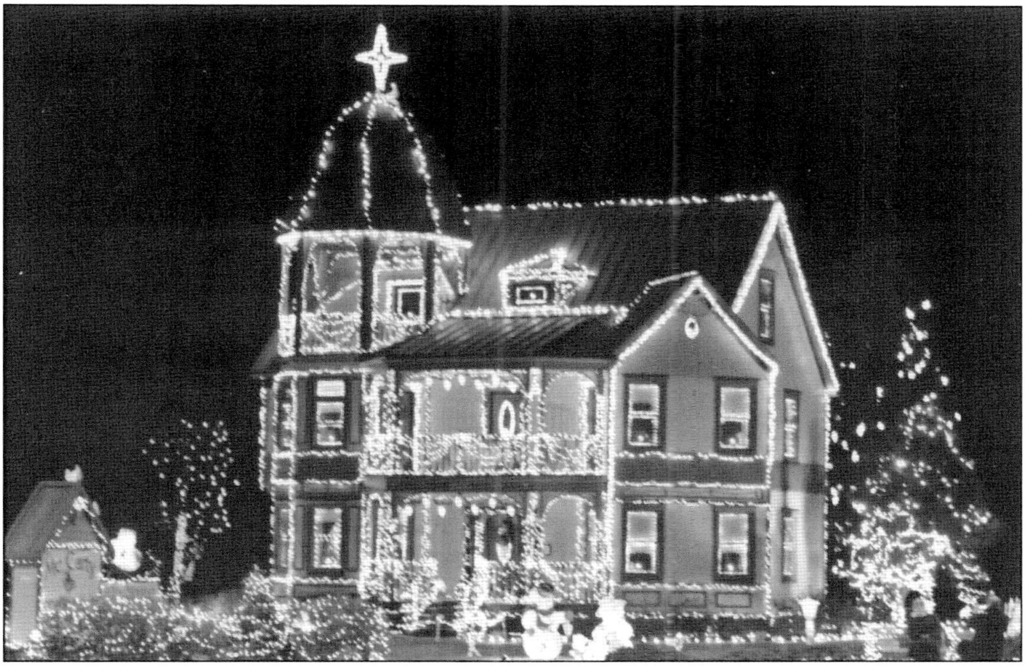

Entering Show Low from the west, the Victorian is a beautiful edifice any time of the year, but at Christmastime, it is spectacular. The McCarty family decorates in big-city fashion, including vintage displays from when sisters Liz, Victoria, and Kathy were youngsters. The house is a period-correct replica, including parlor and kitchen, although the house was constructed as offices for the family business and never used as a home. On the walls hang many early photographs of Show Low and the White Mountains. (McCarty family.)